Andrew Seccull grew up in a family of gardeners and now runs Jenny Smith Gardens, a design business started by his mother. He is a regular contributor to a range of newspapers and magazines, and has been the gardening editor at *The Age*. He also co-hosted the popular 'Sunday Gardening Show' on 3AW for many years.

Andrew lives in Melbourne with his partner and four dogs.

the perfect garden

Andrew Seccull
photography by Simon Griffiths

LANTERN
an imprint of
PENGUIN BOOKS

LANTERN

Published by the Penguin Group
Penguin Group (Australia)
250 Camberwell Road, Camberwell, Victoria 3124, Australia
(a division of Pearson Australia Group Pty Ltd)
Penguin Group (USA) Inc.
375 Hudson Street, New York, New York 10014, USA
Penguin Group (Canada)
90 Eglinton Avenue East, Suite 700, Toronto ON M4P 2Y3, Canada
(a division of Pearson Penguin Canada Inc.)
Penguin Books Ltd
80 Strand, London WC2R 0RL, England
Penguin Ireland
25 St Stephen's Green, Dublin 2, Ireland
(a division of Penguin Books Ltd)
Penguin Books India Pvt Ltd
11 Community Centre, Panchsheel Park, New Delhi – 110 017, India
Penguin Group (NZ)
Cnr Airborne and Rosedale Roads, Albany, Auckland, New Zealand
(a division of Pearson New Zealand Ltd)
Penguin Books (South Africa) (Pty) Ltd
24 Sturdee Avenue, Rosebank, Johannesburg 2196, South Africa

Penguin Books Ltd, Registered Offices: 80 Strand, London WC2R 0RL, England

First published by Penguin Group (Australia), a division of Pearson Australia Group Pty Ltd, 2006

10 9 8 7 6 5 4 3 2 1

Copyright © Andrew Seccull 2006
Photography copyright © Simon Griffiths 2006
Simon Griffiths' photograph of the knot garden at Retford Park (page 63) is reproduced
by kind permission of James Fairfax

The moral right of the author has been asserted

All rights reserved. Without limiting the rights under copyright reserved above, no part of this
publication may be reproduced, stored in or introduced into a retrieval system, or transmitted, in
any form or by any means (electronic, mechanical, photocopying, recording or otherwise), without
the prior written permission of both the copyright owner and the above publisher of this book.

Design by Adam Laszczuk © Penguin Group (Australia)
Typeset in Gramond 3, Perpetua and Meta by Post Pre-press Group, Brisbane, Queensland
Printed and bound in China by Bookbuilders

National Library of Australia
Cataloguing-in-Publication data:

    Seccull, Andrew.
    The perfect garden.

    Includes index.
    ISBN 1 920989 27 7.

    1. Gardening. I. Griffiths, Simon (Simon John). II. Title.

    635

www.penguin.com.au

This book is dedicated to Jenny, without whose help and guidance over the years it would not have been possible.

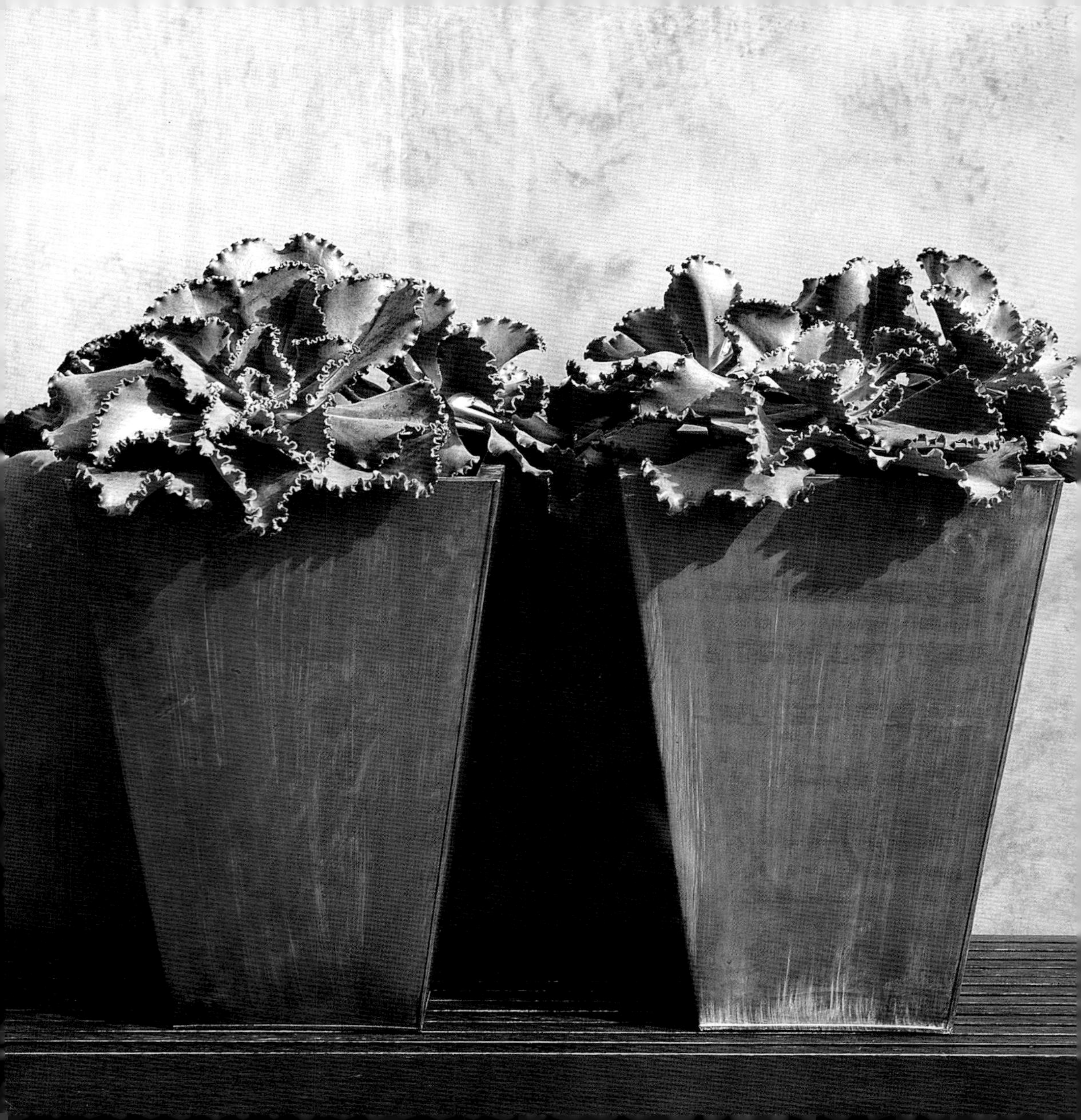

introduction

The perfect garden doesn't need to be large — today many of us live on small blocks with limited open space. But whatever the size of your plot or pot, it does need suitable plants, colour, perfume, structure, texture, decoration. And it needs to be interesting all year round.

This book brings together gardening hints and anecdotes I've collected over the years as a hands-on gardener, writer and broadcaster. During my years on talk-back radio I was asked the same questions over and again: 'When is the best time to prune?' 'What should I plant to attract birds to my garden?' 'How can I hide an ugly fence?' 'Why haven't my bulbs flowered this year?' There were many more, of course. I've always wanted to write a book that answers questions like these as well as providing all sorts of other practical tips and design inspiration. Finally, here it is.

I've really enjoyed 'harvesting' the information and ideas you'll find in these pages. And I hope you will enjoy browsing for inspiration as well as looking for solutions to problems when you get stuck — which every gardener does from time to time. (You might like to copy the calendar on pages 60–1 and stick it in the shed or on the fridge, so that you don't forget when to cut back the lavender or plant the lettuce.) Most of all, I hope that what you find here will encourage you to be creative in cultivating your own perfect garden, not just once but many times in your life.

agapanthus

The erect flower stems of these perennials carry large heads of small, trumpet-shaped flowers in white as well as various shades of blue and pink. Endemic to coastal regions, they thrive in difficult, dry conditions and are invaluable for their strong foliage and abundant, showy flowers. Most are evergreen, but there are also a number of deciduous cultivars that have the advantage of being more frost-tolerant.

Agapanthus flower best in full sun and are traditionally used in clumps in front gardens or to line driveways. But they will also tolerate light shade and make excellent pot plants.

- *Agapanthus praecox* subsp. *orientalis* is the most commonly grown larger species, boasting flower stems to 90 cm with large blue clusters.
- Those looking for something different might try 'Guilfoyle' with its large dark-blue flower heads, or 'Purple Cloud', another beauty.
- A number of long-flowering dwarf varieties are now available – 'Streamline' is one of the better blues and 'Perpetual Peace' is a lovely white.
- 'Alba Roseus' has 40 cm flower stems that commence white but fade to a soft pink.

In some areas, agapanthus have naturalised to the extent that they are listed as environmental weeds, so it is important to cut off the spent flower heads and dispose of them before the seeds ripen or get spread by the birds.

See also: **seaside garden; summer garden**

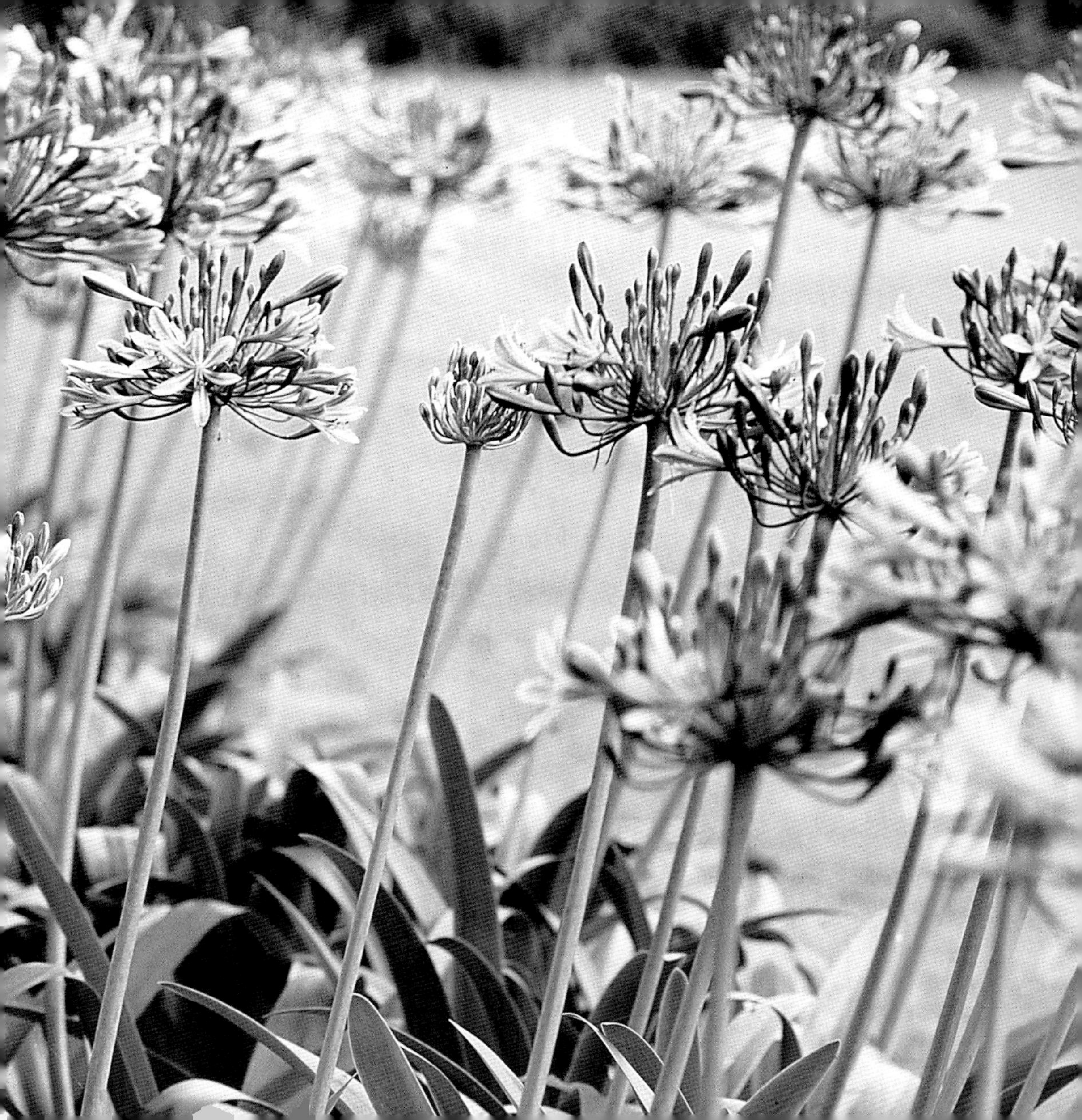

annuals

Annuals are plants with a lifespan of a year or less. They include ornamental plants such as alyssum, pansies and petunias; most vegetables; a number of herbs; and many weeds and ornamental grasses.

Annuals are invaluable for the home gardener. Use them to fill spaces between more permanent plantings such as perennials and shrubs, and for massed colour displays in feature beds and under roses. Some annuals, such as forget-me-nots (*Myosotis* spp.), Californian poppies (*Eschscholzia californica*), alyssum and campions (*Silene* spp.), will self-seed and pop up in unexpected places, which all adds to the fun. Do make sure you keep them under control, though, or they can take over.

Annuals are ideal for brightening up your garden for a special occasion, but bear in mind their short life. For instance, if you're planning a garden wedding in early spring, plant white or pale-pink primulas a little later than usual and they will be looking lovely for the big day. But soon afterwards they will start to look tired and will have to be pulled out. If you then plant petunia seedlings, it will be at least two months before they are looking nice. During this 'in between' period, the only way to get a good display is to buy ready-grown bloomer pots. These, however, are generally expensive and seldom look as good as a massed planting.

> For petunias in pots, the more you pinch them back and liquid-fertilise, the bushier and healthier they will be. Just remember to stop pinching back in time to have them flowering beautifully for the special occasion.

See also: **colour in the garden; pots**

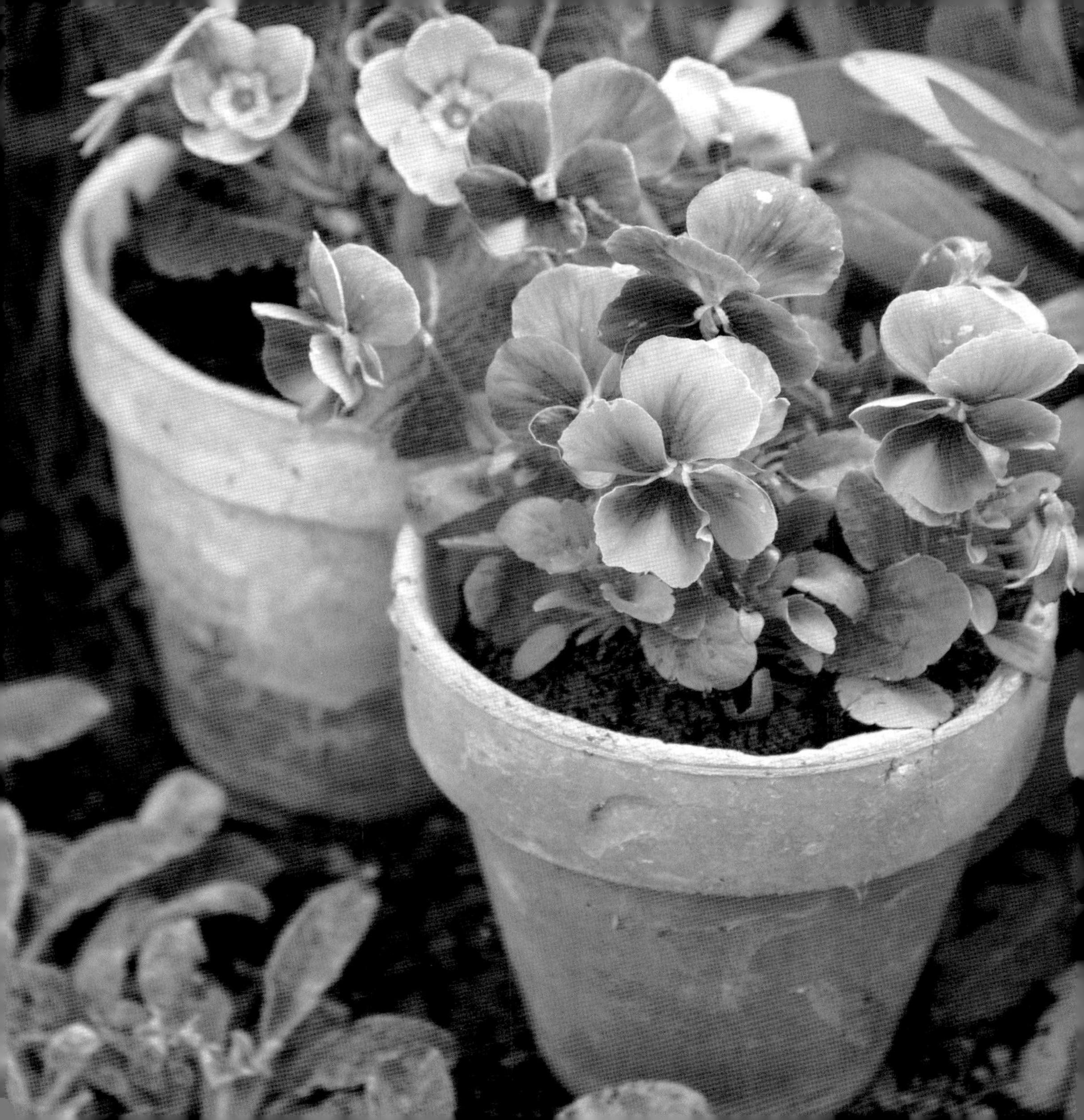

apples

Apple trees flower in late spring, and their pink or white blossom is quite beautiful. If grown without interference, an apple tree can reach a height of 10–15 m, but most people keep their trees to half this size by pruning. If you only have a small garden or a courtyard, dwarf varieties are available, or you can easily espalier your tree onto a fence or wall.

Many gardeners choose crab-apples, but while decorative they bear only small, sour, inedible fruit. There's nothing better than having edible apples available from your own tree and, like tomatoes, home-grown apples taste infinitely better than those grown commercially. Varieties such as 'Golden Delicious', which are pedestrian at best from a supermarket, are positively ambrosial when picked straight from the tree! Growing your own apples also allows you to sample varieties such as snow apples, 'Cox's Orange Pippin' and 'Gravenstein', seldom seen in shops now.

Like most deciduous fruit trees, apples prefer a sunny, well-drained location that is not too dry over summer and experiences cold nights in winter. Most apples need cross-pollination in order to fruit well; Jonathan is a good choice as it will pollinate most other varieties.

It is easy to tell when the apples on your tree are ripe. Pick one that appears to be ripe and slice it in half horizontally. Immediately push the two halves together again and hold the apple up by the stem so that one half is underneath the other. If the apple is ready to pick, the two halves will stick together without falling apart.

See also: **espaliers; fruit trees; organic garden; pruning**

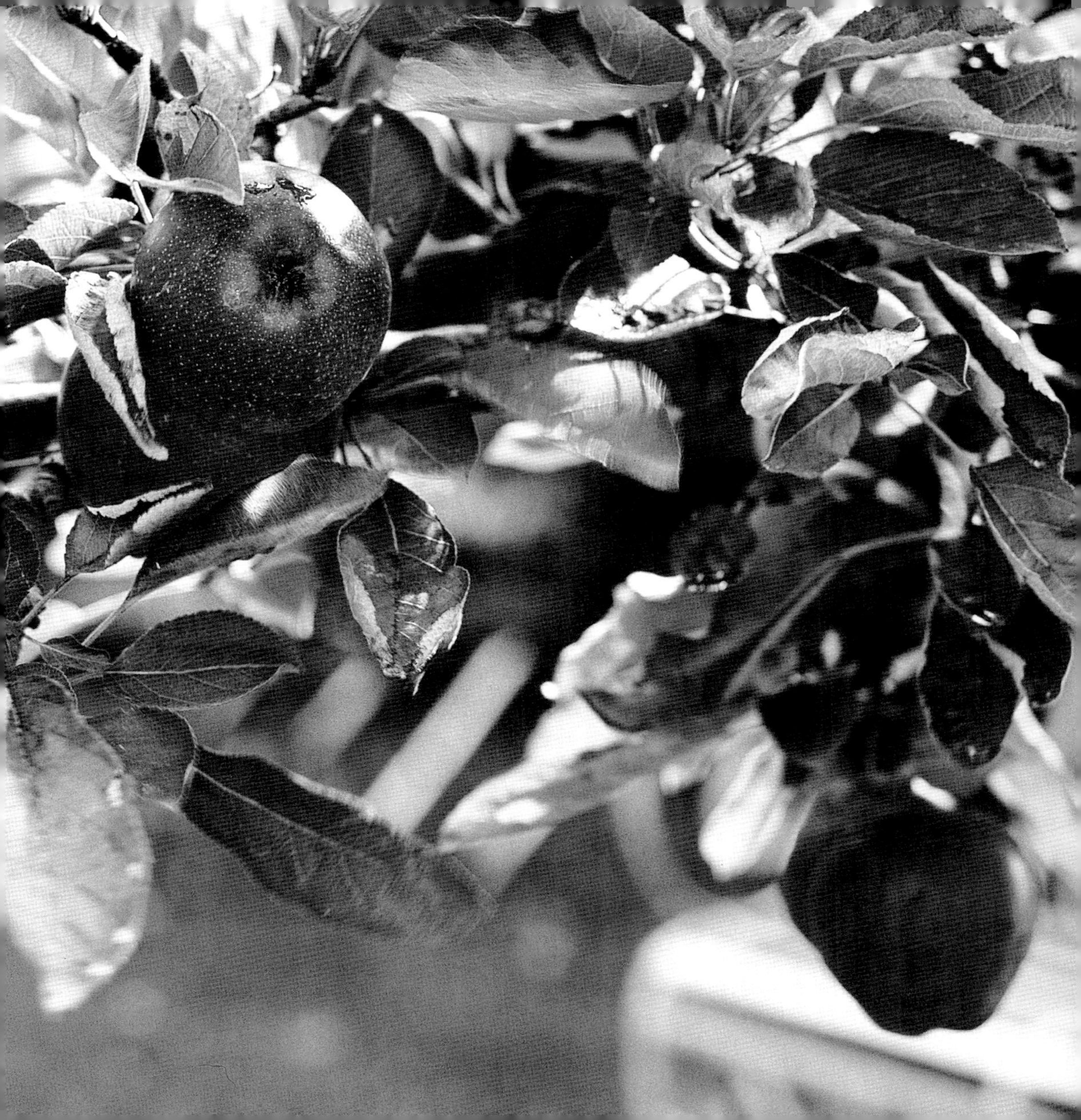

autumn garden

In autumn, summer foliage starts to fall apart and exposes any structural weaknesses the garden may have. Now is the time for the added interest of foliage colour and the beautiful effect of fruit, berries and hips – the 'accessories' of a garden.

My brother has planted a hedge of quinces along one side of his garden. In autumn their large, pendulous yellow fruit are magnificent. The autumn display of rosehips on the old-fashioned roses covering his big pergola is equally impressive. In my previous garden, I had a hedge of Mexican hawthorns along the back; in autumn, they were a mass of small orange-yellow berries.

Ornamental grasses start to dry off in autumn and, whether used en masse, by themselves or combined with other plantings, their soft colours can really lift the garden. Choosing the right deciduous trees will also give you good autumn colour, as well as providing interest for the rest of the year. If you want a large tree, a pin oak (*Quercus palustris*) or a golden ash (*Fraxinus excelsior* 'Aurea') is a good choice. For a smaller space, you might consider a Japanese maple (*Acer palmatum*), a crepe myrtle (*Lagerstroemia indica*) or a Mount Fuji cherry (*Prunus* 'Shirotae').

Autumn jobs
- **Trim back and fertilise violets**.
- **Cut back winter iris foliage** to allow sun into the centre of the clumps; this will encourage more flower buds to form.
- **Plant sweet pea seed** around Saint Patrick's Day (17 March).
- **Top up mulch** to keep the ground warmer through winter and to help control weeds.

- **Plant spring-flowering bulbs** such as tulips, daffodils and freesias.
- **Inspect the garden** for plants that have not coped well with summer conditions and consider replacing them with plants that are more drought-tolerant.
- **Look out for passionvine hoppers** (small, brown, papery, moth-like pests that damage leaves and flower buds on chrysanthemums, dahlias and passionfruit).
- **Plant new lawns** from mid-March onwards. (Wait until the really hot weather has passed, but plant while it is still warm enough for the new grass to establish itself before winter. Mix seed in a bucket with some light sandy soil – this will make it easier to spread. To encourage a better strike, spread lawn starter, or another phosphate-rich fertiliser, at the same time.)
- **Dress existing lawns** with a thin layer of topsoil or sandy loam, lawn starter and seed. If you have a large number of weeds in the lawn, water two weeks prior to top-dressing with a broadleaf herbicide.
- **Divide perennials**, but only those that are showing new green shoots. Do not divide perennials that die back in winter.
- **Spread snail bait** regularly, as slugs and snails love autumn conditions.
- **Divide and replant liliums and strawberries**.
- **Control oxalis** using a glyphosate-based herbicide before it takes hold.
- **Identify any particularly wet areas** and deal with drainage problems before the winter sets in and the soil becomes waterlogged.
- **Collect autumn leaves** for your compost heap or to use as mulch.

See also: **bulbs; dry spaces; drainage; grasses; perennials; roses; snails**

bamboo

With the increased popularity of Japanese gardens, bamboo is becoming more common everywhere. These beautiful, low-maintenance structural plants represent one of the larger plant families in the world. They vary greatly in size and growth rates; some of the taller tropical species reach over 40 m high, while others only grow to a few centimetres.

Many people are fearful of planting bamboo because of its invasive habits, but there are plenty of non-invasive, clumping varieties available. Those that I have had great success with include:

- giant timber bamboo (*Bambusa oldhamii*) – a tough, tall-growing species that can be hedged or left to grow to its full height of around 15 m (it makes an excellent screening plant)
- Buddha's belly bamboo (*B. ventricosa*) – by placing this species under a bit of stress, you can not only limit its height to around 2–3 m, but also cause attractive internodal swellings to form at the base
- hedge bamboo (*B. multiplex*) – another good hedging variety, though it can also be kept smaller in pots
- miniature sacred bamboo (*Nandina domestica* 'Nana') – although not my favourite, with its almost fluffy leaves and strange colour mix, this dwarf form is very popular.

As a rule, bamboos prefer moist, rich soil. But given the number of species available, there is a bamboo suitable for almost any situation.

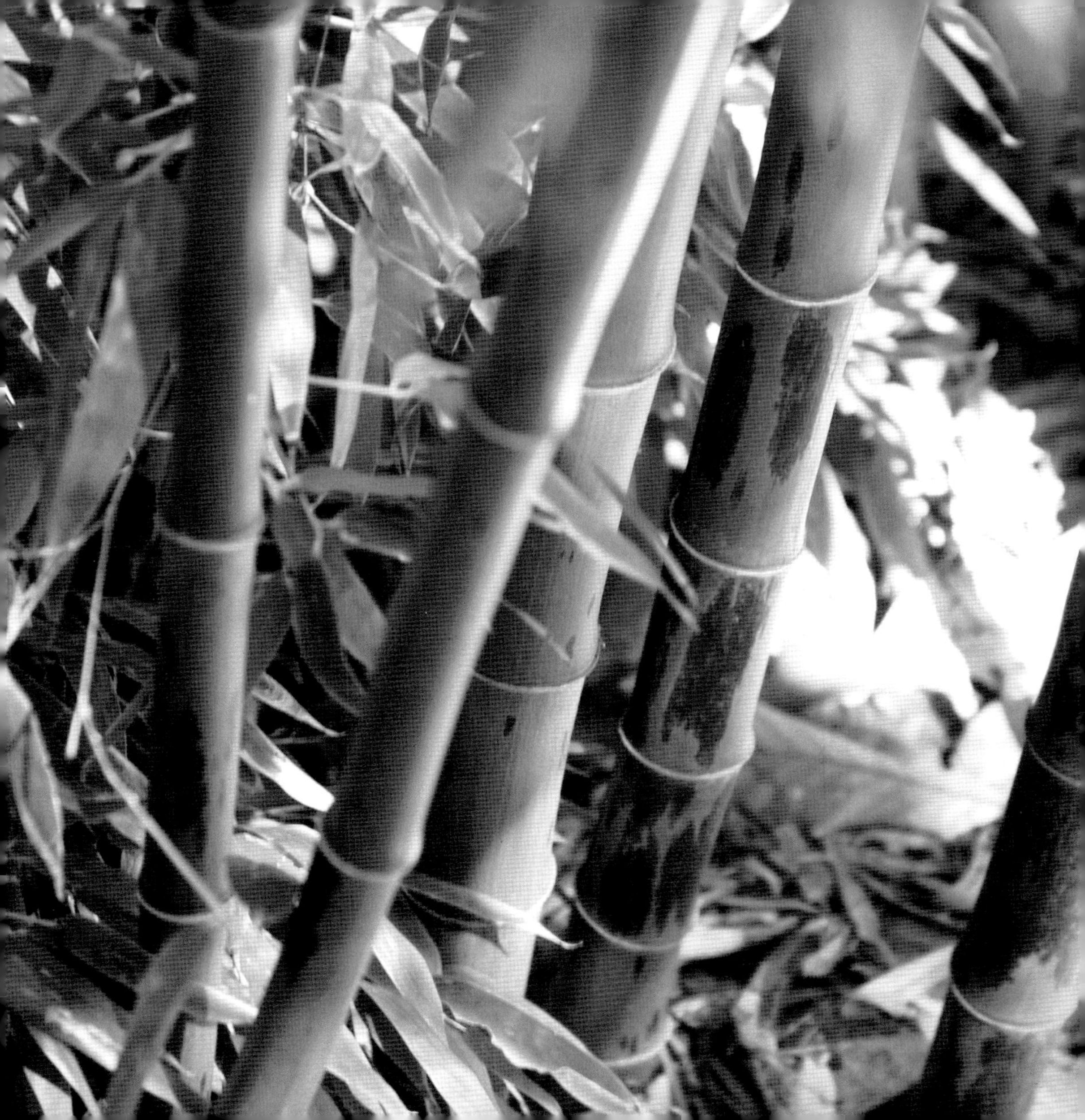

bark

Gardens in colder parts of the northern hemisphere are often reduced to their 'bones' in winter. But even in temperate regions where gardens never become completely dormant, bark is vital in the overall garden scheme. Eucalyptus trunks, for example, can look just as spectacular as silver birches and will survive much better under tough conditions. My top trees for beautiful bark:

- snow gum (*Eucalyptus pauciflora*) – the trunk is striped in beautiful colour variations and has rumpled joints like a rhinoceros's armpit
- silver princess gum (*Eucalyptus caesia* subsp. *magna*) – a small, weeping tree with juvenile branches that look as if they have been dusted with icing sugar; as the tree ages, the bark changes to a rough dark-brown, but trim off a couple of branches each year and you will be able to retain some beautiful white bark
- lemon-scented gum (*Corymbia citriodora*) – with its smooth, grey–green, almost fluorescent trunk, this is the quintessential eucalypt
- Sydney red gum (*Angophora costata*) – similar to *C. citriodora* except that the bark is a pale salmon-pink
- Chinese elm (*Ulmus parvifolia*) – a spreading tree with flaking orange and brown bark
- crepe myrtle (*Lagerstroemia indica*) – as this tree ages and when the branches are bare, the smooth, dappled trunk becomes like a piece of garden sculpture.

See also: **decorative elements**

beans

Easy to grow and generally liked by most family members, beans are a perfect summer or winter crop. Also, as a legume, they introduce nitrogen into the soil via root nodules and are a valuable soil-conditioning plant. Good, rich soil is essential for quick growth; slow growth can result in a poor yield and small, tough pods.

Dwarf and climbing French beans are some of the most rewarding summer vegetables. In subtropical climates they can be grown throughout the year; in other areas, they can be sown from September to February only. They grow particularly well when planted in rotation after cabbages or cauliflowers, for which the soil needs to be generously fertilised. Apply a complete fertiliser before planting the beans.
Climbing beans, especially 'Purple King', which has long purple pods that turn green when cooked, look great growing up tripods.
Broad beans are cold-climate vegetables that enjoy cool, moist growing conditions, although – like all vegetables – they require as much sun as possible. They are propagated by seed sown from April to June and fill the gap when French beans might not be available. Dwarf cultivars are less susceptible to wind damage and more compact. Broad beans are heavy feeders and grow best in soil improved by compost and manure.

> Beans are prone to aphid and red-spider attack so plant with a suitable insecticidal companion plant such as pyrethrum or nasturtiums if possible.

See also: **companion planting; fertiliser**

berryfruits

As well as plenty of sunlight, you need quite a bit of space to grow berryfruits. For most berries, a trellis is necessary once the canes are about 1 m high. (Strawberries, which are low, clump-forming plants that can be grown just about anywhere sunny, and mulberries, which grow on a tree, are exceptions.) If you only have space for one berryfruit, raspberries are probably your best bet as they are easy to grow, arguably the nicest to eat, and expensive to buy in punnets from the greengrocer. But hybrid blackberries (which are non-invasive), loganberries, boysenberries, gooseberries and blueberries are also popular.

Raspberries fall into two categories: early and late (indicating the time of year that they fruit). The early, summer-fruiting varieties generally prove more successful in warmer climates. To grow tasty raspberries:

1. Enrich the soil with plenty of organic matter before planting.
2. Plant seedlings in neat rows to make trellising, picking and pruning easier.
3. Water regularly during the summer.
4. Keep the plants under control by cutting out all the old canes, and any weak new canes, at ground level immediately after harvesting. (Raspberries are a biennial – the canes grow for one season, fruit, then die off in the next season.)
5. Keep the rows tidy by pulling out any stray suckers and mulching well each winter.
6. Weed by hand rather than with a spade or fork, as raspberries are surface-rooted and resent any root disturbance.

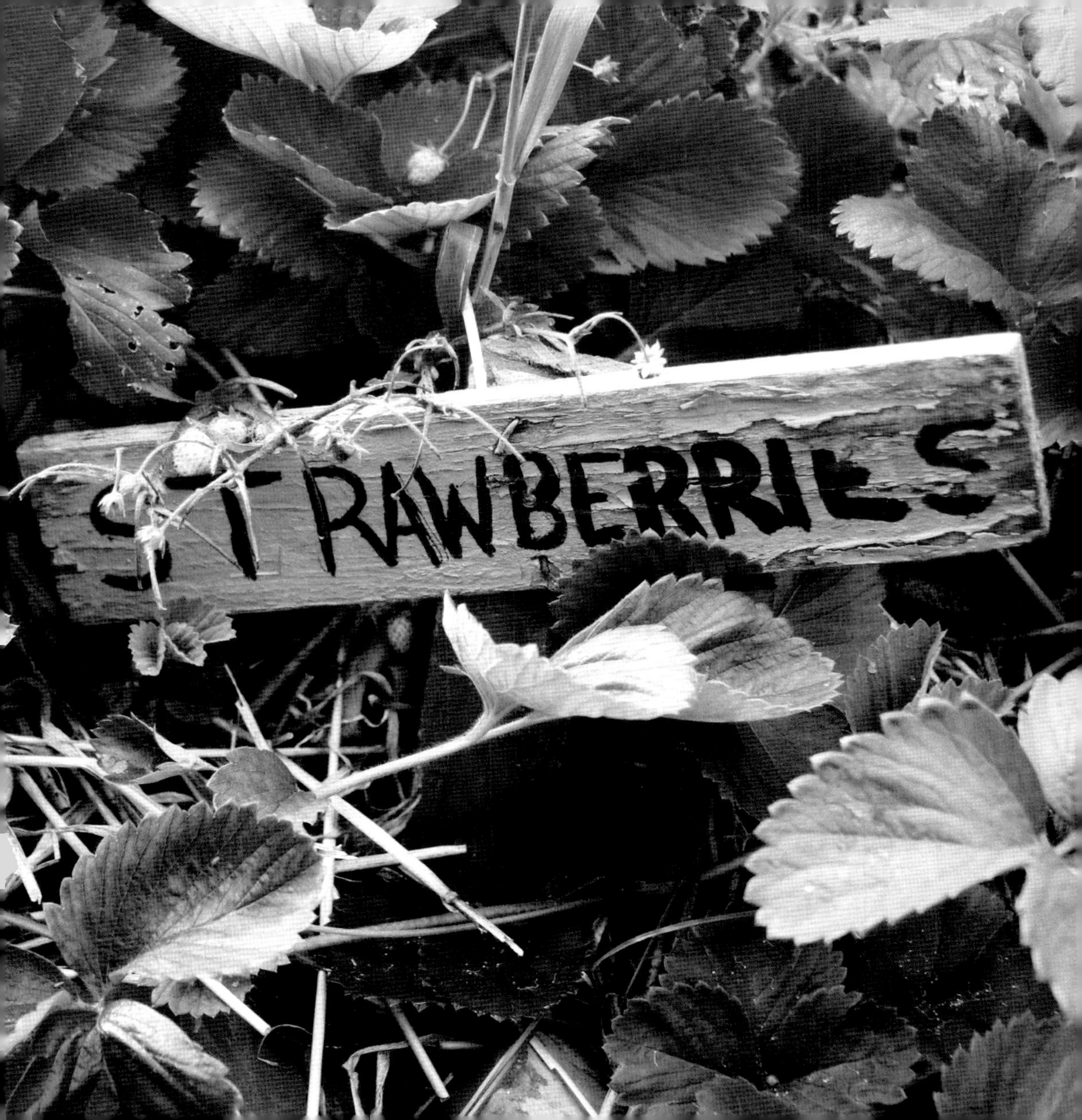
STRAWBERRIES

birds

The essential ingredients for attracting birds to your garden are food (flowering, fruiting and seeding plants), water (especially through the summer months) and shelter. Different birds have different requirements, and the more habitats you can create, the more species you will attract.

- Banksias and grevilleas are particularly attractive to wattlebirds and lorikeets. But if you include other, smaller species in another part of your garden, they will provide food and nesting shelter for honeyeaters, silver-eyes and thornbills. Blue wrens also prefer to nest in small, dense bushes.
- Honeyeaters like anything they can get their beaks into, and they don't mind whether it is a native or an exotic. They love correas, with their nectar-rich, pendulous flowers, as well as kangaroo paws, fuchsias, kniphofias and any other bell-shaped flowers. Chinese lantern bush (*Abutilon* spp.), butterfly bush (*Buddleja* spp.) and camellias are other nectar-rich bushes.
- Native grasses are a good source of food for seed-eating birds such as firetails and finches.

For water, a birdbath or a shallow bowl is generally more appealing than a pond. The birdbath in my mother's garden is so popular with the local bird life that there is often a patient little queue of bathers lined up on the pergola awaiting their turn.

> In a more European style of garden, birds love eating the seeds from ash trees. Fruit trees, grapevines, berry bushes and rosehips will also be an attraction.

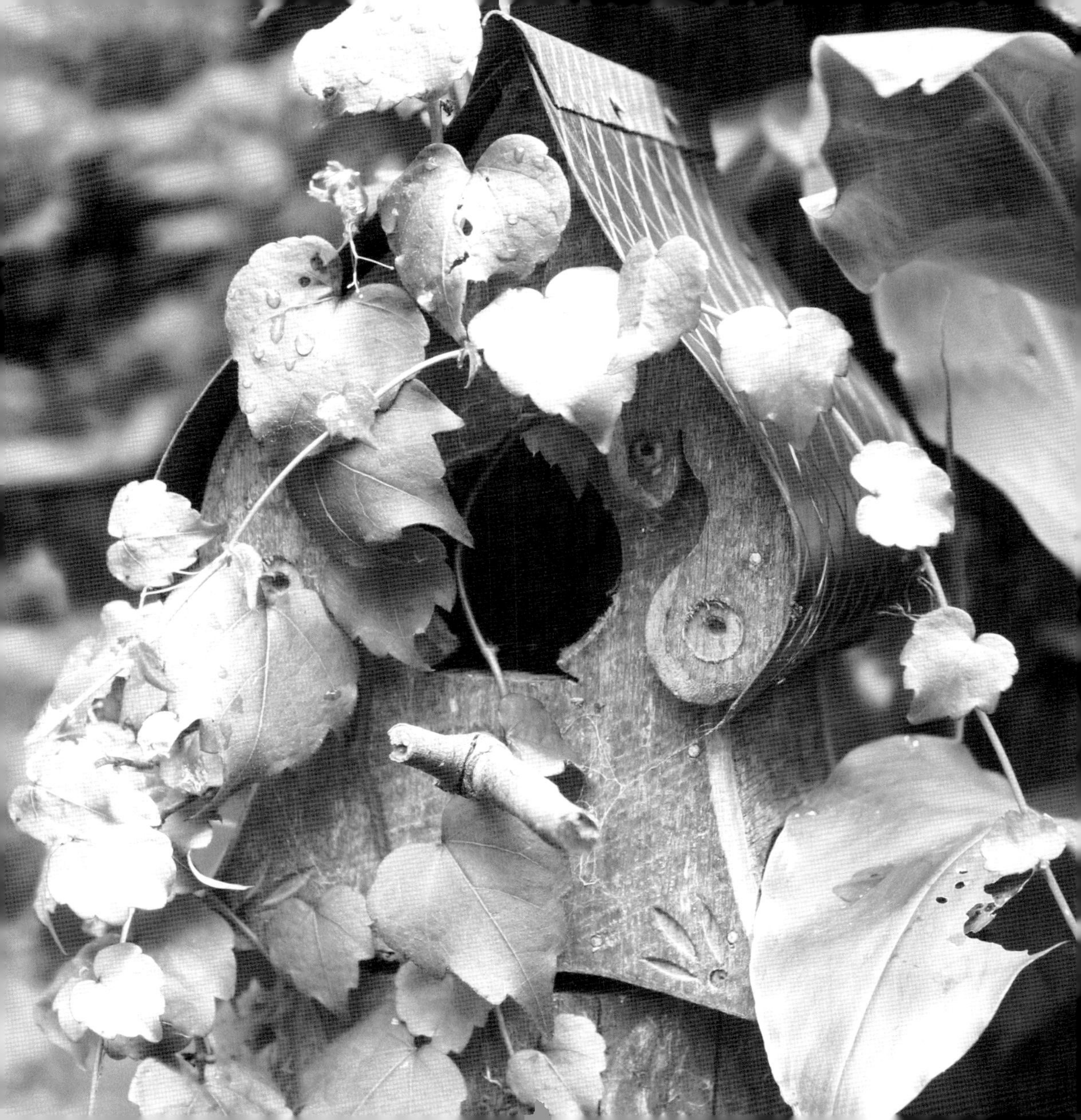

blossom

The ethereal beauty of blossom trees is always a welcome indication that spring is around the corner. A quandary faced by many gardeners is whether to plant trees that flower at a similar time, so that all the flowers appear in one spectacular display, or to plant a variety of trees and shrubs, to extend the garden's blossom season. If you prefer a progressive display, many gardening books include a chart detailing the flowering sequence of various species. But do remember that these charts are a guide only; their accuracy can be affected by seasonal and climatic variations as well as aspect.

You might include three or four blossom trees in a medium to large garden, but a single tree can be used as a feature even in a courtyard. As a rule of thumb, blossom trees prefer full sun, although some northern-hemisphere natives such as dogwoods and magnolias do need some protection from hot conditions.

My favourite blossom trees (in order of flowering sequence):

- Japanese apricot (*Prunus mume*)
- common almond (*Prunus dulcis*)
- flowering crab-apple (*Malus floribunda*)
- Mount Fuji cherry (*Prunus* 'Shirotae')
- Bechtel's crab-apple (*Malus ioensis*)
- white lilac (*Syringa vulgaris* 'Mme Lemoine').

See also: **apples; fruit trees; spring garden**

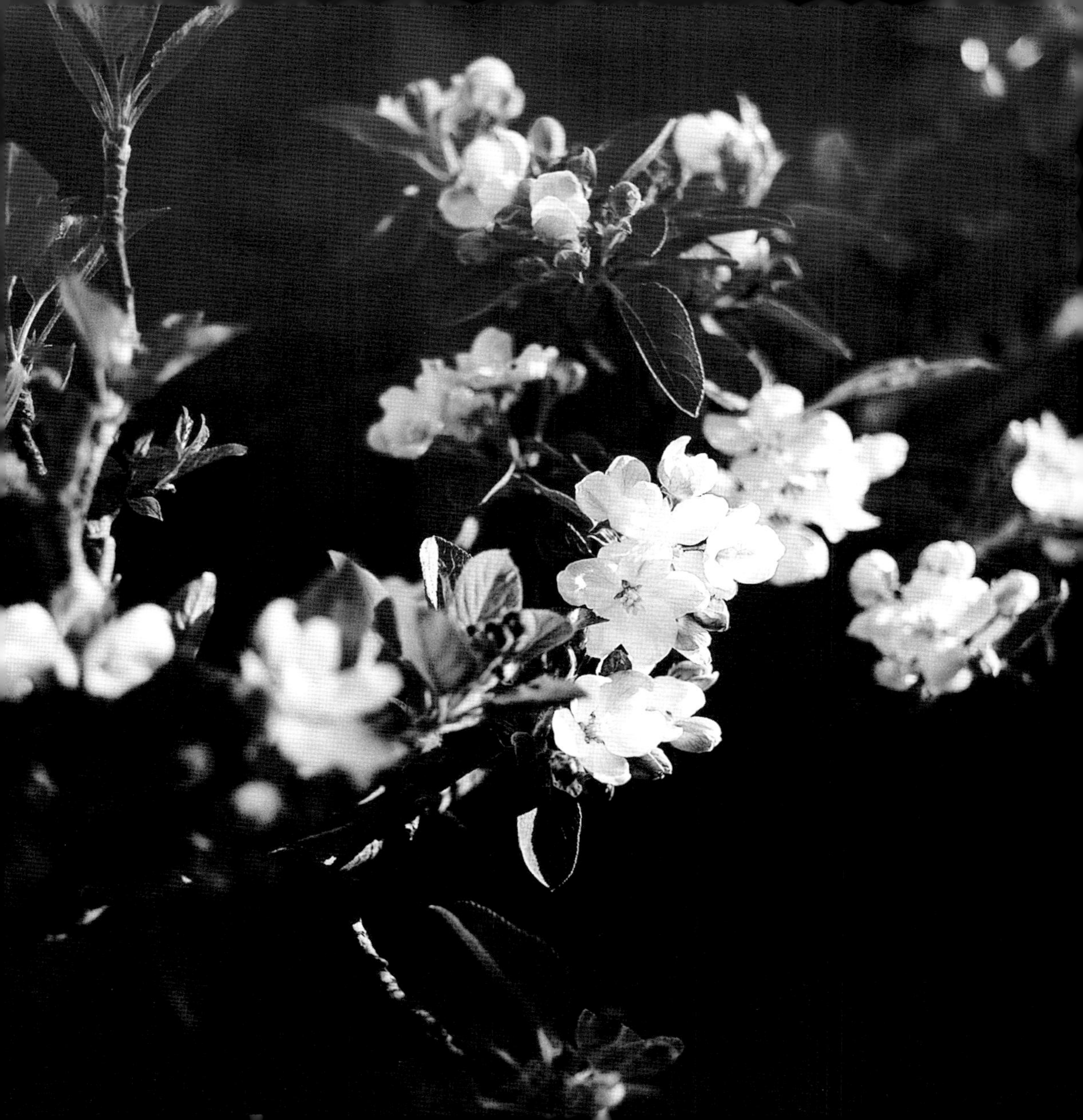

blue flowers

Blue works with almost every other colour and is one of the easiest colours to use in the garden throughout the year.

Winter – *Alyogne hueglii* bears blue hibiscus-like flowers not only in the depths of winter but almost continuously throughout the year. At the end of winter, *Echium candicans* becomes covered with huge blue horns of flowers.
Spring – blue irises bloom in every imaginable shade.
Summer – agapanthus, hydrangeas and the magnificent *Jacaranda mimosifolia* (the best blue display of all) show their true colours.
Autumn – asters start to bloom just as the garden is looking a bit tired at the end of summer, and the inky-blue flowers of *Iochroma cyaneum* add an unusual element.

Red tulips growing out of a sea of blue forget-me-nots, or a huge clump of blue echium flowers contrasting with yellow kniphofias, can be dramatic. Californian lilac (*Ceanothus* spp.) is in bloom at the same time as the lime-green flower heads of *Euphorbia characias* subsp. *wulfenii*; both plants revel in full sun and make a spectacular display when planted together.

The semi-prostrate rosemary 'Blue Lagoon' looks good contrasted with orange and yellow Californian poppies, or with gazanias and African daisies (*Arctotis* spp.); all have low water requirements and flower at around the same time.

> A bit of repetition is a good thing when it comes to colour. If you are planting a large bush with striking blue flowers, balance it by planting another blue-flowering plant elsewhere in the garden.

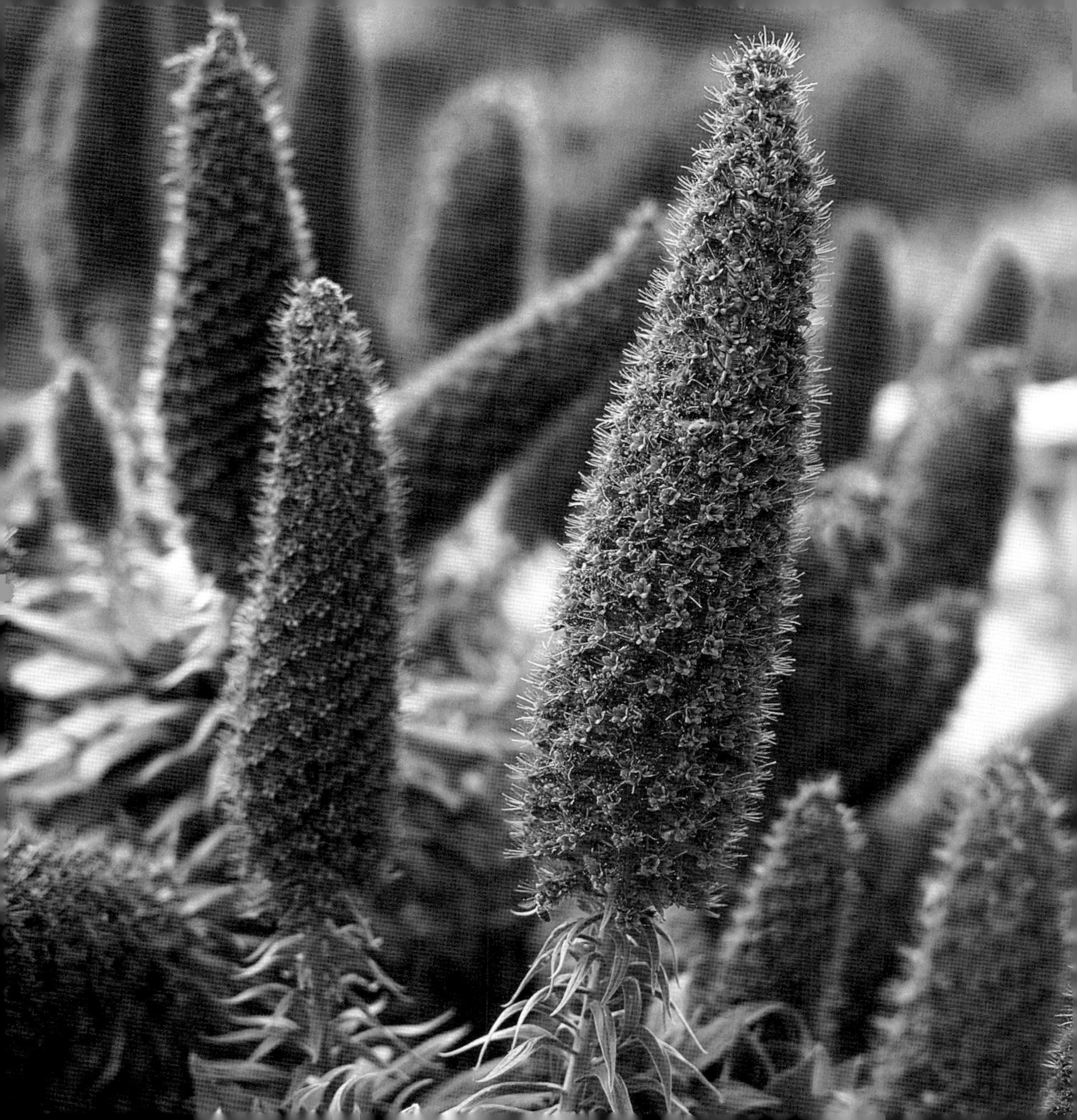

borrowed landscape

I once designed a garden that included several trees with crimson autumn foliage. In late autumn, I received a call from the delighted garden owner, complimenting me on my choice; the huge elms in the street had golden autumn foliage that contrasted splendidly with the crimson within the garden. Without realising it, I had made use of a borrowed landscape. Over the years I have become increasingly aware of how important the landscape beyond the garden can be, and how much we can benefit from a design that draws distant views into our garden setting.

Many large European gardens include borrowed landscapes of adjacent valleys or city views. And in England you will often see a ha-ha (a wall or fence sunk in a ditch or depression) around a country garden; below the level of the lawn or garden bed, the ha-ha is invisible from the house and the garden seems to flow out into the landscape beyond. Similarly, a wet-edge swimming pool built on the edge of a cliff seems at one with the sea. But borrowed landscapes can also be extremely useful in making small gardens seem larger. For example, a mirrored door in a garden wall can appear to lead to a garden beyond, creating an illusion of a much larger space.

In North Queensland, where I used to live, a friend lived next to the local botanic gardens. Rather than separating his garden, he moved his lawn and planted his plot to give the appearance that the botanic gardens were an extension of his own.

Although visually wonderful, the downside of my friend's borrowed landscape was that groups of people would wander through his garden at odd times of the day, thinking they were still in the botanic gardens.

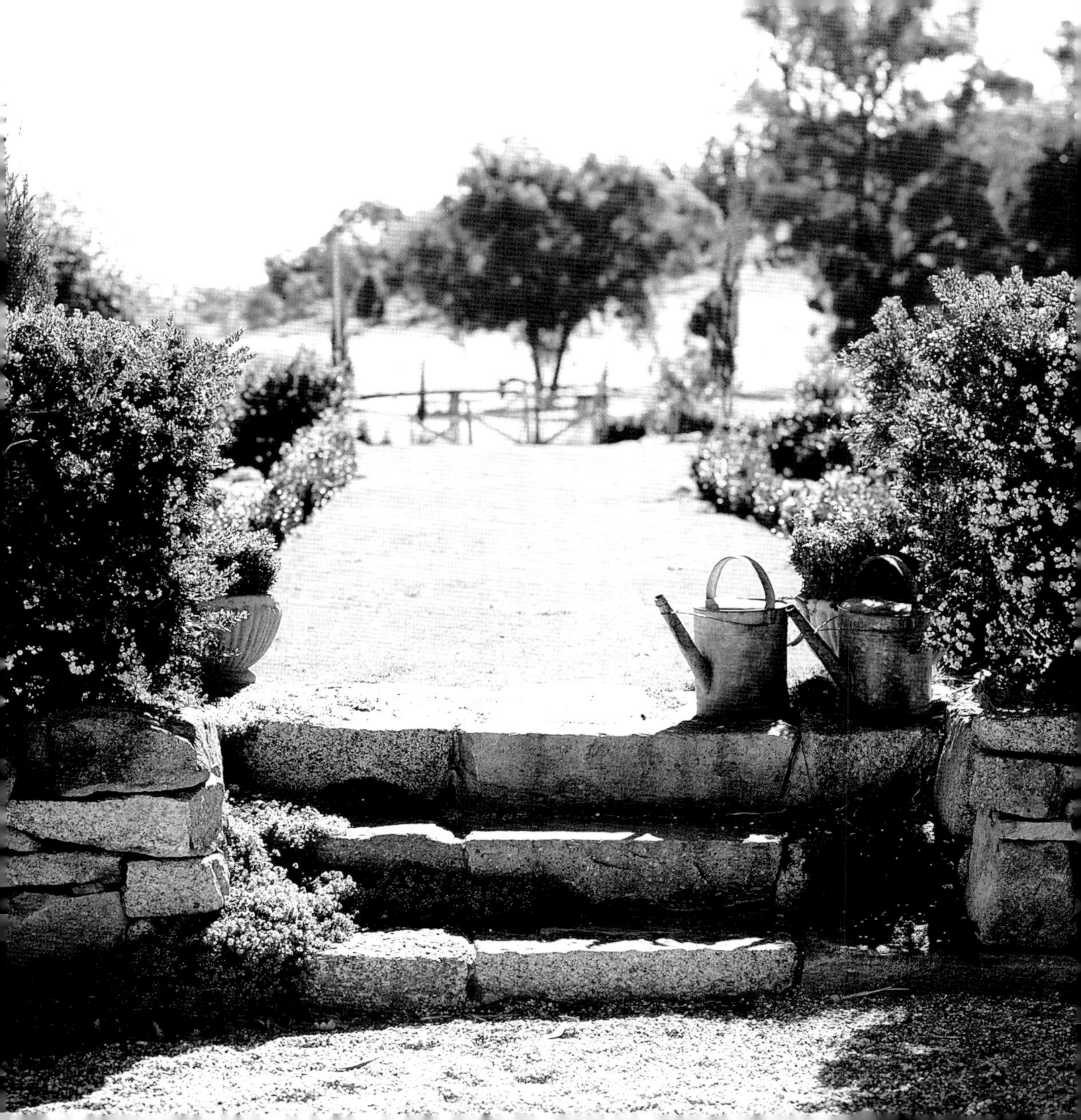

bulbs

Bulbs are the novice gardener's best friend. They arrive properly prepared with next year's flower neatly packaged inside; all you have to do is plant them the right way up. But many gardeners ask why their bulbs flower beautifully the first year and only produce an occasional flower the next. The reason and the solution are simple.

All bulbs need a period of dormancy to recharge their batteries. For spring-flowering bulbs such as daffodils (*Narcissus* spp.), lack of flowers is almost always a result of over-watering during summer and autumn, when they are dormant. In contrast, summer-flowering bulbs such as storm lilies (*Zephyranthes candida*) and Asiatic lilies (*Lilium asiaticum*) don't like too much water during winter. Over-watering problems most often arise in gardens with automatic sprinkler systems.

The solution is to either lift your bulbs when they have died down after flowering, or turn your sprinklers off during their dormant times. If you lift them, store them in a paper bag in a cool, dry, dark place. But remember that bulbs are a 'use 'em or lose 'em' proposition; left unplanted, few will survive more than one season.

Do not lift your bulbs or cut back the foliage while it is still green, as these leaves are the bulbs' solar receptors and collect energy for next year's flowering. Also, resist the temptation to tie the foliage in knots as it dries off. Instead, take a leaf and tie it loosely around the others – a bit like a hatband. If growing your bulbs in pots, feed them with a slow-release fertiliser and keep them in a cool, shaded position.

> To bring out the best in your tulips, store the bulbs in a paper bag in the crisper part of your fridge for 4–6 weeks before planting.

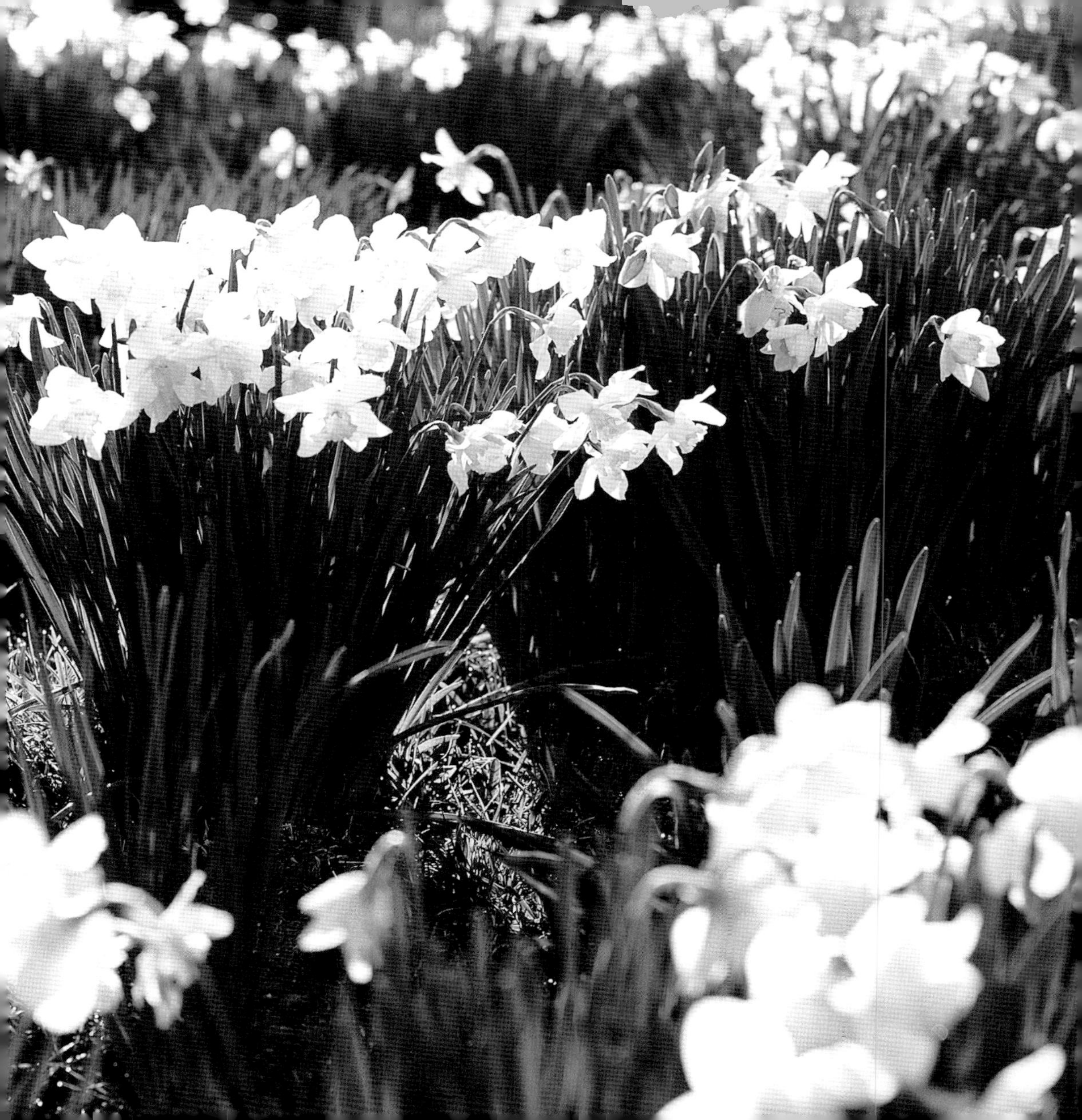

camellias

With almost 300 species and innumerable cultivars, camellias are probably the world's most popular cultivated plant, after roses. Famous for their glossy green foliage and beautiful flowers, these natives of the mountainous regions of East Asia flower during the cooler months of the year. Camellias are a lot hardier than many people give them credit for, and will survive quite happily in all but the coldest or driest climates.

Most gardeners would be familiar with the many *Camellia japonica* varieties, but it would be a shame to miss out on the numerous other species available.

- Many of the *C. sasanqua* and *C. hiemalis* varieties have the most exquisite perfume, particularly *C.* × *hiemalis* 'Showa-no-sakae'. Although its dusky-pink flowers do not present well in a vase, they make an attractive table centrepiece floating in a small bowl of water. Other cultivars with similar habits are 'Shishigashira' (with its deeper pink flowers) and the beautiful white variety 'Mine-no-yuki' (spectacular in flower but lacking perfume).
- Some of the smaller species such as *C. lutchuensis* and *C. tsaii* also have a lovely scent.
- The later-flowering *C. reticulata* varieties make up for any lack of smell with larger and more spectacular flowers.
- 'Magnoliiflora' (or *C. japonica* 'Hagoromo') has sublime, creamy-pink magnolia-like flowers. ('Hagoromo', in Japanese, describes the raiment of an angel – a good description, in my opinion.)

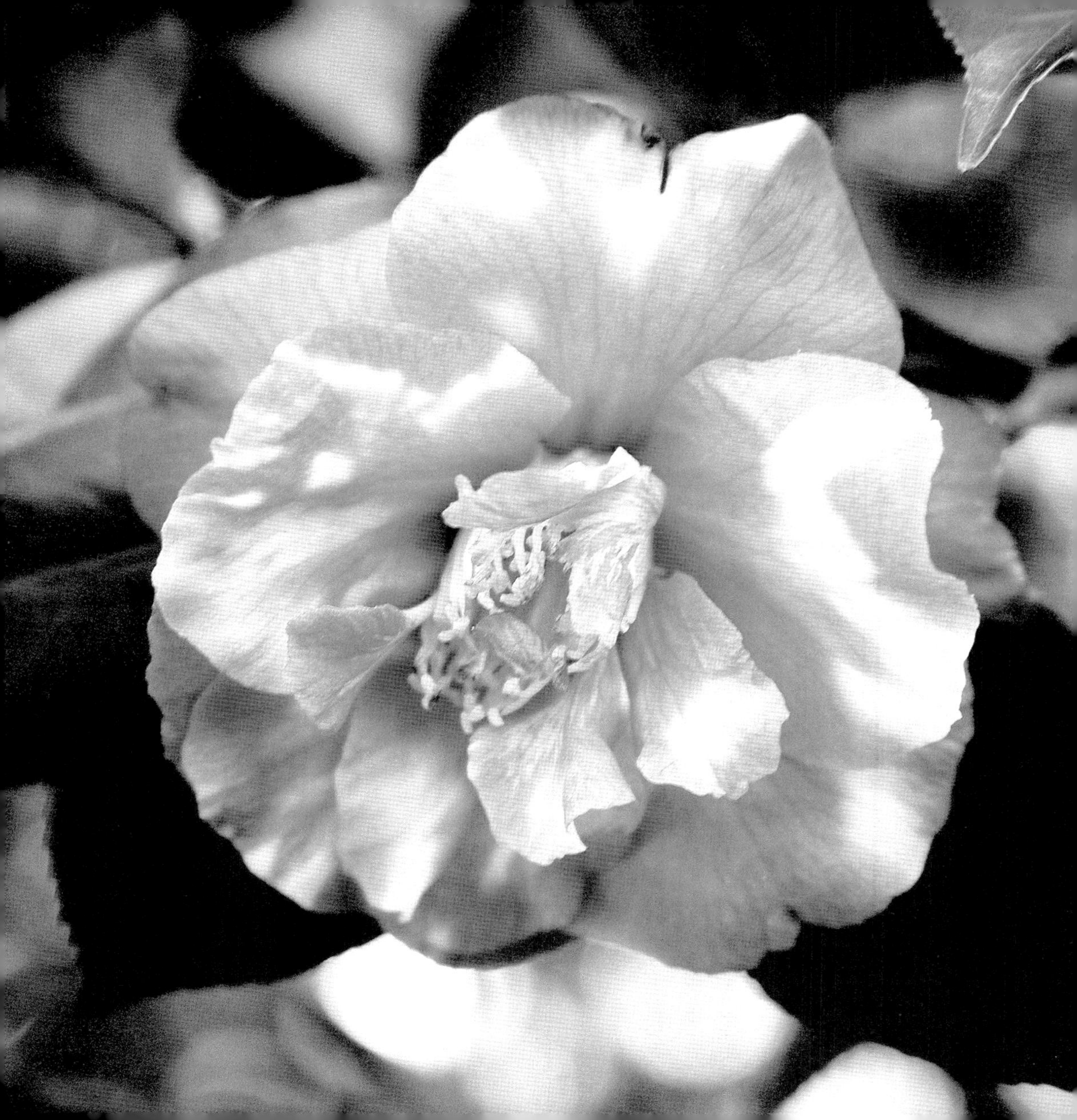

children's garden

More often than not, children from gardening families grow up to love gardening themselves. The scent as I brush past tomatoes, the taste of freshly picked strawberries and peas straight from the pod, and the feel of pulling carrots, all bring back vivid and happy childhood memories of time spent in my grandmother's vegetable garden.

A great way to encourage a love of gardening is to make space for children to have their own little vegetable plots. Carrots, radishes and lettuces are fast-growing and don't take up too much space; they can even be grown successfully in pots or polystyrene boxes. Strawberries, always a winner, can also be grown in containers. And if you haven't room for fruit trees, you could always espalier them on a fence or wall.

When designing a garden for a family with young children, I try to amalgamate a play area into the overall scheme. A low hedge in front of the area means that the children can still be seen while their toys are hidden from view behind the hedge. Pelargonium hedges work well – they are hardy enough to take a bit of bashing, and they regrow quickly. Also, children love scented plants, and the leaves of various pelargonium species carry the scent of rose, apple, lemon, peppermint and nutmeg, making them an ideal choice for a bit of sandpit cookery!

Elements that help to create a sense of adventure in the garden are paths that lead through the back of beds, safe climbing trees and small areas of privacy.

See also: **lettuce and other leafy greens; no-dig garden; root vegetables; tactile garden**

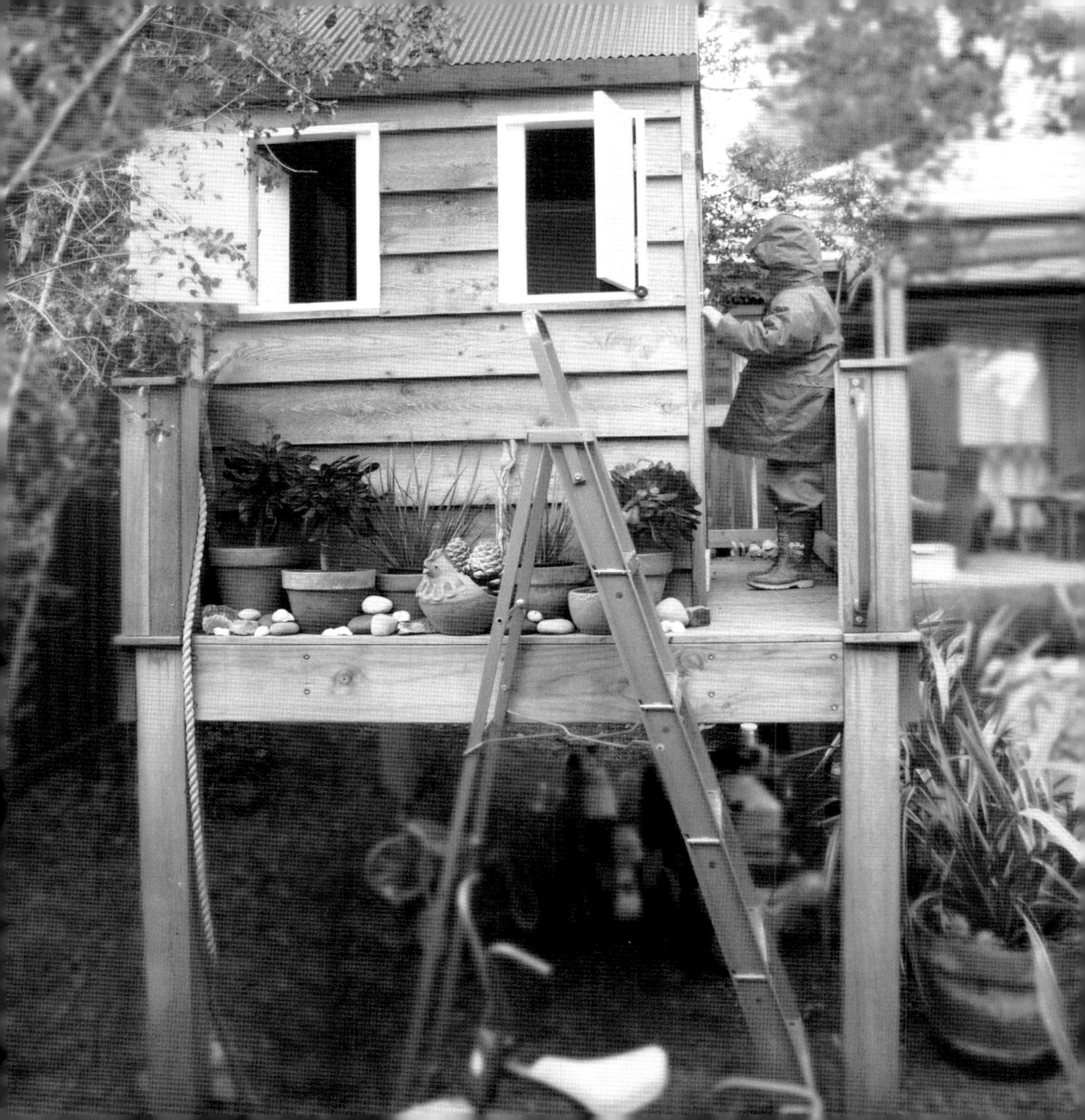

climbers

I think of climbers as the curtains in a garden room. They can cover ugly fences, grow up trellises to provide privacy, climb over pergolas to give shade in summer, and generally add a softness to the garden as a whole.

Summer shade can be provided by a deciduous climber such as wisteria, or a grapevine over a pergola that is attached to the back of the house. During the winter the branches are bare, allowing winter sun into the back rooms. I particularly like the crimson glory vine (*Vitis coignetiae*), an ornamental grape that is quite vigorous but easy to control with pruning. It has huge leaves that turn a brilliant shade of scarlet in autumn.

Screening is best achieved with a fast-growing evergreen. Potato vine (*Solanum jasminoides*), with its lovely white flowers, is excellent but does need to be clipped regularly. It flowers continuously, even in quite shady positions.

Fences can be clad with edible climbers such as passionfruit or kiwifruit (bearing in mind that kiwifruit requires both male and female plants to produce fruit). It is not necessary to tack up wire netting on the fence or wall; strong wires about 45 cm apart will be adequate to tie up your climbers.

Jasmine is available in many varieties, all of which are sweetly scented. *Jasminum polyanthum* is one of the true harbingers of spring. It is a tough plant and needs hard cutting back after flowering. *Jasminum azoricum* is slower growing and not so invasive; it flowers for an extended period from early summer to autumn.

See also: **perfumed plants; screening; walls**

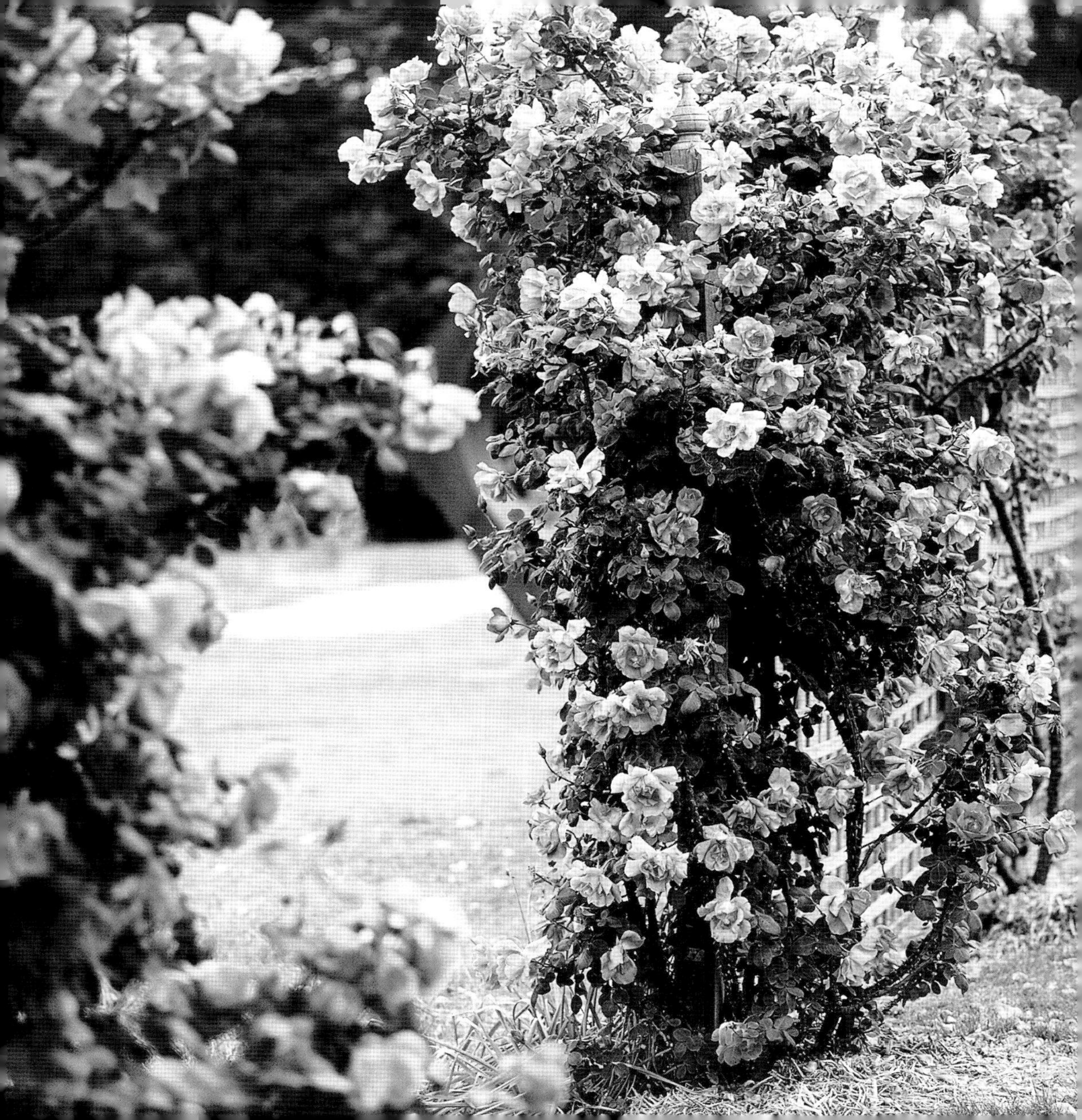

clivias

For the last 50 years or so, clivias have been the poor relations – neglected under trees in old gardens and relegated to the tip when the garden is rejuvenated. But now that strong colours are fashionable again and drought-tolerant plants are appreciated not only for their hardiness but for their aesthetic qualities, clivias have regained their rightful place in the garden-plant hierarchy.

Native to South Africa, clivias thrive in dry, shady conditions where most other plants would turn up their toes. They do, however, need to be protected from frost. They generally flower from late winter through to early spring and, after flowering, produce bright-red seed heads that are almost as beautiful as the colourful orange, red or yellow flowers. They also make excellent pot plants.

- *Clivia miniata* is the most commonly grown and showiest variety. Growing to around 45 cm in height, it bears clusters of predominantly orange tubular flowers.
- Many cultivars have now been developed and a number of hybrid forms are available with bigger, brighter and bolder blooms. For those who really can't stand orange in their garden, more yellow, cream and red varieties are being bred. In particular, *Clivia miniata* 'Aurea' is a lovely yellow variety.
- *Clivia nobilis* is a slightly smaller and more slow-growing variety. It bears pendulous, trumpet-shaped pale-scarlet flowers tipped with green.

Propagate clivias by dividing them after flowering. They will grow from seed, but these plants can be very slow to flower.

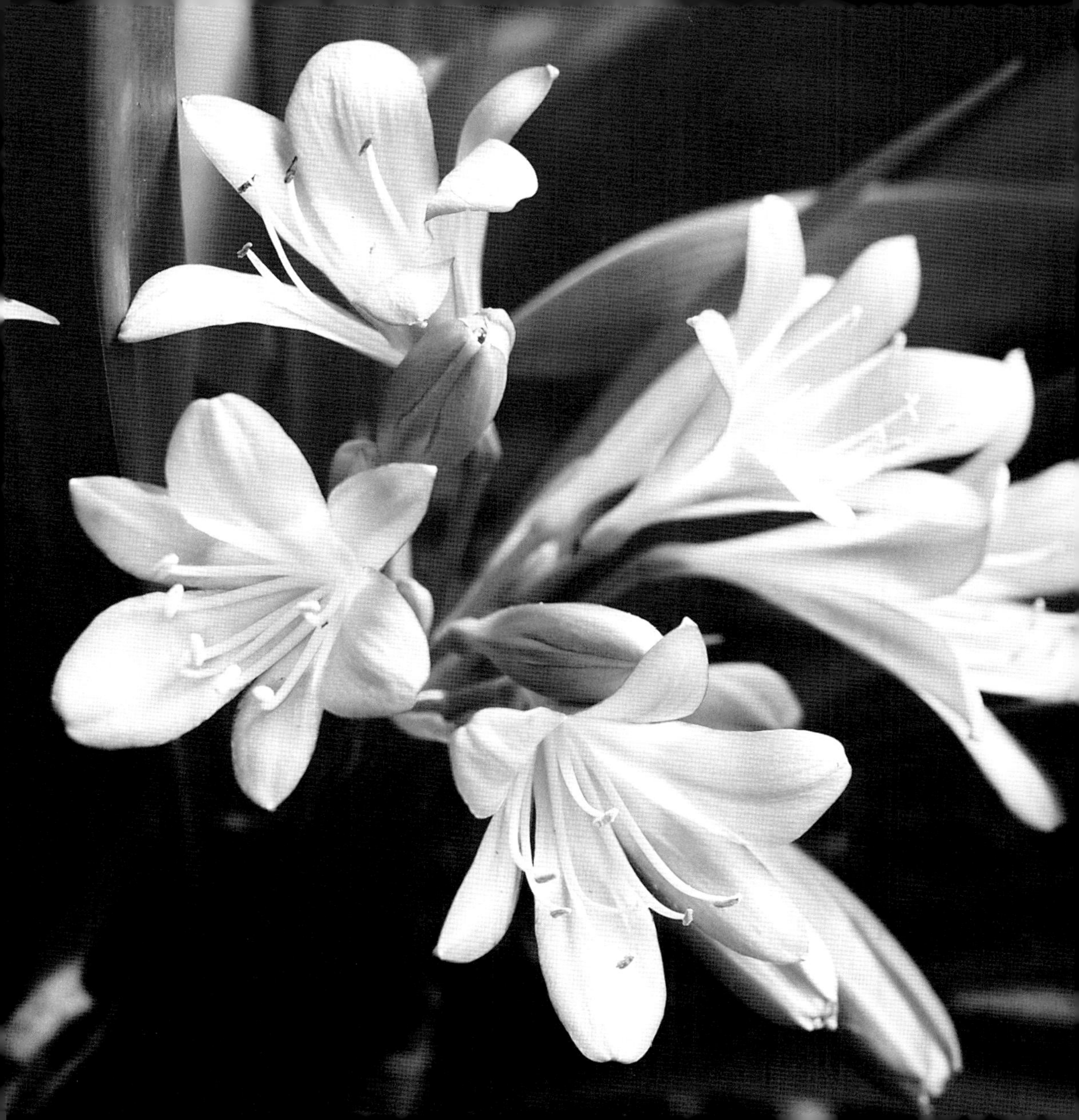

colour in the garden

As it is elsewhere, colour in the garden is a matter of taste. Treat your garden as you would the interior of your house; choose a colour scheme and work within it.

My mother's garden is terraced up a hill. From her kitchen window, her vegetable garden is quite close, on the other side of a path and at eye level. She has decided to include in it only plants with flowers of orange, yellow or blue – strong colours that stand out and make a kind of stage of the garden. 'Blue Lagoon' rosemary, orange and yellow marigolds, and Californian poppies carry on the colour scheme in the shrubbery behind.

I'm always surprised at the proliferation of pastel colours in Australian gardens. In England and Europe, these colours are more appropriate because the diffused light means that brighter colours can appear gaudy. But in Australia and other countries with a similar climate, the scope for variability is greater and we should not be afraid to take advantage of it. Particularly in the city and suburbs, we need to be more courageous in our choice of garden plants!

> In a recent garden design, I included bright-red canna lilies and deep-yellow daylilies in front of a large sweep of palm grass (*Setaria palmifolia*), beneath a jacaranda. The oatmeal-coloured heads of the palm grass and vivid red and yellow of the lilies made quite a statement against the deep blue-grey of the fence behind, with the blue of the jacaranda an added bonus.

See also: **daylilies; white flowers**

companion planting

Companion planting involves growing particular plants together to achieve better results. It works by increasing the productivity and health of the soil and the plants that grow in it. Nowadays, with the emphasis on high-yield production and single-plant crops, the balance of nature tends to be overlooked in the commercial world. But we can still practise this beneficial routine in our own garden plots.

- Some plants act as nurturers by stimulating the growth of their neighbours – foxgloves, marigolds, marjoram and oregano.
- Others increase flavour and productivity – borage improves the flavour of tomatoes.
- Some attract beneficial insects – squash and strawberries attract bees.
- Others repel destructive insects by masking the scent of their companion plants – garlic helps keep aphids away from roses and grapes, and is also said to improve the perfume of roses; nasturtiums planted under fruit trees deter codlin moth grubs, woolly aphids and ants; rosemary repels sap-sucking insects and is a perfect choice for a hedge around your vegetable garden; basil is a good companion plant for most vegetables (especially tomatoes), as it helps deter aphids and whitefly.
- Diseases can also be fought with companion plants. Horehound grown under peach trees is reputed to help fight leafcurl, while chives under apple trees help control scab.

See also: **herbs; organic garden; tomatoes**

compost

If you want to make good compost, a recipe is a must. The one I use was pioneered many years ago by Sir Albert Howard, the founder of the organic farming movement. To contain the heap and keep the layers level using Howard's method (below), make your compost in any solid structure with three sides and an open front.

1. **Pile** garden waste (this might consist of anything that was once alive, although care should be taken if using meat scraps, as they can attract blowflies and other scavengers) to about 15 cm.
2. **Add** about 5 cm of animal manure.
3. **Add** 1 cm of topsoil, a sprinkling of garden lime and perhaps a little blood and bone or another high-nitrogen fertiliser.
4. **Repeat** 1–3 until you have a heap about 1 m high.
5. **Turn** the heap after two or three weeks, and then again after another five weeks, so that what was on the bottom is now on the top.
6. **Leave** the heap for another two months or so, or until it has degraded sufficiently that the original components are no longer recognisable. Your compost is now ready for the garden.

Troubleshooting compost:
- If your compost smells, it may not be getting enough air; turn the heap to give it more oxygen. Or, it may be too wet; improve drainage under the heap or add some dry material such as dry grass clippings.
- A heap that includes fresh animal manure and green waste is unlikely to become too dry, but you can sprinkle it with a hose if necessary.

- The temperature of the heap should get to about 82°C. In winter, it may be necessary to cover the compost with something to retain warmth.
- Theoretically, the heat of most compost heaps should take care of any diseased plant material that is included, but I prefer not to tempt fate; either burn diseased material or discard it with the rubbish.
- Dog droppings take longer to break down than most other material in the heap, and I think they're better dealt with by a worm farm or a smaller, stand-alone compost pile.
- Try not to introduce invasive weeds such as morning glory, oxalis or tradescantia to the heap – you may end up transplanting them all over the garden.
- Anything too coarse added to the heap is unlikely to break down; a suitable shredder is a good investment for the compostoholic.

Stinging nettles and valerian hasten the process of breakdown in the heap and are extremely beneficial in making good compost.

See also: **fruit trees; mulch; soil; worms**

courtyards

Courtyards have been a feature of homes for thousands of years, particularly in warmer countries conducive to outdoor living. For the growing number of people living in townhouses and apartments, courtyards are often their only private outdoor space. If you can, include the elements below in your courtyard.

Walls necessarily enclose a courtyard so you may as well make the most of them. Ornamental latticework and timberwork, painted or rendered finishes and laser-cut steel can all be used to great effect.
Water trickling is the most relaxing sound on a warm summer's night. Along with more traditional styles, there are many fabulous modern water features available.
Night-scented flowers are a boon if you spend most of your day at work. Plant your courtyard with species such as angels' trumpets (*Brugmansia* spp.), frangipani (*Plumeria* spp.) or night-scented jessamine (*Cestrum nocturnum*), and jasmine or honeysuckle for the walls. Citrus trees in pots also look good and the scent of their blossom is a bonus.
Furniture must be chosen carefully because everything in a space as small as a courtyard is under scrutiny. It is worth saving up to buy something that looks good, and is long-lasting and comfortable. The same is true for pots, which are a fabulous addition if they look good but undermine the space if not.

See also: **fruit trees; walls; water features**

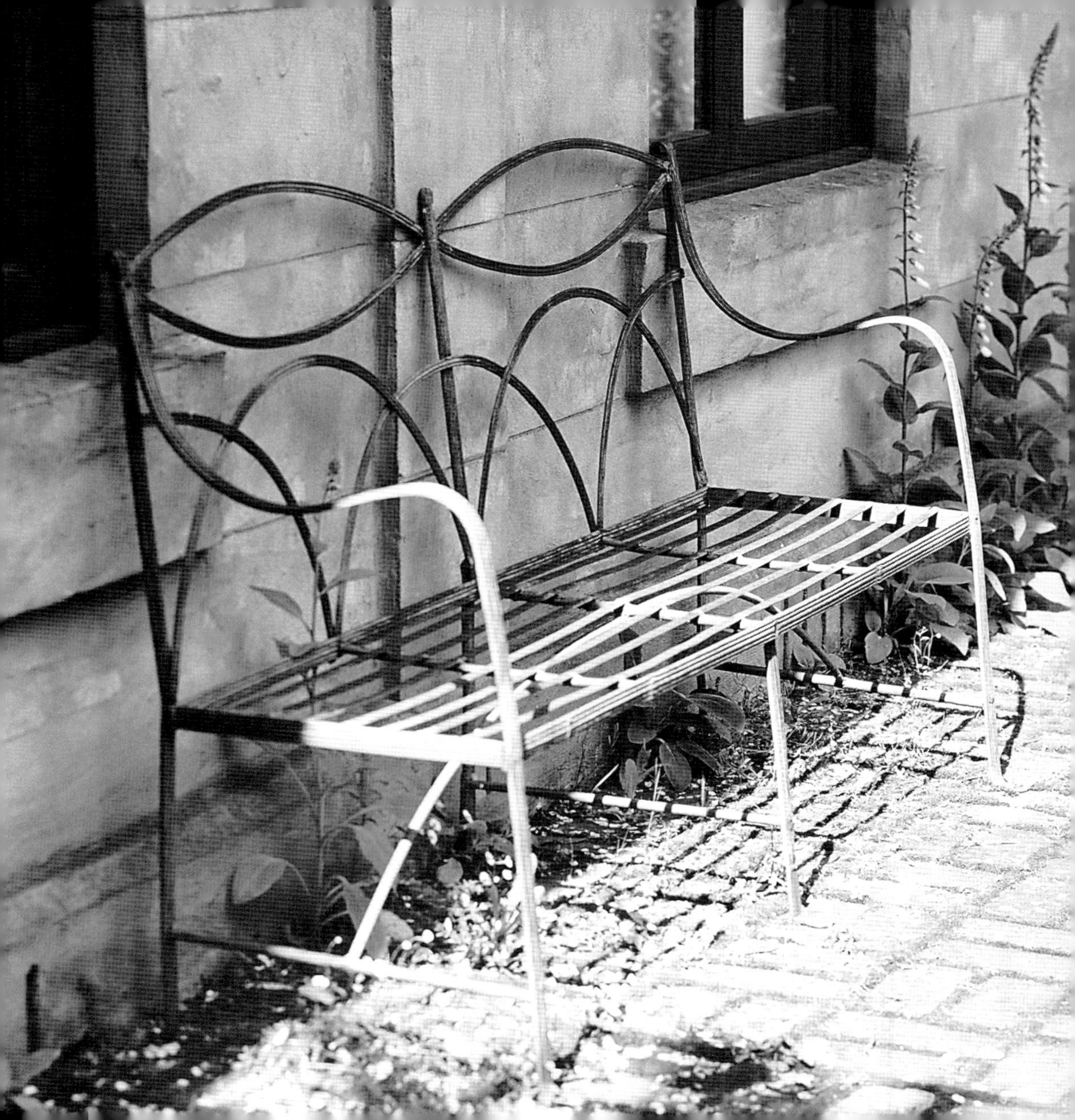

cut flowers

There is nothing more disappointing than arranging a vase of beautiful flowers only to find them flopped all over the place a couple of days later. There are several things you can do to ensure that your cut flowers last longer:

1. **Pick** the flowers first thing in the morning, before the heat of the sun has caused evaporation. If you can't arrange them straight away, at least put them in water.
2. **Cut** the stems cleanly and on an angle, above the cut you made when you originally picked them.
3. **Seal** the stems of flowers such as dahlias, Iceland poppies (*Papaver nudicaule*) and hellebores over a gas stove, or by quickly dipping the stems into boiling water and then plunging them into cold water. Lilac and hydrangeas don't seem to last as well unless you hammer the cut stems.
4. **Use** cut-flower solution (below) to preserve the flowers longer. Sugar feeds the flowers, vinegar keeps the water slightly acidic, and bleach prevents the build-up of bacteria (which makes the water smell and kills the flowers).

cut-flower solution

2 tsp sugar

4 tsp vinegar

4 drops household bleach

Add the above to one litre of water for your vase. Top up the water as necessary.

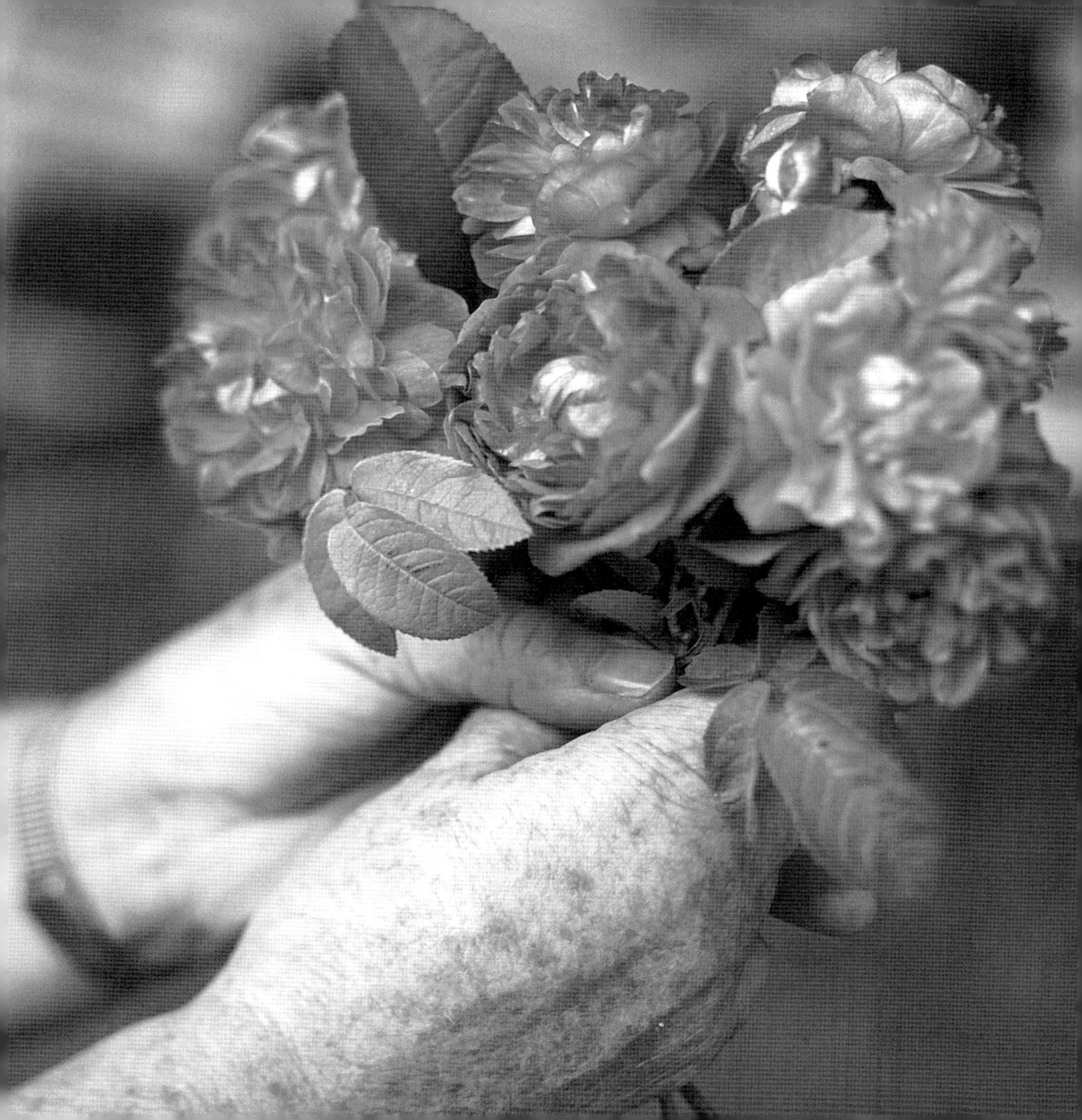

daylilies

Daylilies (*Hemerocallis* spp.) are not a lily, in fact, but a fibrous-rooted perennial. They work well in mixed or herbaceous borders, and dwarf daylilies are ideal for small gardens or pots.

The plant has been around for over 2000 years. Its name comes from the Greek 'hemero', meaning day, and 'callis', meaning beauty, because the blooms on the original species last only for a day. Modern hybrids, however, can flower almost continually for months on end; while each individual bloom still lasts only a day, each stem can have up to 30 buds, and each clump might have quite a few of these flowering stems. In all, this adds up to a lot of flowering days! Similarly, daylilies used only to come in shades of yellow, orange and red, but with hybridisation it is now possible to get them in almost any colour except blue.

Daylilies are tough, forgiving plants that will grow virtually anywhere except in deep shade. Although originally native to temperate East Asia, modern hybrids are tolerant of extremes of heat and cold, and will deal with both dry and wet conditions. They are relatively free of pests and diseases; the only real problems are aphids, which can easily be hosed off, and spider mite, which may require periodic spraying with an insecticide such as Confidor.

> Like irises, daylilies need lifting and dividing every three to four years to keep flowering well. They are one of my favourite plants and I use them extensively in most gardens that I design.

See also: **irises**

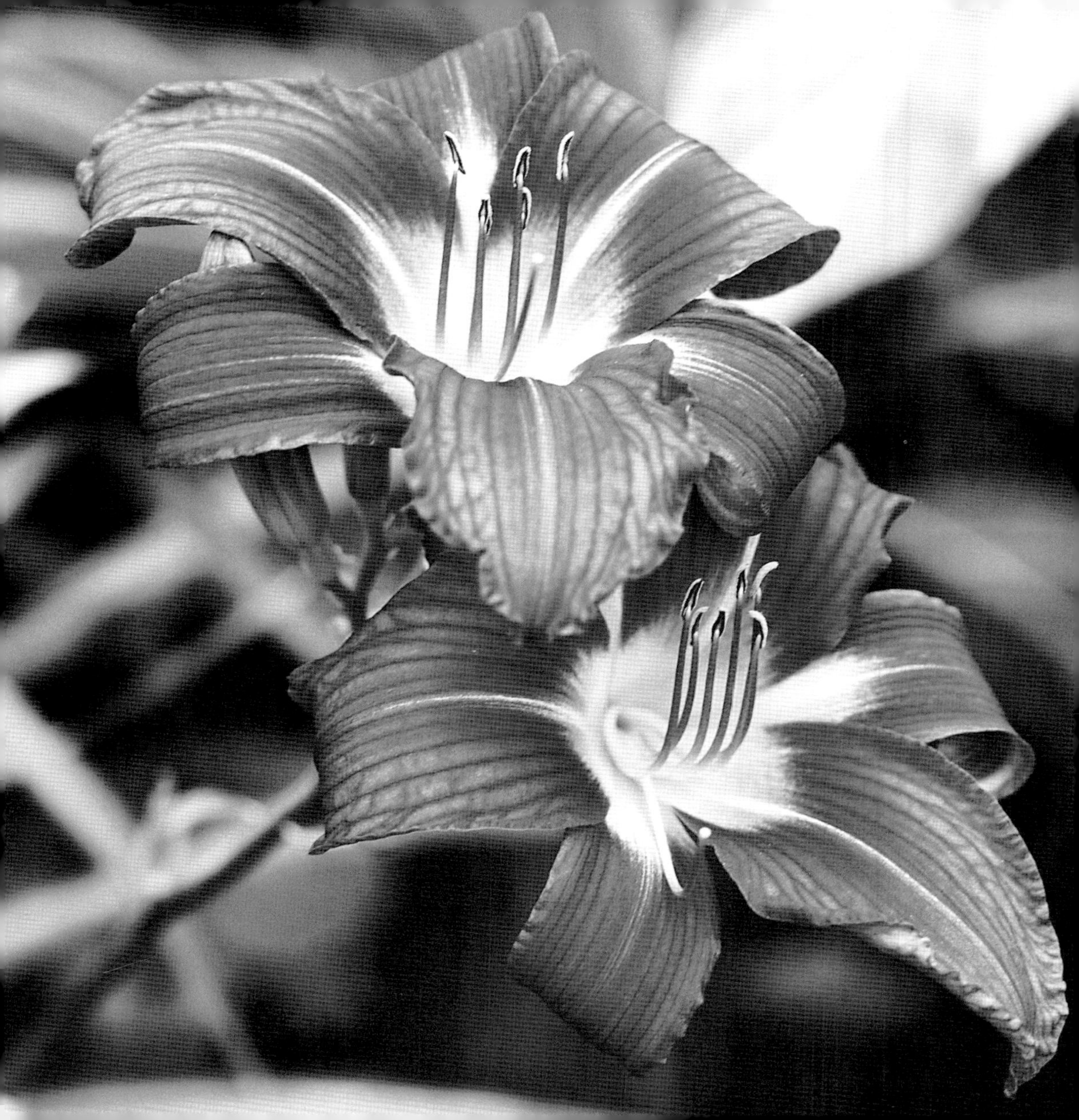

decorative elements

Decorative elements in your garden are like the artworks and finishes that complete your home. But they must be chosen carefully to ensure that they enhance the space. For example, a rustic timber seat will not necessarily suit a formal courtyard, while wrought-iron chairs might fit perfectly; and a rusted metal gate is likely to work better than an ornamental lattice design in a modern seaside garden.

Stone is a key element of many different types of garden. Huge granite boulders look magnificent in larger native gardens and were used extensively in the 1970s. Chinese gardens are often based around stony outcrops, and stone is one of the foundations of Zen garden design, which is becoming increasingly popular in smaller inner-city gardens.

The increased availability of an extensive selection of local and imported natural stone at a competitive price means that it has regained its place as a favoured paving material. It has the benefit of being more durable and colourfast, and ageing better, than manufactured cement pavers.

For walls, modular stone is now available in almost any type. So, those beautiful stone walls you often see in older country gardens may not be out of financial reach after all. Look at any of the gardens by Australian designers Edna Walling and Ellis Stones and be inspired by their beautiful stone walls and steps.

Wood is another cornerstone of garden design in terms of both construction and aesthetics. Australia is fortunate in having some of the most beautiful and durable timbers in the world; what was once a fairly basic jarrah or treated pine deck can now be constructed from larger planks of such lovely recycled timbers as ironbark, tallowwood, spotted gum or grey box. Individual timber features such as sculptures, gates, fences, or even simple logs and stumps, can all be used to great effect in any style of garden.

And we mustn't forget the natural beauty of the trunks of larger trees, and the beneficial branching effect of some of the smaller deciduous species. My personal favourite trunk is the snow gum (*Eucalyptus pauciflora*); it not only develops the most wonderfully twisted shapes but also has exquisitely coloured bark.

Glass is a material much favoured in modern garden design. Sculptors such as Rudi Jass and Warren Langley use glass to stunning effect in their water features and other garden sculptures. Colourful ground glass can be used as path toppings or pond features, or even incorporated into the hard surfaces of swimming pools, walls or paving details. And coloured glass screens can both protect and enhance areas of the garden that are subject to strong winds.

See also: **bark; walls; water features**

drainage

Drainage is to a garden as a foundation is to a house; if it is not adequate, there will be trouble. Like foundations, drainage cannot always be seen and can be very expensive, so there is a temptation to ignore it when creating a garden. But gardeners should never underestimate the importance of drainage as there are few plants that will cope well with soggy conditions.

The need for drainage is not always dictated by the topography of a site. Run-off from other properties and water transferred underground between layers of impervious clay can appear where you least expect it, whether your land is flat, terraced or sloping.

Retaining walls — drainage pipes must be laid behind the walls to prevent build-up of water that will not only have a detrimental effect on your plants but can cause loading stress on the walls.

Paving or other hard surfacing — if you are doing this yourself, use a spirit level to ensure that it is angled away from the house towards a drain.

> Some gardens contain low points from where water cannot drain away. In these cases you have only a few options: build a pit and use a sump pump to draw out the water; dig a deep hole and fill it with scoria to allow the water to dissipate slowly into the soil; or plant a bog garden.

See also: **wet spaces**

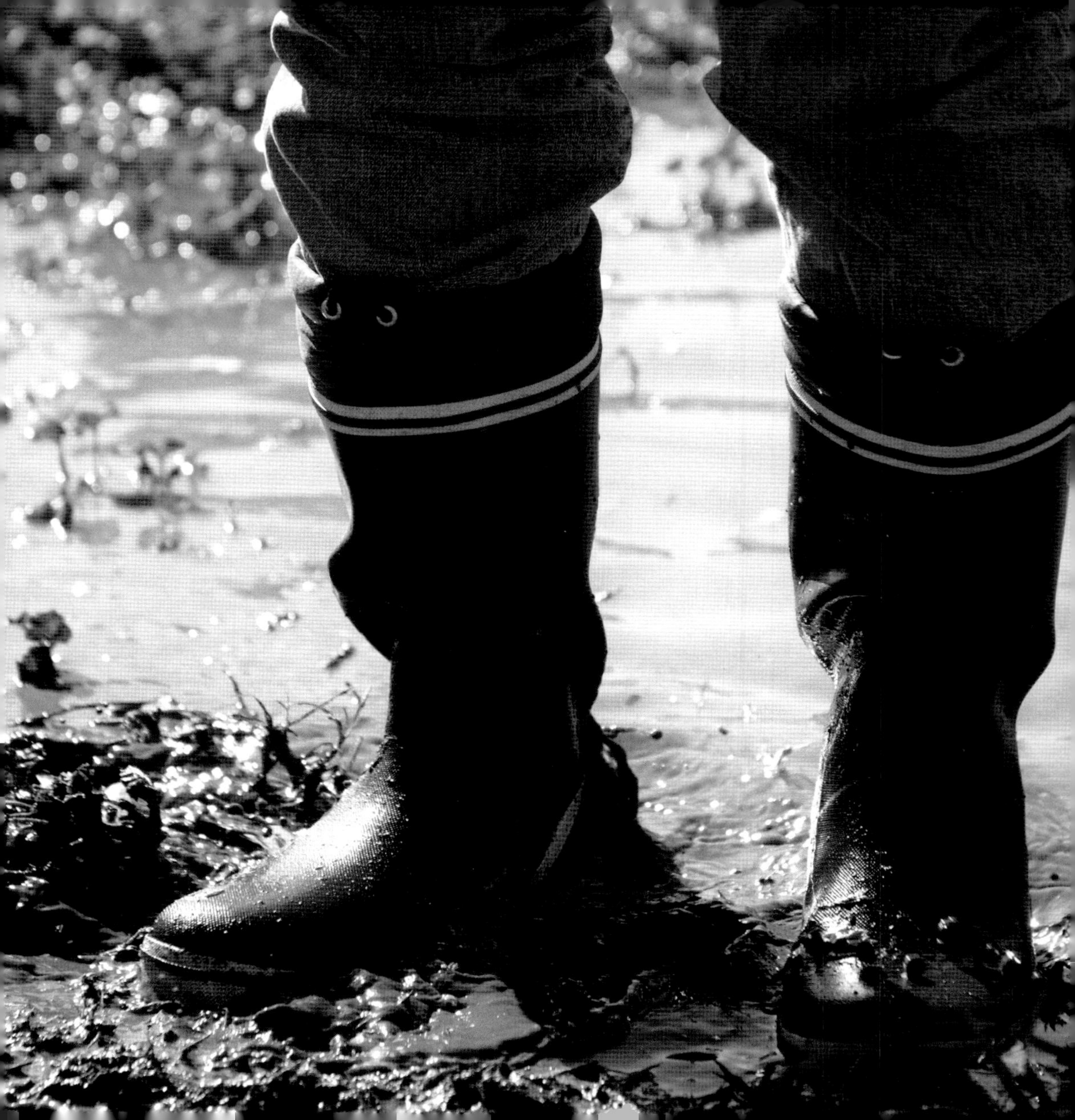

dry spaces

Almost every garden has dry spaces and these spots often let the rest of the garden down. But there are plenty of plants, indigenous to low-rainfall areas, that thrive in dry conditions. Try some of those listed below and the dry spaces in your garden might become its most attractive spots:

- dietes – a tall to medium strappy-leafed perennial that tolerates poor, dry soils and bears iris-like flowers from spring to summer
- succulents – choose between the bright red–orange spikes of *Aloe arborescens*, the grey–blue of the ground-covering *Senecio serpens*, the slightly taller *Cotyledon orbiculata*, the stately *Agave americana* or the grey–green rosettes of echevaria (ideal for rockeries or filling small spaces, its pinkish-orange, yellow-tipped flowers are an added bonus in spring)
- veldt daisy (*Osteospermum* spp.) – comes in shades of pink and mauve as well as a white variety that has a navy centre and dark blue on the underside of the petals; 'Buttermilk' is pale yellow but is more like a small shrub and doesn't spread as obligingly as the other varieties
- African daisy (*Arctotis* spp.) or gazania – the vivid orange, red, yellow and cream spectrum of these species will provide a similar effect to veldt daisy
- *Clivia miniata* – grows well in dry, shady spots and produces huge bracts of orange, red or yellow flowers on short stems in early spring
- plumbago – in summer, its lovely blue or white flowers will cover a dry, shady area under trees very satisfactorily (although it does prefer a bit more sun)

- spiny-headed mat rush (*Lomandra longifolia*) – a hardy Australian native that will handle almost all conditions and produce fragrant cylindrical flowers in yellow or cream during summer
- kniphofia – a hardy, colourful plant that is a favourite with native birds
- *Plectranthus ecklonii* – one of the few plants that will grow happily in dry shade, it is hard to go past in autumn, with its tall spikes of deep purple
- yucca – makes a spectacular pot plant but can also look marvellous planted en masse in a dry area of the garden; in summer, it produces huge, metre-tall, creamy-white flower spikes
- *Iris germanica* – distinctive for its pale, sword-like foliage and stunning flowers that come in almost every colour imaginable, this tough, rhizomatous perennial is happy in almost any sunny situation.

See also: **agapanthus; clivias; irises; kniphofias; native garden; roses; succulents**

espaliers

Espaliering is a method of training and pruning trees or shrubs against a wall or frame to achieve a particular shape. The practice can be traced back to the ancient Egyptians (there is a detail of an espaliered fig on the tomb of the commander-in-chief of the Egyptian army during the reign of Pharaoh Amenophis II). Lemons, apples, pears, cherries, figs, peaches, apricots, plums – all can be espaliered with ease. But the method is not limited to fruit trees; it works with any plant that responds well to pruning.

Espaliering works particularly well in colder areas, where the tree benefits from the reflected warmth of a wall. But wherever they are located, espaliers tend to produce trees with more, and larger, fruit. They make picking fruit and monitoring its health considerably easier, take up less room and are aesthetically attractive.

Shapes can be as diverse as your imagination, provided that the basic tenet of growing is adhered to, i.e. sap rises, so shapes that involve training branches downwards are unlikely to work. Classic shapes are fan or 'informal' (stone fruits seem to espalier best this way, without a central leader); tiered or 'horizontal cordon'; and candelabra. But if you really want to impress your friends, try the striking palmette verrier, or even a latticed espalier fence (apples and pears work best for these patterns).

See also: **fruit trees; walls**

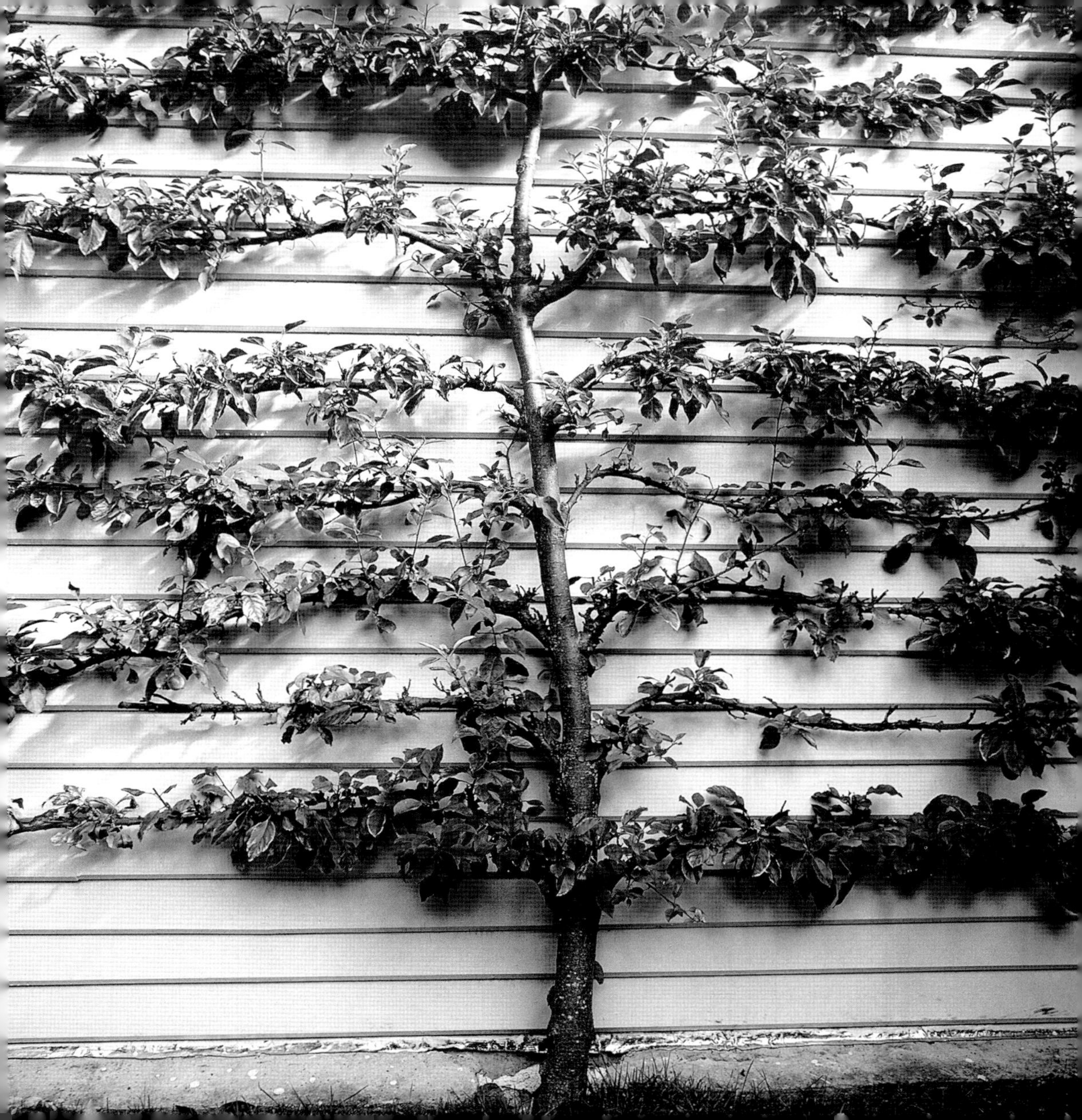

euphorbias

Commonly known as spurges, euphorbias constitute an enormous genus with close to 2000 species of annuals, perennials, shrubs and strange, cactus-like succulents.

- *Euphorbia characias* subsp. *wulfenii* is a large perennial shrub with blue–grey foliage. Happy in full sun or semi-shade, it is drought-tolerant and produces masses of huge, brain-like bracts of yellow–green flowers in spring.
- *E. rigida* is a smaller plant with paler foliage. It prefers full sun and starts to produce its yellow–green flower heads a bit earlier in the year. It makes an excellent edging plant, particularly in dry areas.
- The delightfully named Mrs Robb's bonnet (*E. amygdaloides* var. *robbiae*) forms a carpet of dark-green leafy rosettes, again with yellow–green flower bracts. It works well as a ground cover in a shady position.
- Poinsettia (*E. pulcherrima*) is a well-known subtropical species that makes a lovely indoor plant in colder areas and is distinctive for its new foliage, which is coloured flame-red and cream.
- African milk tree (*E. trigona*) is a mid-sized, spiny upright succulent that makes an excellent pot specimen.
- *E. horrida*, *E. obesa* and *E. misera* are less commonly grown; their names might suggest why.

The one thing that all euphorbias have in common is a caustic, milky sap that can cause skin irritation and, if rubbed in the eyes, cause temporary blindness in some people. They are also likely to cause severe discomfort if eaten.

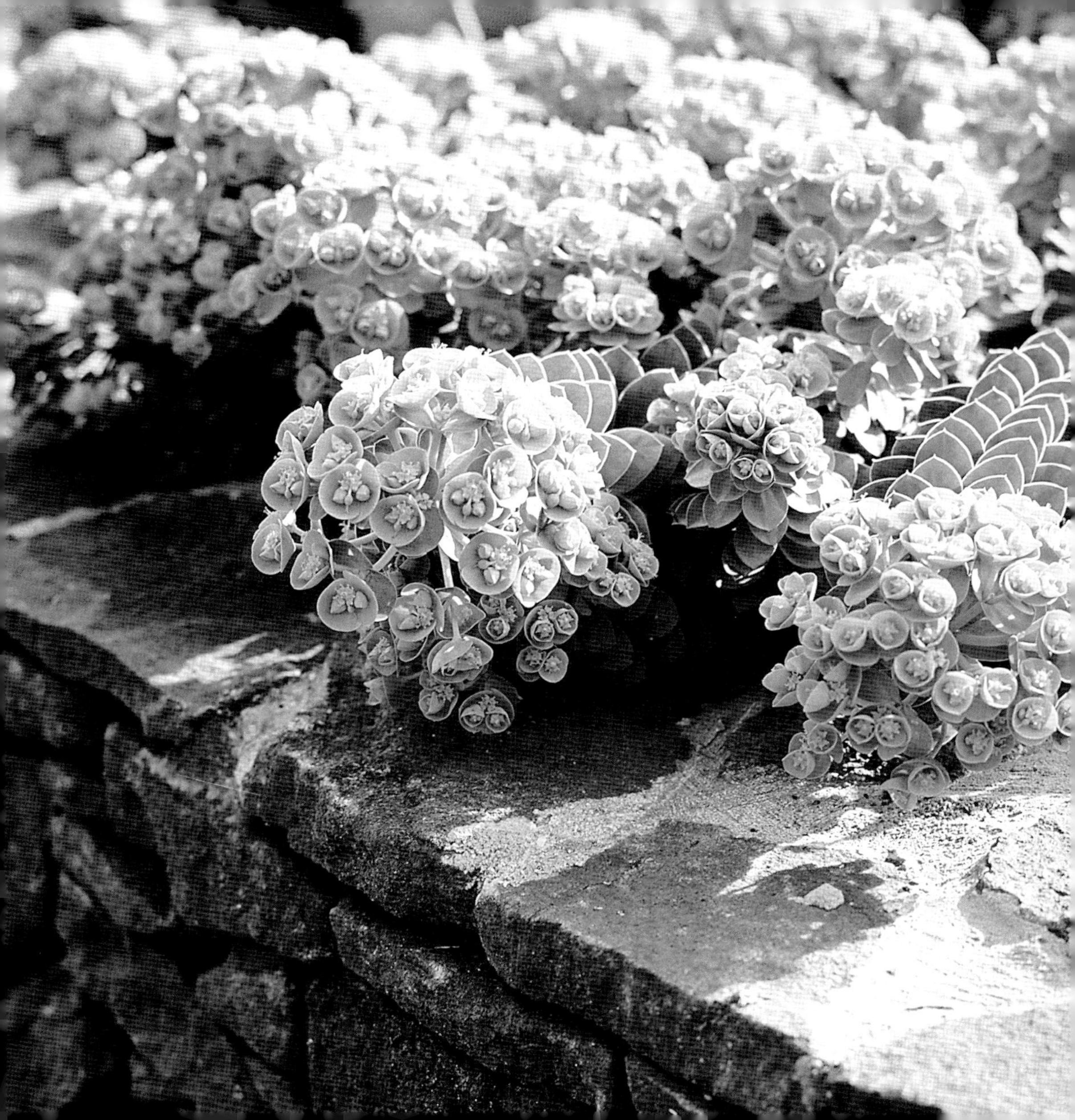

fertiliser

Plants need a wide range of trace elements and nutrients in order to grow. Most of these are already found in variable quantities in garden soil. But the primary growing requirements of nitrogen, phosphorus and potassium (potash), or NPK as they are jointly referred to, are used in greater quantities than the rest and need regular replacement.

Nitrogen aids green-leaf development, phosphorus helps root development, and potash promotes flower and fruit development. The NPK ratio on a bag of fertiliser tells you what percentages of the elements the fertiliser contains. For example:

- urea (38:0:0) contains a lot of nitrogen and virtually nothing else, making it suitable for green-leaf development in cases such as yellow lawns or yellow citrus in pots
- complete garden fertiliser (6:3:10) is suitable for most plants, encourages flowers and fruit, and strengthens and improves colour
- lawn starter (16:10:8) has a high phosphorus content to aid root development
- sulphate of potash and other soluble flower- or fruit-promoting fertilisers (0:0:48) do just that!

In normal situations, gardens only need to be fertilised with a complete fertiliser twice a year. I use a blood-and-bone-based mixture with added potash in a ratio of 3:1.

> Look after your garden's diet as you do your own: all things in moderation. Feeding your garden solely with a high-potash fertiliser thinking you will get fabulous flowers is like eating nothing but carrots and thinking you will have fabulous eyesight.

foliage

Many gardeners put much more thought into the flowers than the foliage in their garden design. But plants only flower for part of the year, while foliage is visible year-round (except for deciduous plants). So, when planning your garden, be aware of the ways in which you can add extra interest through clever use of foliage.

- A garden with a good combination of 'spikes and mounds' will always look appealing, even when nothing is in flower. Locate strappy-leaf plants such as irises or daylilies (spikes) next to softer plants like lavender or gardenias (mounds).
- Contrast gold or grey foliage against plants with shiny green leaves, and plants with huge leaves beside plants with tiny, dainty leaves.
- Light up a dark corner under trees with a massed planting of something that has either grey, gold or variegated foliage. The sunlight filtered through the branches will catch the foliage and give the area a whole new dimension.
- Clip shrubs such as box (*Buxus* spp.), westringea and privet (*Ligustrum* spp.) into balls or mounds; these shapes can add interest individually or be used as border plantings to retain whole garden beds.

I love the look of flag iris bordering a path. They are spectacular when in flower, but their grey, sword-like foliage remains interesting year-round. Combine this border with a low lavender hedge; the lavender flowers later than the iris and can then be clipped back into either a straight hedge or round humps.

fruit trees

Fruit trees are making a comeback as we realise the many benefits of home-grown produce. Stone fruit (peaches, plums, cherries, apricots and nectarines) don't ripen once removed from the tree, so the best-flavoured specimens will always be those from your garden. And these fruits will grow in most temperate regions, providing there is adequate drainage and at least some cold nights.

In a small garden, what could be better than a tree that bears blossom in spring and fruit in summer? Fruit trees are good specimens for espaliering, perfect for small courtyard gardens or narrow beds, and even grow well in pots. Plus, contrary to popular opinion, they are easy to look after if you follow these simple rules:

- prune stone fruit in summer after they have fruited (rather than in winter, as is traditionally recommended)
- if you have enough space to plant more than one tree, allow plenty of room between them and prune to give good airflow between the branches
- be vigilant in removing any rotten fruit and diseased branches
- do not compost the leaves if they show any signs of disease or fungal infection
- control pests with an organic spray and, in the case of stone fruit, an application of Bordeaux mix at bud swell.

Many fruit trees require cross-pollination with another variety; check before deciding what to plant. Nectarines, peaches and apricots don't usually require cross-pollination but plums and cherries usually do.

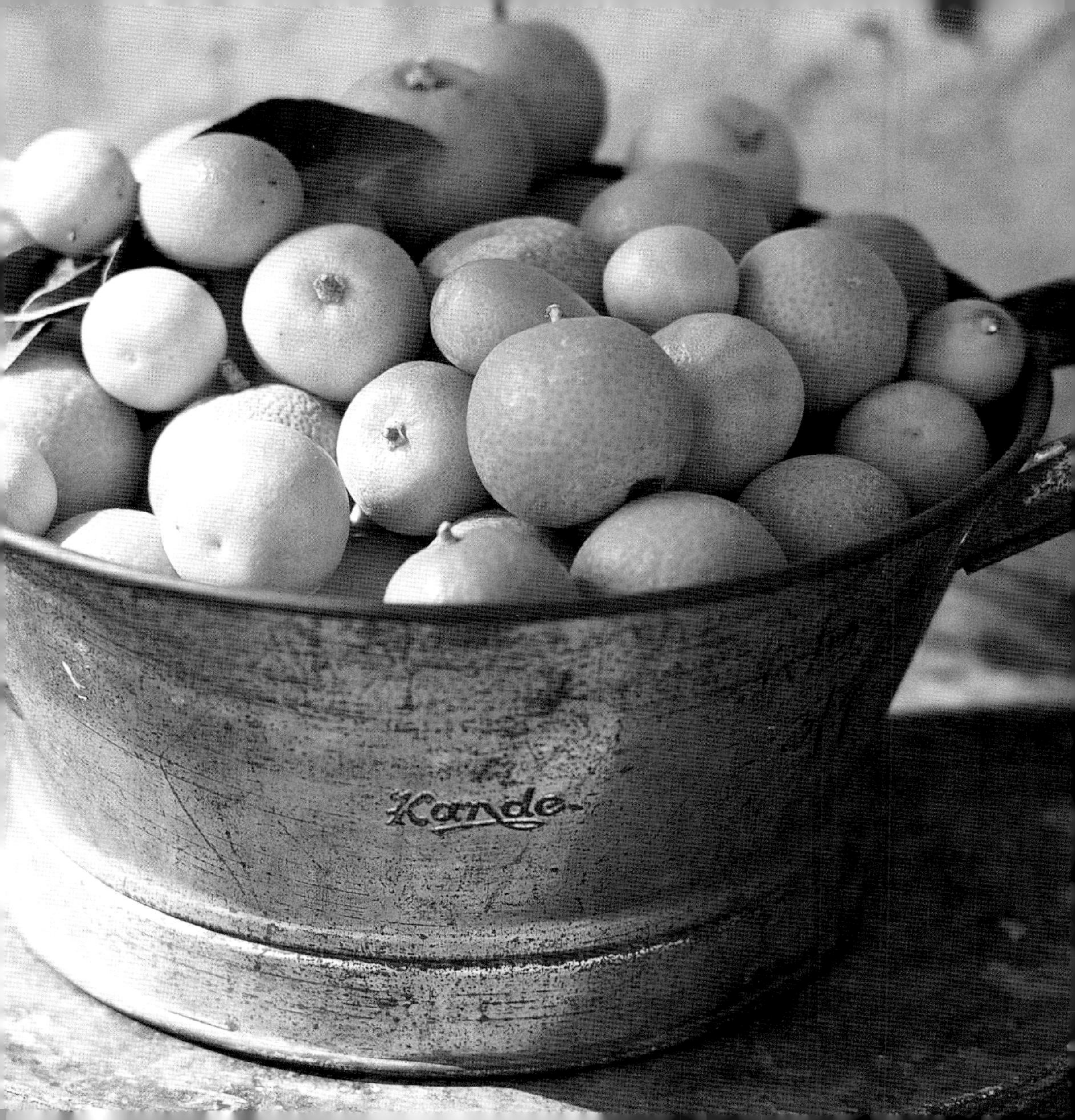
Kande

garden bounty

It can be disheartening to see the results of your efforts in the garden going into the compost bin or rotting on the ground simply because of a lack of time or energy. But a little lateral thinking can go a long way when you find yourself with an over-supply of a particular fruit, vegetable or herb.

- Your large parsley crop *could* be the source of a never-ending supply of tabouli and parsley butter . . . or you could use some of it for decoration. A large jug or vase of any sort of herb looks wonderful in the kitchen.
- Arrange winter vegetables (such as squash and zucchini) or lemons in a wire basket in the centre of the kitchen table.
- If you prefer to use your excess lemons for something more productive than table decorations or gin and tonics, try the simple lemon cordial recipe below. It will be a sure winner with the kids, especially if they are allowed to help make it.

lemon cordial

2 kg sugar
30 g Epsom salts
30 g citric acid
60 g tartaric acid
grated rind of 4 lemons
500 ml lemon juice
1.8 litres boiling water

Put all ingredients into a large stainless steel saucepan and stir over heat until all the sugar dissolves. Don't let the mixture boil as this will spoil the colour. Strain and pour into warm, sterilised bottles. Cap when cold.

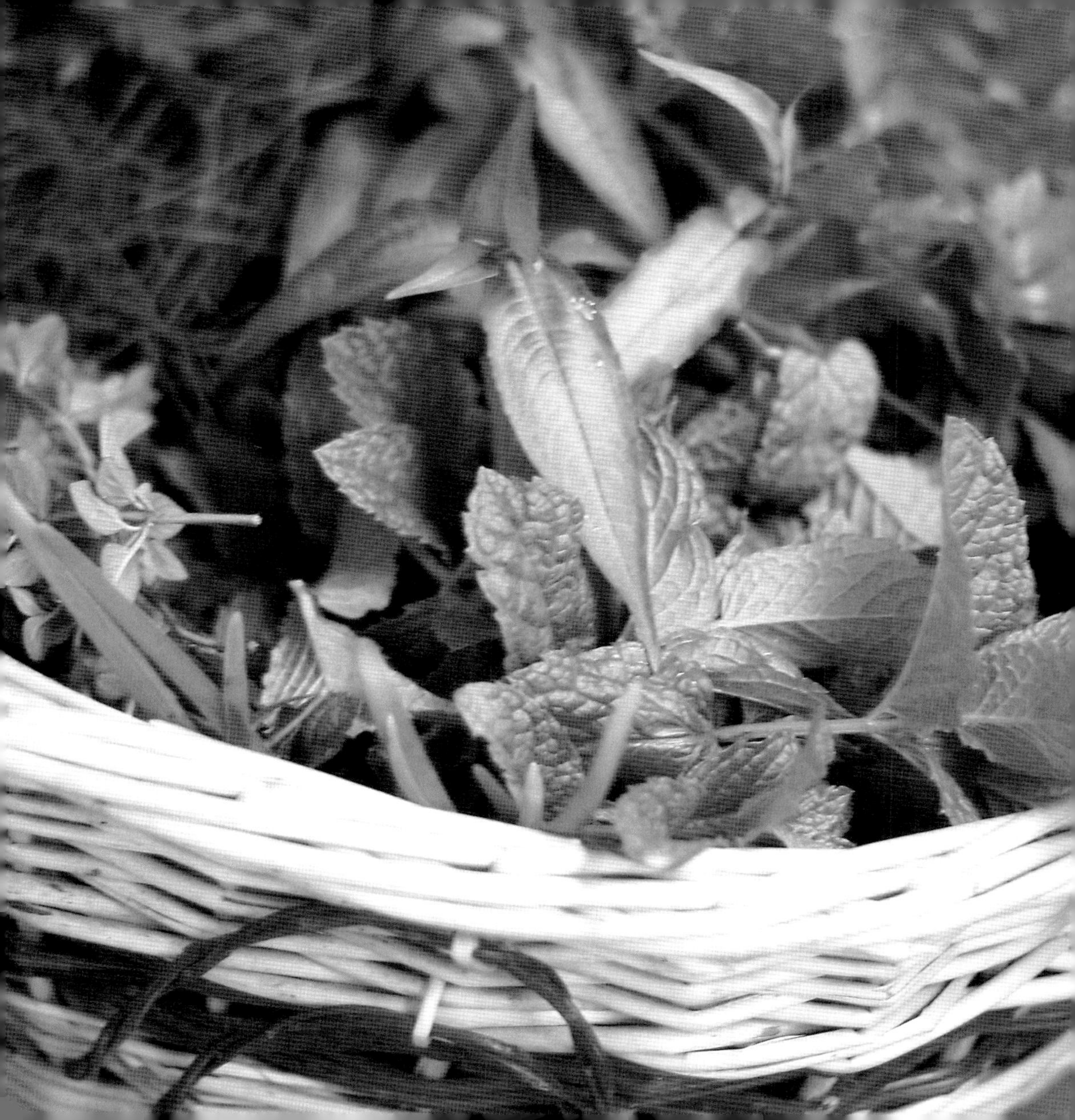

garden calendar

What better than a holiday or a sporting event to remind us of what is due to be done in the garden? (Keep in mind that this calendar is specific to Australia.)

- **New Year's Day**: Prune French lavender
- **Australia Day weekend** (late January): Dig and divide flag irises
- **First week of school** (late January/early February): Mulch; give roses a light summer prune; plant brussels sprouts and turnips
- **St Valentine's Day** (14 February): Re-pot cyclamen and polyanthus; start planting peas
- **Blue Diamond Stakes** (late February): Cut back English lavender; prune geraniums; start planting winter broccoli and spinach; start planting onions; fertilise fruit trees; plant coriander and primulas
- **Grand Prix weekend** (early March): Order bare-rooted roses
- **St Patrick's Day** (17 March): Cut back ferns; plant sweet pea seeds, watsonias, broad beans and winter lettuce
- **April Fools' Day** (1 April): Put tulip bulbs in a paper bag in the refrigerator crisper for 4–6 weeks; divide violets; plant more coriander
- **Good Friday**: Fertilise lawn with a complete lawn fertiliser, watering well before and after application
- **Anzac Day** (25 April): Plant ranunculus and daffodils; stop fertilising orchids
- **May Day** (1 May): Divide lilies
- **Mother's Day** (mid-May): Cut back dahlias; plant tulip bulbs

- **Queen's Birthday** (mid-June): Prune hydrangeas and fruit trees
- **American Independence Day** (4 July): Prune roses; lift dahlias
- **Bastille Day** (14 July): Plant raspberries and bare-rooted roses
- **First day of spring**: Plant petunias, celery, cucumber and eggplant; bed out begonias
- **Start of AFL finals** (early September): Fertilise, aerate and lime lawns; prune hibiscus
- **Father's Day** (mid-September): Prune passionfruit; plant leeks, summer lettuce, beetroot, cabbage, capsicum, carrots, silverbeet and parsnip; clean out lily ponds; plant gladioli; re-pot and start fertilising orchids
- **AFL Grand Final** (late September): Plant tomatoes, zucchini, dwarf beans, climbing beans, impatiens and petunias
- **Caulfield Cup** (mid-October): Divide chrysanthemums
- **Halloween** (31 October): Mulch; plant dahlias
- **Melbourne Cup** (early November): Plant basil
- **Remembrance Day** (11 November): Prune lilacs
- **Start of school holidays** (mid-December): Water lawns with a wetting agent to improve water penetration and avoid dry spots
- **Boxing Day**: Check roses for black spot and, if necessary, spray with Triforine.

garden layout

Have you noticed that some gardens just don't work, even if there's nothing ostensibly wrong? Perhaps corners of beds stick out where you want to walk, paths are too thin, or there are not enough trees – or too many! Then there are other gardens that look as if they were put together after a drunken barbecue but nonetheless have a certain feeling of rightness about them; simply being in them makes you feel good. The difference between these gardens is almost always in their use of space.

There are no hard and fast rules governing the use of space, but the secret is balance. The most common mistake occurs when gardeners copy an idea from another garden without allowing for the fact that their own garden is usually of quite different proportions. This is exacerbated when gardeners try to combine a whole lot of ideas in their own little plot, ending up with a dog's breakfast. There's nothing wrong with copying, but ideas need to be adapted to our own situation.

It is easy to waste space in a garden, and as house blocks become smaller, it is increasingly important to use space wisely. For example, the traditional front lawn is becoming redundant. If you have a front garden, make use of it however you can. If it is shady during summer and a sun trap during winter, you might like to build a high wall around it to make it an alternative private space. Or if you have a low front fence, or no fence at all, you might create a loose woodland effect to give you privacy from the street and a prettier aspect from your front windows.

See also: **borrowed landscape; paths; screening; walls**

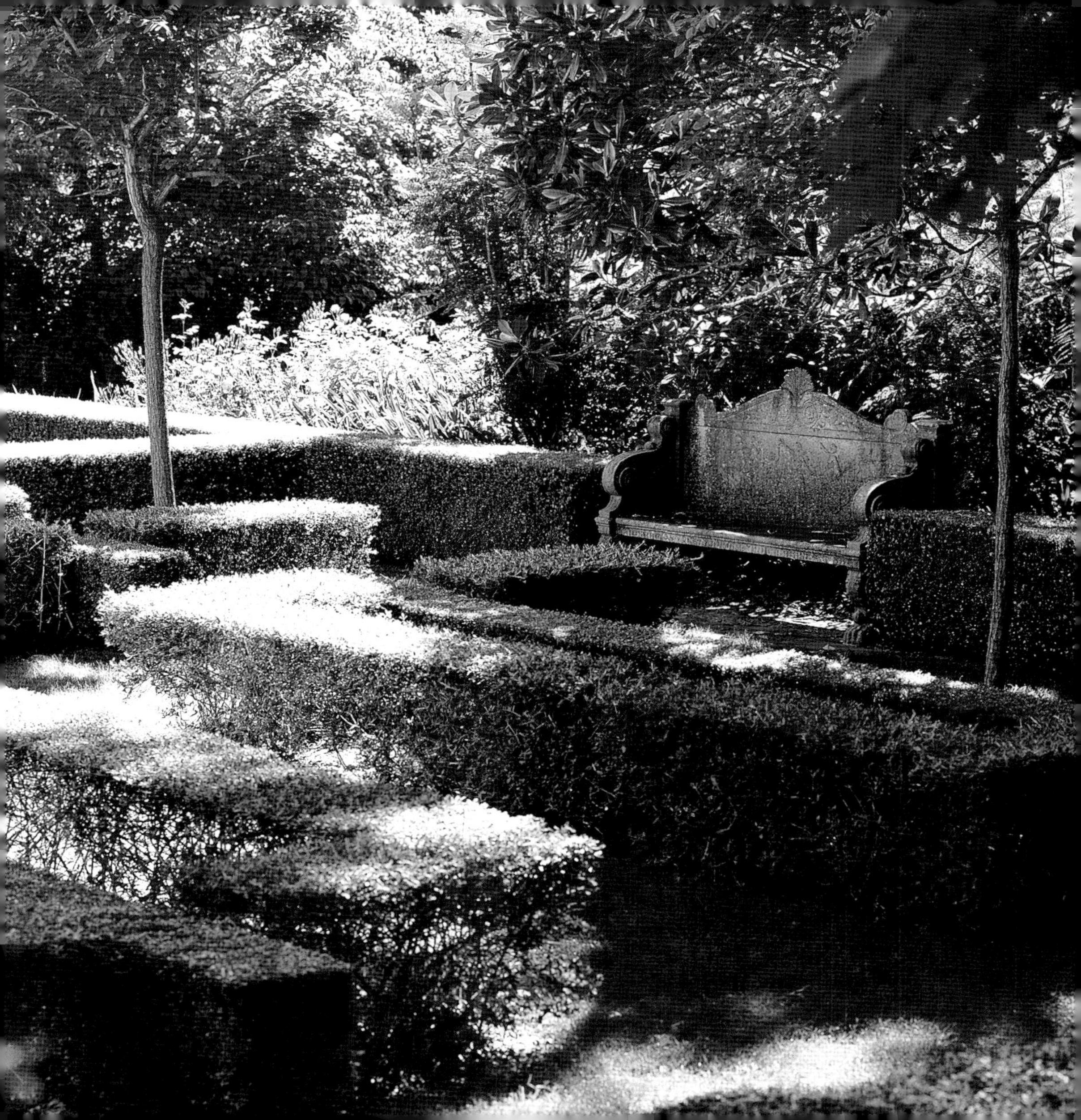

gardenias

Gardenias, with their bright-green foliage and scented, showy flowers, are not as difficult to grow as most people believe. Although they are native to warm climates and frost-tender, they will flower in a sheltered position in a temperate climate as long as the area is frost-free. They thrive in light shade but will also cope with full sun if the soil is kept moist.

- *Gardenia augusta* 'Florida', which has an exceedingly long flowering period over summer, is the most popular variety. Picking the beautifully scented blooms is the best way to prune and to encourage continuous flowering.
- 'Magnifica' bears fewer but much larger flowers.
- 'Radicans' is almost prostrate and bears many smaller flowers.
- Tree gardenia (*G. thunbergia*) is, in my view, the queen. Although slow-growing, it will eventually reach a height of 4 m or more. In summer, the scent from the spectacular, fragrant white flowers will fill your garden.

Yellowing leaves and bud drop can cause angst among gardenia growers. Yellow leaves are most likely the result of cold temperatures or a lack of iron in the soil (an application of chelate of iron, available from nurseries, can help). Bud drop is generally caused by irregular watering. Gardenias are shallow-rooted so they appreciate moist soil, regular fertilising and, most importantly, mulch.

> The best way to offset the effects of a frost is to get up at sunrise and wash any frost off the leaves of your gardenia before the sun hits them.

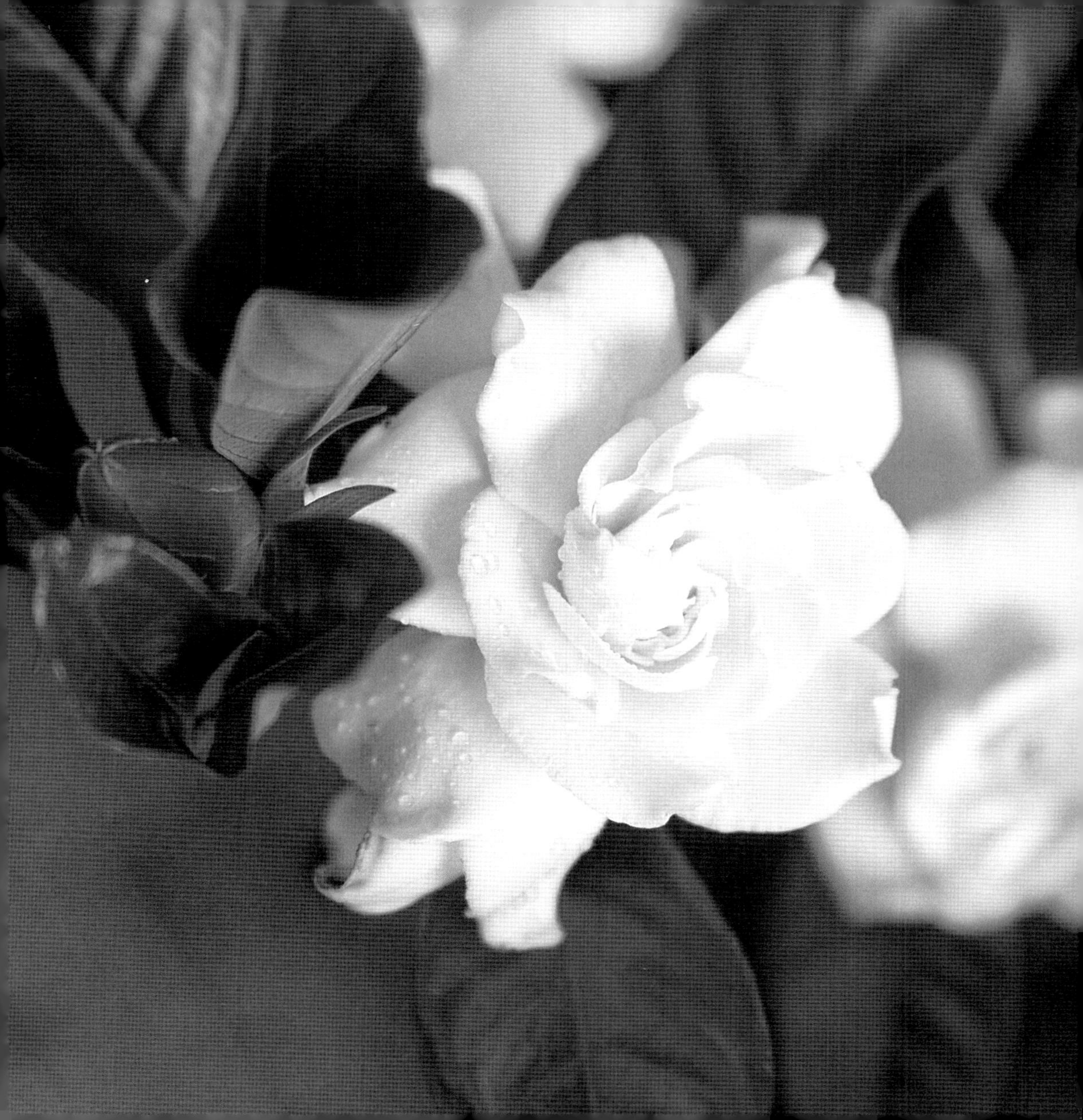

grasses

Grasses are part of the modern minimalist look. But they can also look amazing when integrated into a traditional herbaceous border. The soft, swaying foliage of a tall grass such as miscanthus or the nodding heads of swamp foxtail grass (*Pennisetum alopecuroides*) make a perfect foil for plants with rounded foliage or habit.

In his large, drought-tolerant garden, my brother has planted a whole bank of grasses bordering a white-gravelled terrace. The effect is fantastic, particularly when the wind ripples through the different species. In other parts of the garden, plants are grouped in large sweeps of one variety; a huge clump of succulents backed by soft grasses is particularly spectacular.

- Some grasses, such as *Miscanthus sinensis* 'Zebrinus', have striped foliage and make an amazing fountain of grass, often as tall as 2 m.
- Others, such as blue fescue (*Festuca glauca*) grow only to around 15–30 cm high and are perfect for the edge of a flower bed. The foliage of this particular grass is an intense silver–blue; plant it in front of sedum, with its glaucous green leaves, for a wonderful effect.
- Japanese blood grass (*Imperata cylindrica* 'Rubra') has strong red foliage.
- Carex species come in many shades including the silvery-white of 'Frosted Curls' and the bronze of *Carex flagellifera*.

A large winery garden I know uses various forms of *Miscanthus sinensis* and smoke bush (*Cotinus coggygria*) as a hedge around its car park; the mixed purples of the smoke bush contrast superbly with the oatmeal of the miscanthus.

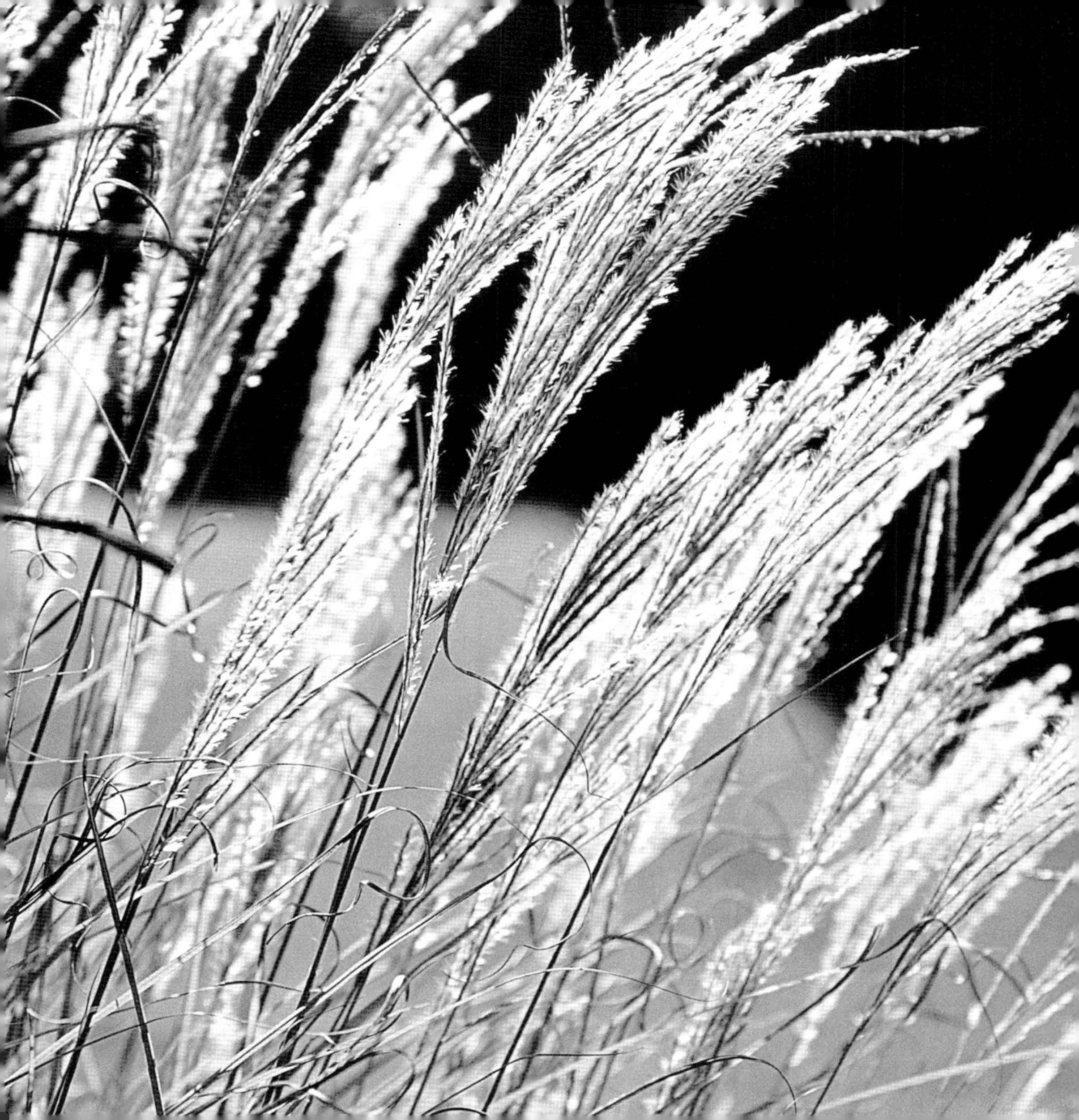

green flowers and foliage

To see what can be achieved using green alone, look at a garden in early spring. At this time of year, my garden is reasonably colourless as far as flowers go, but the interest generated by a few blooms in different shades of green combined with their various foliage forms is magnificent . . .

- In one corner, a snowball tree (*Viburnum opulus* 'Roseum') is covered in lime-green buds like little broccoli florets, while underneath there is the everlasting display of green goddess lilies (*Zantedeschia aethiopica* 'Green Goddess').
- A Manchurian pear (*Pyrus ussurensis*), with its new avocado-coloured leaves, sets off the street tree outside – a pear of a different variety.
- Four sprawling *Camellia sasanqua* hold onto last year's dark-green foliage, while the *Gordonia auxilaris* is covered with new brown–green growth. Underneath, the new mid-green leaves of Japanese anemones (*Anemone hupehensis* var. *japonica*) provide a wonderful foil for the pale blades of watsonia, the darker spikes of *Dietes bicolor*, and the strong serrated leaves of *Helleborus orientalis*.
- Lurking in the furthest corner is the ubiquitous *Acanthus mollis*; with its dark, glossy leaves, it has managed to resist all attempts at elimination.
- Two little box bushes (*Buxus sempervirens*) in square tubs already have their spring dusting of lime-green growth.
- Clipped *Helichrism petiolatum* in urns maintain their silvery-green presence as an ongoing companion to the mixed campanula and violets fighting for attention around the bases.

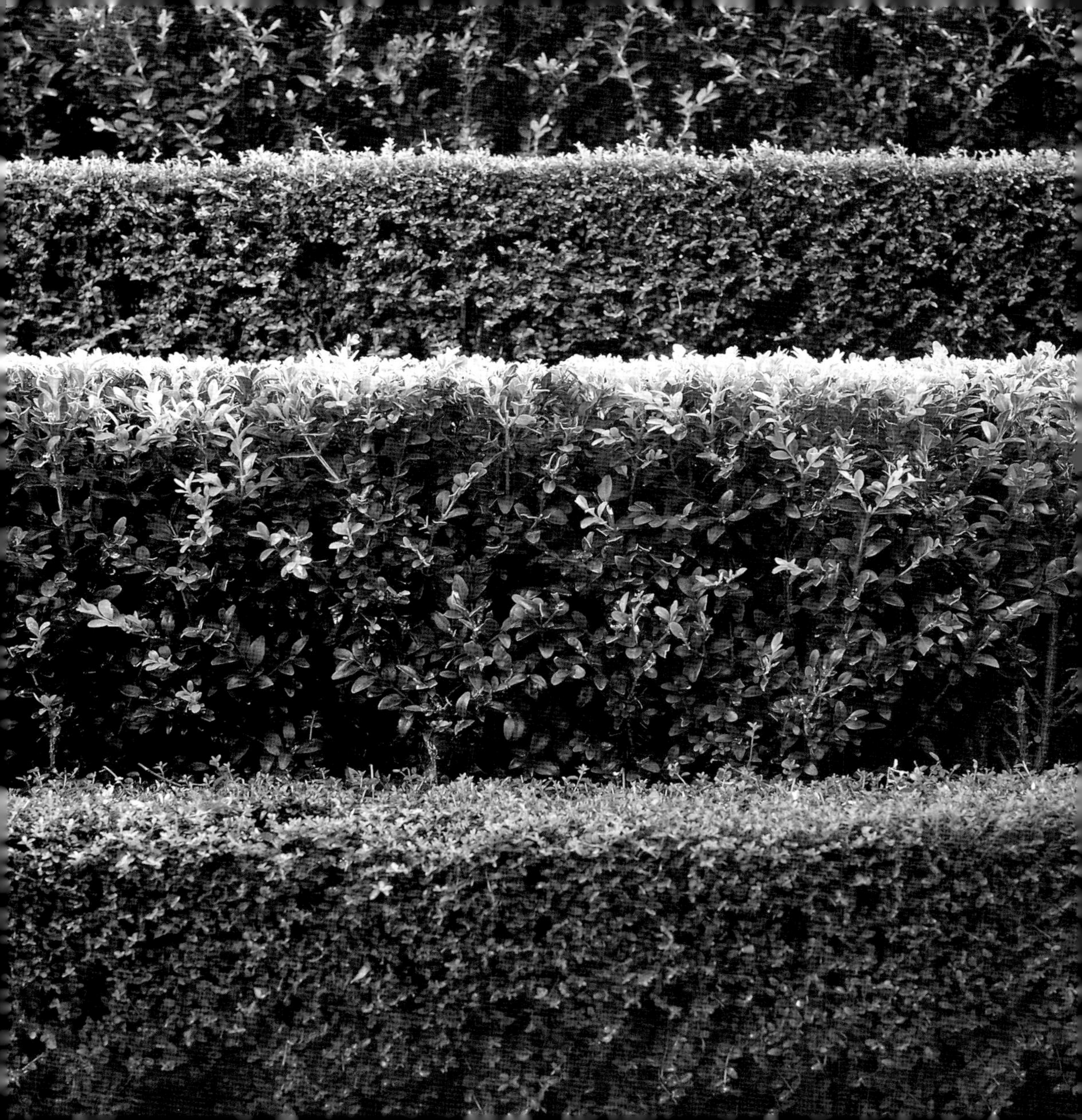

greenhouses

An authentic greenhouse can look lovely in a large garden, but most of us do not have the space, money or need for a structure like this. Plastic 'igloos' are a cheaper way to achieve the same effect and are handy for people in colder regions who want to grow orchids, begonias, poinsettias and the like. Igloos can be bought in kit form and are easy to erect (look in the *Yellow Pages* for suppliers).

In countries such as Australia with extreme light intensity, greenhouses need to be covered with shadecloth or whitewashed seasonally to protect plants in the hotter weather.

The cheapest and easiest way to get your summer vegetables going early, protect frost-sensitive seedlings or strike cuttings is to use miniature greenhouses.

Miniature greenhouses can be made by cutting the bases out of two-litre plastic milk or orange juice containers. Turn the bases upside-down and they become the mini greenhouses. Cover your new seedlings with the greenhouses both day and night until the days become warmer and the plants stronger; then, take the houses off during the day. This way, the plants acclimatise gradually.

> Originally referred to as orangeries, greenhouses were introduced into the gardens of Europe so that the exceedingly wealthy could show off to their friends by indulging in out-of-season fruits and flowers.

See also: **tomatoes**

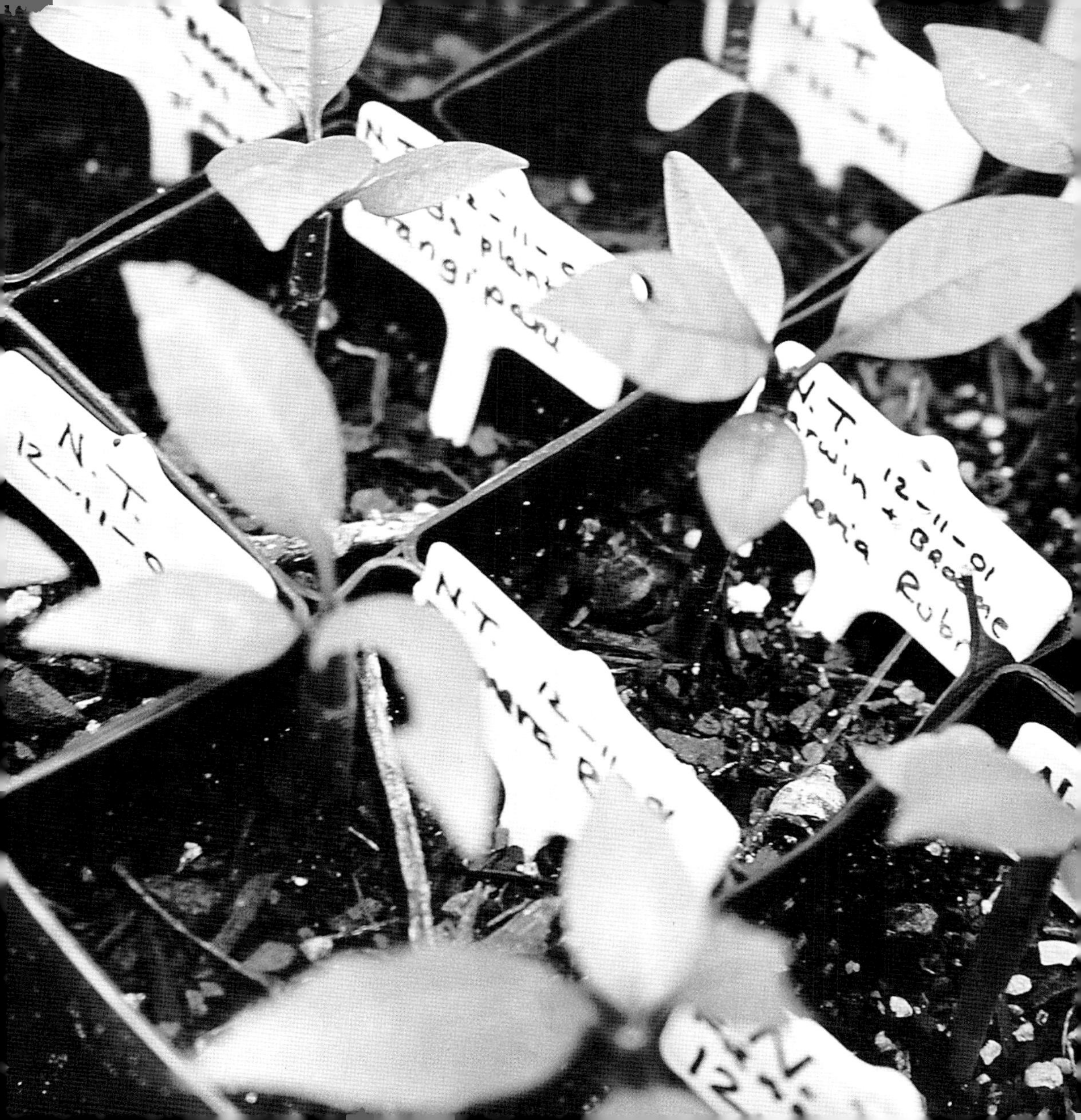
N.T.
12-11-01

ground covers

No garden is complete without ground-covering plants; think of them as the rugs and throws that add comfort and warmth to your house. There are ground covers suitable for virtually any conditions.

Hot, dry areas — tough, free-flowering ground covers such as gazanias, arctotis or osteospermums can turn a barren wasteland into a colourful display throughout the year. If the spot is really inhospitable, pigface (*Carpobrotus* spp.), blue chalk sticks (*Senecio serpens*) or one of the ground-covering grevilleas will do the trick.

Shady areas — under trees, periwinkles (*Vinca* spp.), violets, persicaria or aluminium plants (*Pilea cadierei*) work well where conditions are a bit dry, while native violets (*Viola hederacea*), Serbian bellflowers (*Campanula poscharskyana*) and kidney weed (*Dichondra micrantha*) do better in moister conditions.

Narrow beds — the vigorous *Convolvulus sabatius* bears pale-blue, white or pink flowers almost continuously; it is a marvellous plant for a bed that runs between the drive and the fence or for spilling over a retaining wall. The white-flowering *Pratia angulata* also does well here.

Herb and gravel gardens — choose from pennyroyal (*Mentha pulegium*), any number of thymes, and snow-in-summer (*Cerastium tomentosum*).

Normal conditions — I am particularly fond of the ubiquitous seaside daisy (*Erigeron karvinskianus*).

> As well as dealing with problem areas, ground covers also act as a mulch, helping to keep the soil cool and moist in summer.

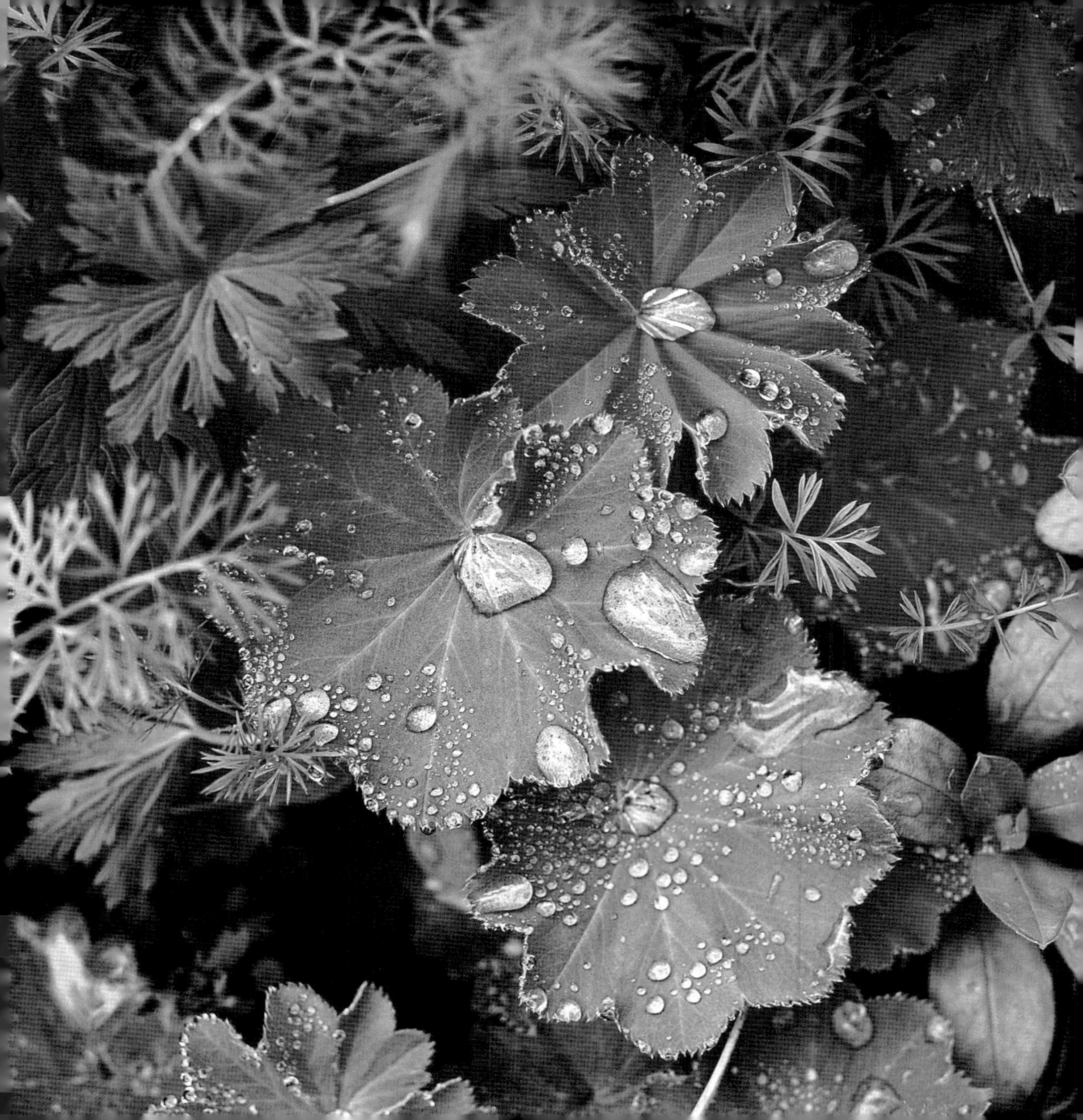

gum trees

When I think of gum trees, the first thing I think of is koalas. After that, I think of *Eucalyptus* (their correct botanical name). Then, I think of the fact that a lot of trees that used to be eucalypts are now classed under a new genus – *Corymbia*. Then I think of the Sydney red gum, which is not a eucalypt at all but a myrtle. After that, it all gets a bit hard and I start thinking of koalas again.

The mention of gum trees usually conjures up images of the larger members of the group – lemon-scented gum (*Corymbia citriodora*), Sydney red gum (*Angophora costata*), peppermint gum (*Eucalyptus nicholii*) and mountain ash (*Eucalyptus regnans*). There are, however, plenty of smaller flowering gums that make perfect garden specimens:

- bell-fruited mallee (*E. preissiana*) – slow-growing but makes an excellent ornamental tree; its large, bright-yellow flowers are quite spectacular
- silver princess gum (*E. caesia* subsp. *magna*) – perfect for a home garden with its lovely pendent habit and magnificent, drooping pink flowers
- *E. macrocarpa* – an outstanding small ornamental gum with frosted white foliage and large crimson flowers 8 cm in diameter
- *Corymbia ficifolia* – of the new, free-flowering hybrid cultivars, 'Summer Red' (red), 'Summer Beauty' (pink) and 'Summer Splendour' (orange) are good examples
- pink ironbark (*E. leucoxylon* 'Rosea') – although a little larger than the others, this long-flowering tree is, like all eucalypts, a favourite with birds.

See also: **bark; decorative elements; native garden; tactile garden**

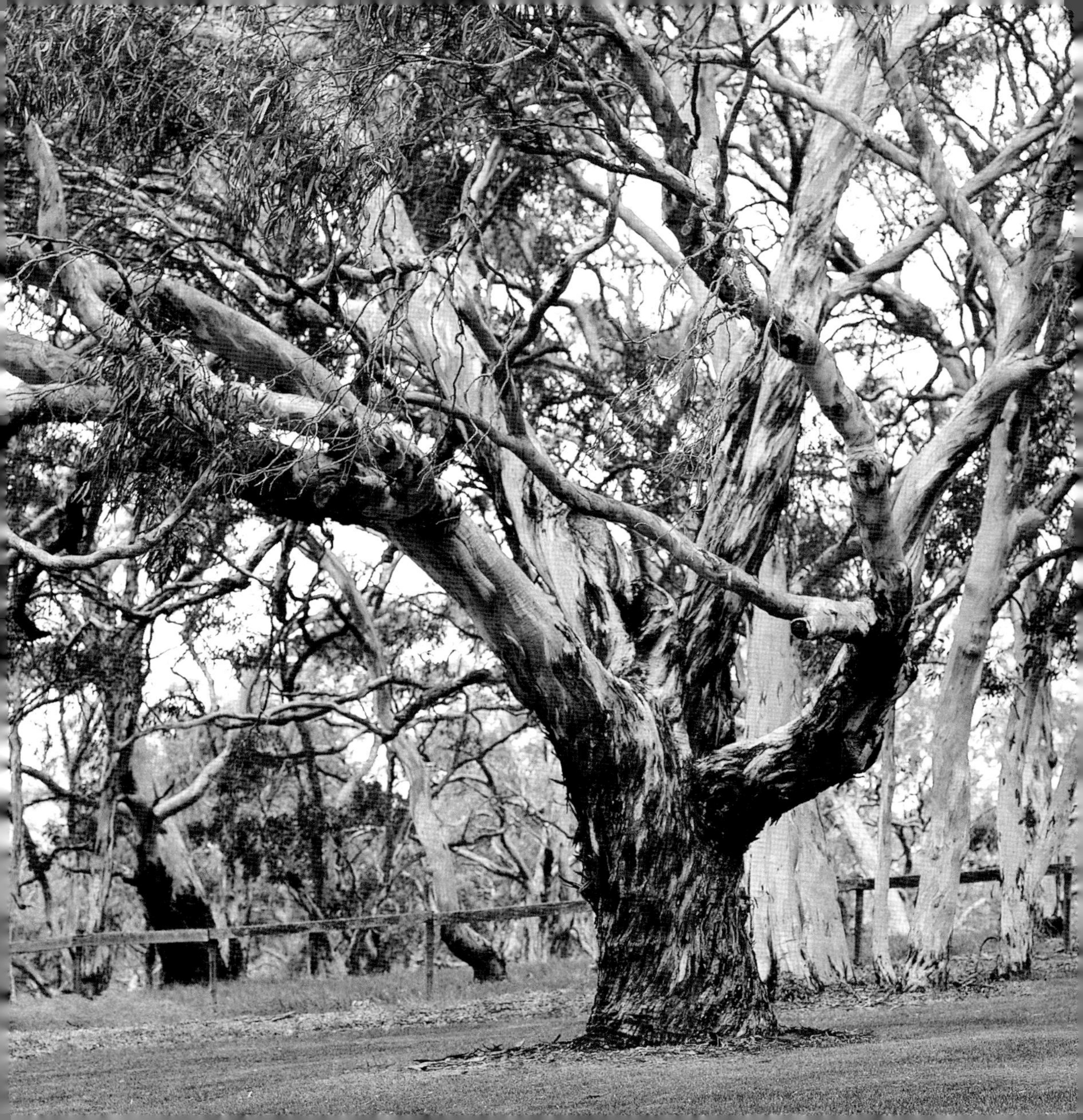

hellebores

These wonderful plants make an excellent ground cover for shady positions, but also grow well in sun. Flowering in winter, they look particularly good under traditional taller shrubs such as camellias and rhododendrons, and deciduous trees such as silver birches. But it is not only their flowering season that makes them so popular; the variety and range of their gentle colours is extraordinary.

- Lenten rose (*Helleborus orientalis*) is the best-known species and flowers profusely, with the seedlings often producing new shades of colour. Being semi-dormant during summer, it survives quite happily through this period without much water, but prefers to be kept moist from autumn onwards.
- Christmas rose (*H. niger*) is a real beauty; its cup-shaped flowers are white with golden stamens and the petals have a faint pink blush on the reverse. It is named after its black root – hellebore roots have been used medicinally for at least 2000 years.
- Bear's foot or stinkwort (*H. foetidus*) is actually a lovely variety, despite its name, with handsome dark-green leaves.
- Corsican hellebore (*H. argutifolius*) is a taller variety growing to 60 cm and is the most sun- and drought-tolerant of the species.
- *H.* × *hybridus* 'Mrs Betty Ranicar' is a double white, a stunner in a winter garden.

As cut flowers, stalks of bear's foot and Corsican hellebores last quite well, but Lenten roses survive better if you plunge the stems into boiling water before arranging them. In a vase, they look particularly good with curly leaf parsley.

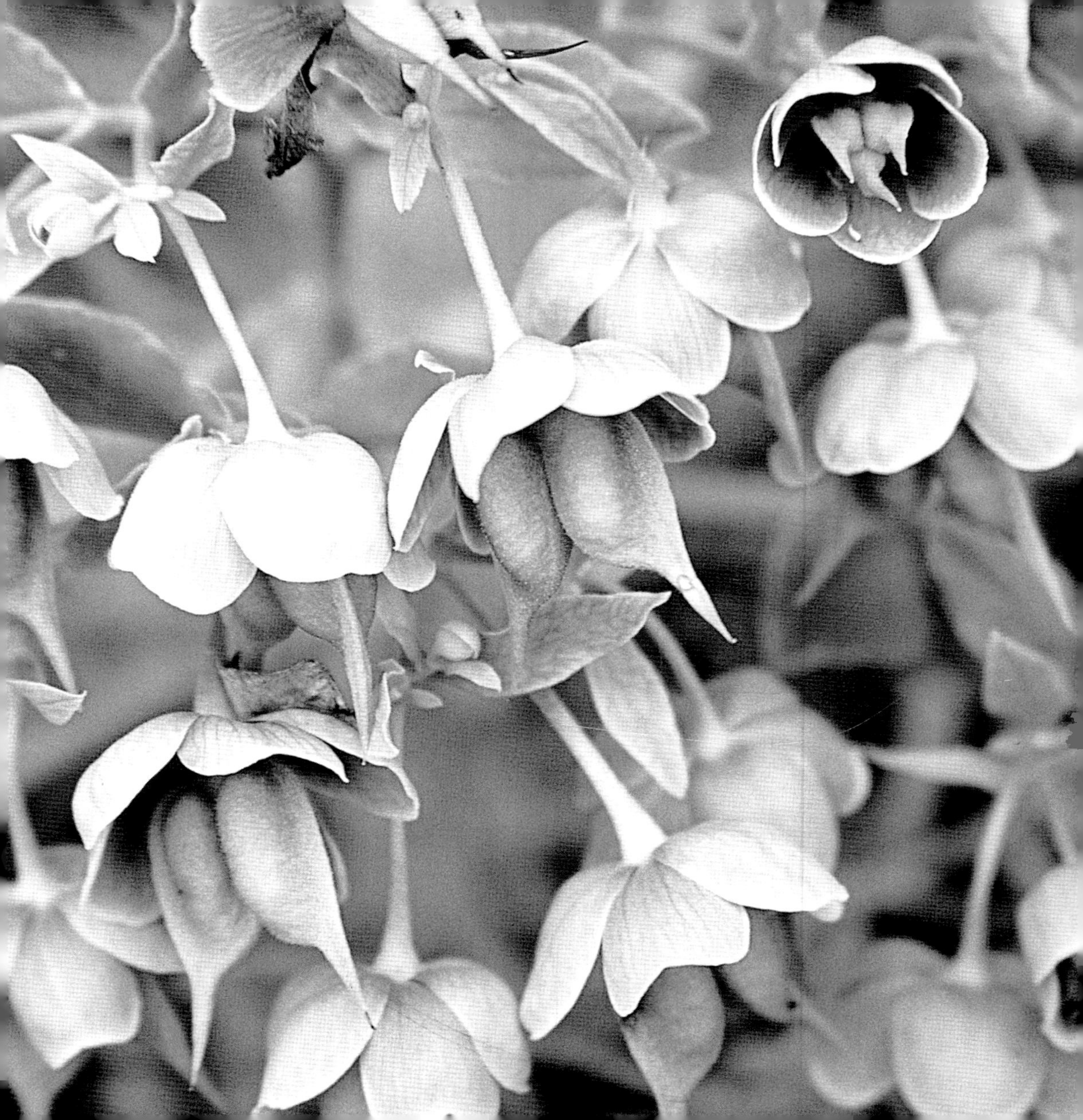

herbs

There is always room for herbs, whether you plant them amongst your other plants, in a separate garden bed, or in a series of pots. The bulk of herbs are perennials and need full sun. If you haven't much room but want a few fresh herbs to cook with, I suggest those below.

Parsley is a biennial plant in Europe but an annual in Australia's warmer climate. Both the curly leaf and Italian varieties self-seed readily; allow it to run to seed each year and you will have it forever. Alternatively, buy a punnet of seedlings and plant them out each year in either autumn or spring.
Basil is a must for summer salads, pesto and any tomato dish. It needs to be planted each year. I prefer to buy a punnet of seedlings and plant them out rather than sowing seed. Don't plant the seedlings until very late spring or early summer, as they don't like cold weather. Basil is caviar for snails so scatter a few snail pellets around the plants.
Oregano and marjoram come from the same family and are very similar in flavour, although oregano may be a little more spicy. I am particularly fond of golden marjoram as it looks spectacular against the grey of sage and the darker green of mint.
Mint is good for summer drinks and tastes lovely with new potatoes or peas, or in a salad.
Thyme adds flavour to casseroles, soups and Italian recipes and, like oregano, is great on pizzas. In an irrigated garden, it does not seem to have a very long lifespan and needs to be replaced every few years.

Rosemary is indispensable in lamb dishes and makes a tasty addition to roasted vegetables. It is a useful plant for hedging around a herb garden (its leaves repel sap-sucking insects) and also looks great in a pot.

Lemon grass is an essential herb for Asian cooking. It is a thirsty plant during the growing season and is best grown near a tap where you can give it extra water.

Chives are the easiest herb of all to grow. The clump just keeps increasing and needs to be divided from time to time.

Coriander is an immensely popular culinary herb. However, it is not commonly grown because of its propensity to run to seed or 'bolt'. To prevent this, vary the planting position depending on the time of year; the hotter the weather, the less sun it needs. If you plant clumps a couple of weeks apart in different parts of the garden, you will have an ongoing supply throughout the year. To do this, let one clump run to seed, collect the seed and re-sow as required. (After the flowers have finished, seed develops in small capsules. Leave the capsules on the plant until fully ripe, then cut the seed heads off and place them in a paper bag. Over the next week, the seed heads will dry off and the seed will be released into the bottom of the bag. Seed viability reduces dramatically as the seed ages, so let at least one crop run to seed each year to produce fresh seed.)

> Most herbs survive well in pots – in particular, bay trees, which have a propensity to sucker in the garden, and mint, which can become invasive if not contained.

See also: **companion planting; garden calendar; silver and grey foliage**

identifying plants

Identifying plants is not easy, especially for beginner gardeners; even if you have a book on the subject, you are unlikely to know where to look in it. And yet nothing can be more frustrating than seeing a plant growing in someone else's garden and thinking it would be perfect for your own, but not knowing what it is or how to get it.

The first step is to make sure you have a sample for identification. Show the sample to anyone you know with some sort of gardening knowledge. (You will find that older people who have grown up with gardening often have a better idea than many younger people, whose experience may be limited to what is currently sold in nurseries.) Failing that, take the sample to your local nursery or even your city's herbarium.

As far as samples go, flowers are the easiest way to identify plants because they are usually species-specific. Make sure your sample includes a flower if possible, or at least a close-up photo of the flower. The shape and make-up of the leaf will also help (particularly in the case of trees), but it is also useful to know what the plant looks like (tall? short? thorny? spreading? leggy? scented?). For example, if you noticed a pale-pink-flowering, glossy-green-leafed shrub that you liked, the size, shape and leaf would indicate whether it was a camellia, escallonia or azalea. But it would be the flower that would tell you the exact variety ('Waterlily', 'Showa-no-sakae' or whatever).

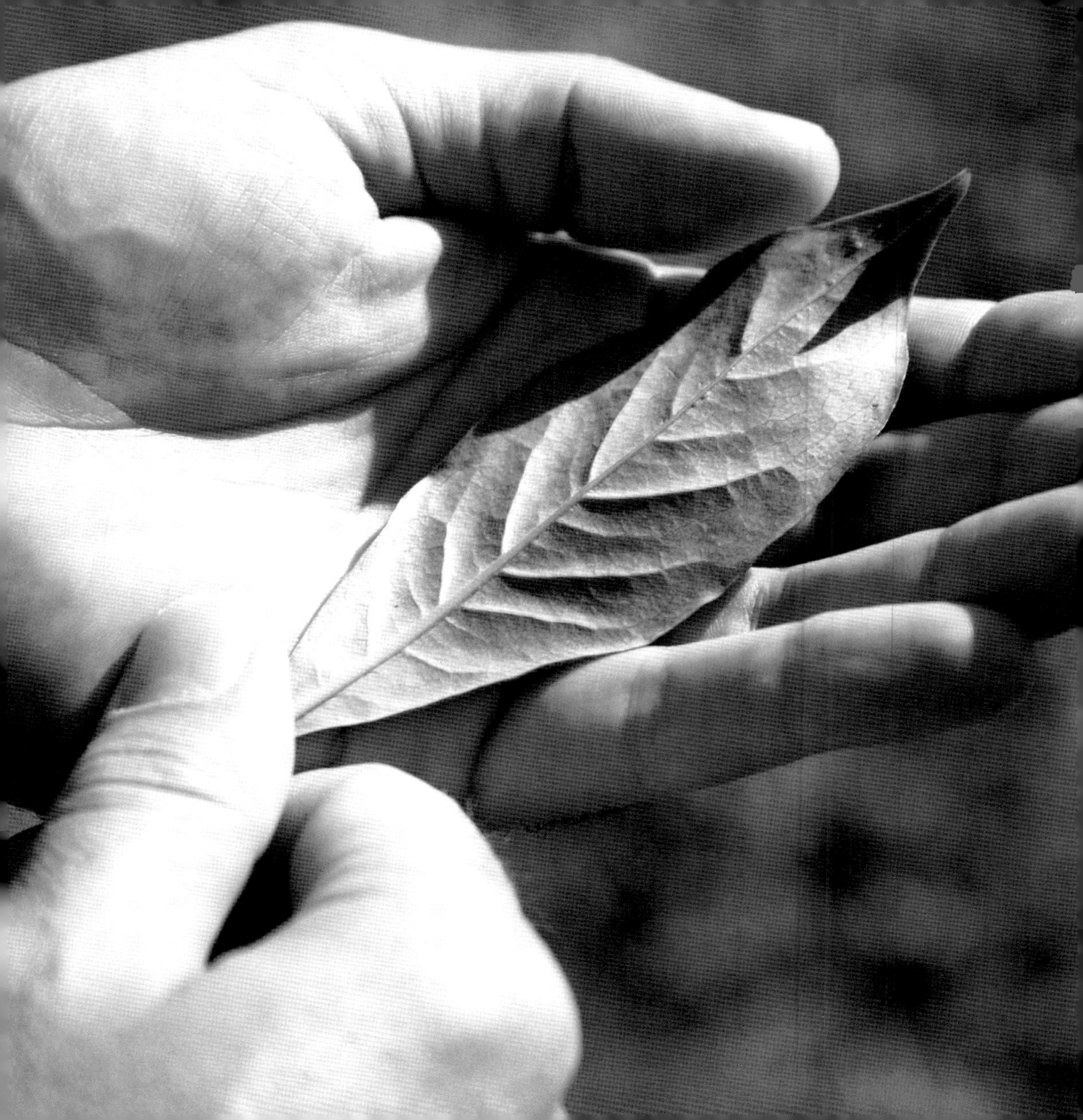

indoor plants

As in everything, fashion in indoor plants changes frequently. Where once you might have found a huge *Monstera deliciosa*, or a fern in a glazed pot, you're now more likely to find a yucca. But no matter what the fashion, indoor plants all need looking after. The death of an indoor plant is most likely the result of one of the conditions below.

Overzealous watering. If pots are placed in a saucer, water tends to collect in the saucer and the plant remains too wet. Avoid this by raising your pots slightly with stone chocks so that they stand above any water sitting in the saucer.
Lack of water. To know when to water a plant, poke your finger into the potting mix; if it feels dry, the plant needs water. In extreme cases, a plant's leaves might begin to show signs of stress by hanging limply or dropping off.
Lack of suitability. Unless they have regular periods of rest and recuperation outside, most plants will eventually die from lack of sunshine. The best way to overcome this is to have several pot plants that you rotate regularly, only keeping them inside for a few days at a time. Also, wipe the foliage of your indoor plants regularly; just like the furniture, they gather dust.

> Cyclamen survives well indoors and certainly cheers up the house in winter. Keep your cyclamen in a cool, light position, and twist off the spent flower stems to prevent them from rotting at the base. If the plant is in a warm room, put it outside at night. Feed it fortnightly with liquid fertiliser and it will flower for months.

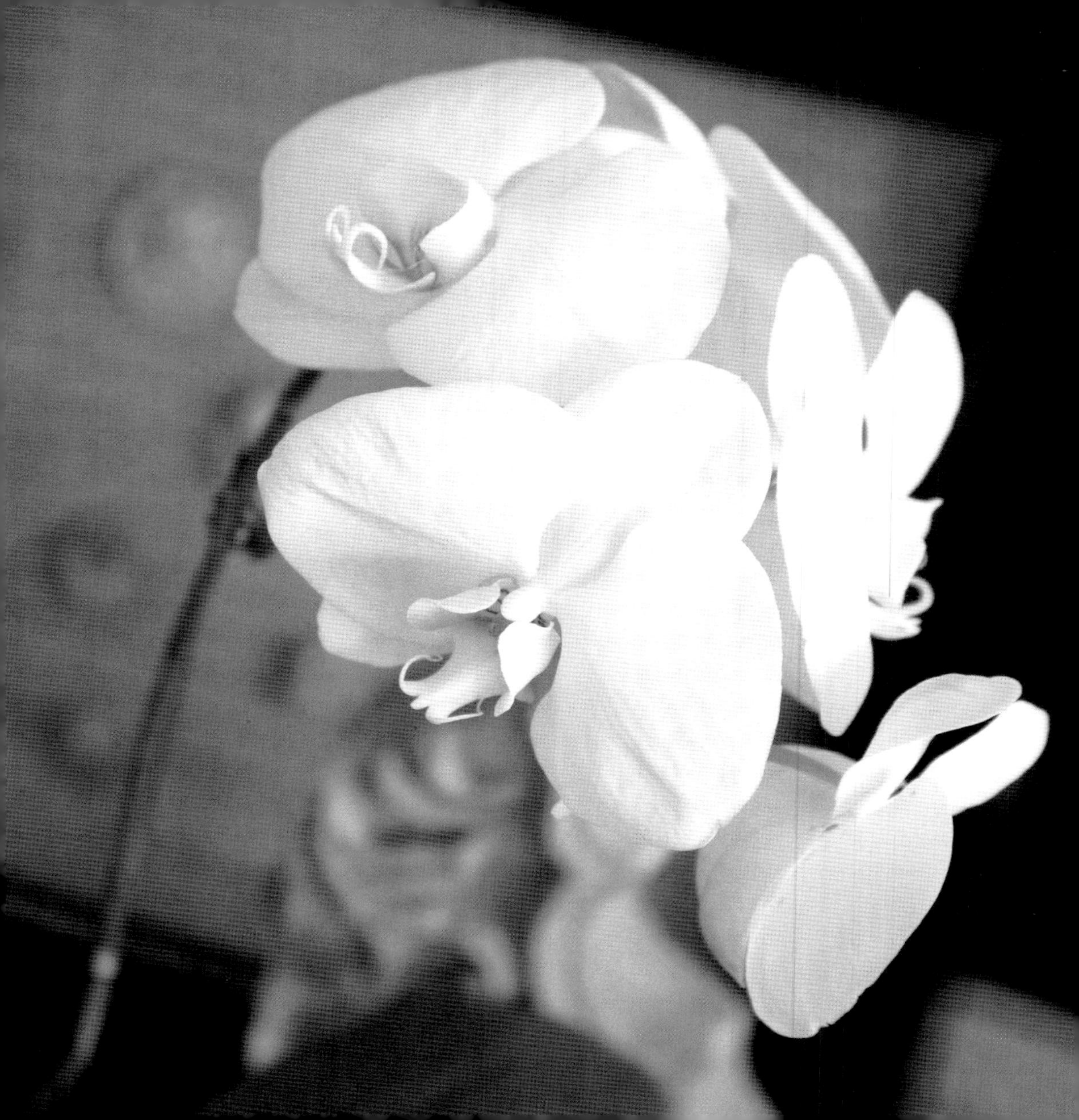

irises

Named after the Greek goddess of the rainbow because they come in every imaginable shade, from the deepest jet to the purest white, irises are native to the northern hemisphere. This is a wide genus of more than 200 species; some are evergreen while others die down in winter. The blooms most often available in florists are the bulbous hybrids known as English, Dutch and Spanish irises, but the variety commonly grown in gardens is the bearded or flag iris (*Iris germanica*).

Bearded irises fall into three classes: tall, intermediate and dwarf. They grow easily from rhizomes and produce a flamboyant display when they flower profusely in late spring. Apart from their exquisite flowers, their pale, sword-like foliage contrasts well with other more rounded plantings. They prefer a sunny position and well-drained soil with a pH of around 7.0. And, like nudists, they like to have their bums in the sun; when you plant them, ensure that the top of the rhizome is just exposed above the soil. Avoid mulching around the rhizomes as this can cause them to rot.

Other iris species worth considering are the beardless East Asian water irises, which include the spectacular *Iris kaempferi*, bred from the Japanese iris (*Iris ensata*), and the showy Louisiana irises, a series of related species that make wonderful pond specimens and are perfect for planting in poorly drained areas. Winter irises (*Iris unguicularis*) are ideal for dry gardens as they thrive on neglect and dislike water during summer, when they are dormant. Their foliage looks good all year, but if you plant them in a sunny position and cut them back in autumn, you will be rewarded by masses of pale-mauve flowers in the middle of winter.

Lifting and dividing bearded irises is necessary every three or four years, otherwise the clumps become congested and don't flower as well. The best rhizomes will be found on the outside of the clump. (Once a stem has flowered, it will never flower again, but will put its energy into developing side shoots; after three or four years, there are unlikely to be rhizomes of any value left in the centre of the clump.)

The preferred planting time is immediately after flowering in late spring or early summer (before the weather gets too hot), or in early autumn. When replanting, choose only the largest, plumpest rhizomes. To encourage new growth, trim back the roots and the foliage by half into a neat wedge (to reduce transpiration). When you have finished, your iris rhizome should look a bit like a yabby wearing a pale-green war medicine bonnet.

If you wish to replant your irises in the same position each year, dig the soil over and fertilise it well with a high-phosphate fertiliser. If you are planting in poorer sandy soil that you wish to improve with compost or manure, sprinkle a 10 cm cover of unmanured soil onto the area before replacing the rhizomes. Then, scratch out a hollow deep enough to set the rhizome in place and tamp soil around its roots without covering its top. Leave about 20–30 cm between each rhizome so that they can clump up again.

kniphofias

Most of us know kniphofias as red hot pokers but, in their native South Africa, they are also known as torch lilies – a more sensible name, for they come in many colours other than orange–red. They are used extensively in English herbaceous borders because of their upright habit of growth and long flowering times. Although they are often relegated to driveways or seaside areas because they are hardy, they can add height and strength to garden plantings and are an absolute boon to anyone wanting to maintain a low-water garden.

- *Kniphofia ensifolia* is a tall, yellow, winter-flowering variety.
- 'Percy's Pride' has green flowers that bloom in late summer and early autumn.
- The enchanting small, creamy-yellow 'Maid of Orleans' flowers all summer.
- The apricot-coloured 'Princess Beatrix' looks good planted beside the soft, mauve flowers of English lavender (*Lanvandula angustifolia*).
- The fabulous orange heads of 'Winter Cheer' tower over the rest of the garden in winter and provide welcome nectar for the birds; plant them near a window, where you can observe the bird life coming and going.

In my brother's garden, which has not been watered for eight years, the kniphofias have crossbred and self-seeded, producing varieties of size and colour peculiar to his garden.

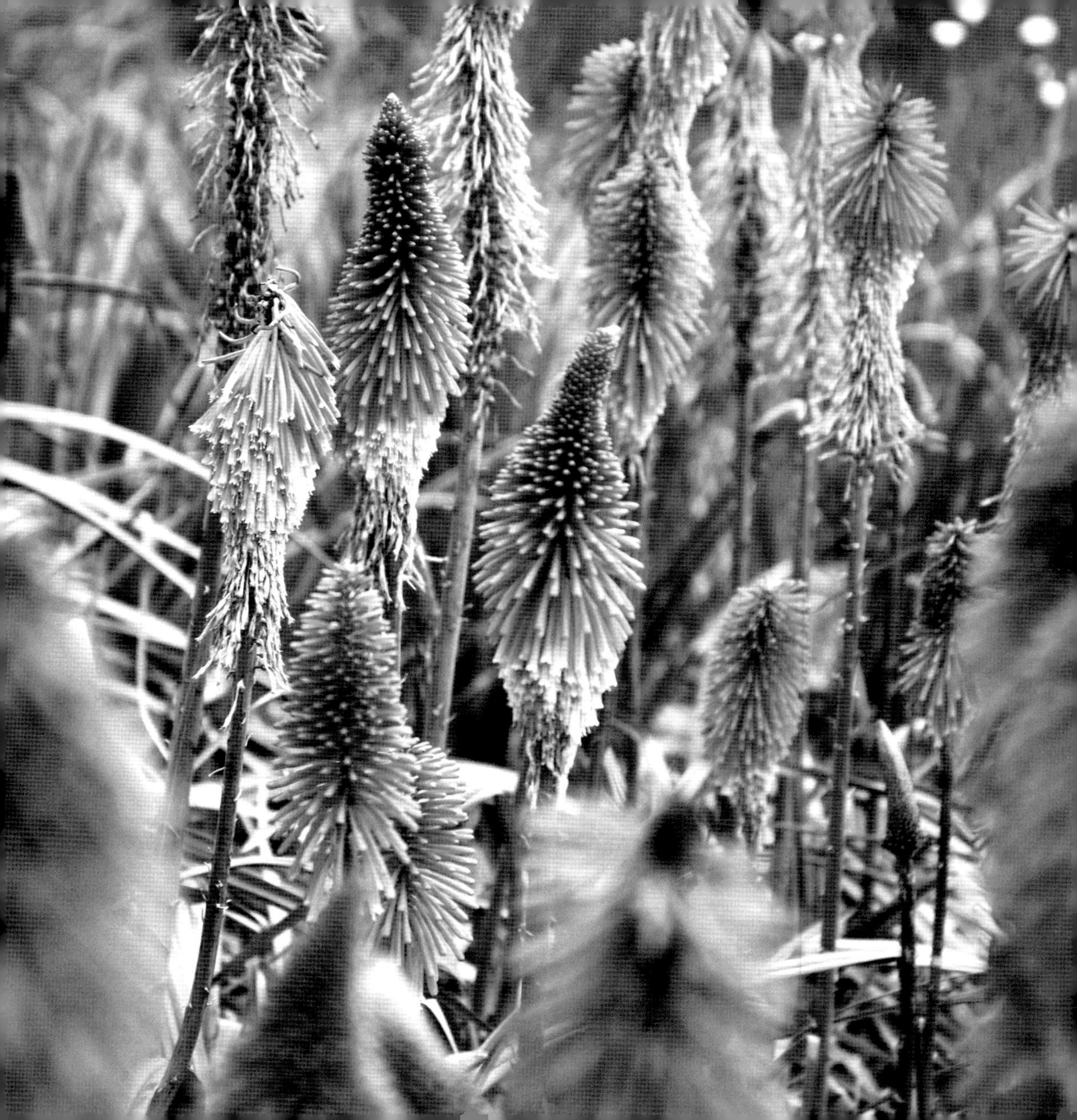

lavender

Lavender (*Lavandula* spp.) consists of around 25 species of grey/green-foliaged shrubs with highly aromatic leaves and flowers. Several species are invaluable to the perfume industry for the pungent oil produced from glands underneath the flower heads. With a new hybrid seeming to appear on the nursery shelves every few months, selecting the right one for your garden might seem confusing. But they all tend to be hardy and like full sun.

- Spanish lavender (*L. stoechus*) – many of the new hybrids have been bred from this species. They require similar conditions to the parents, but they flower more heavily and for a longer period.
- English lavender (*L. angustifolia*) – despite its name, this species is not native to England, but it is much used in English gardens for edging paths and flower beds. Its flowering period is comparatively short, but it clips beautifully and looks good all year.
- French lavender (*L. dentata*) – probably the toughest of all lavenders and moderately frost-resistant. It flowers so consistently throughout the year that it is difficult to find a time to trim it back, which is nevertheless necessary to prevent it from growing woody and out of shape. Midsummer is probably the best time, so that it is in full flower during the winter months. It makes an excellent, slightly taller hedge.
- Allard's lavender (*L.* × *allardii*) – although this species has rather boring, peppery-scented flowers, it clips magnificently.

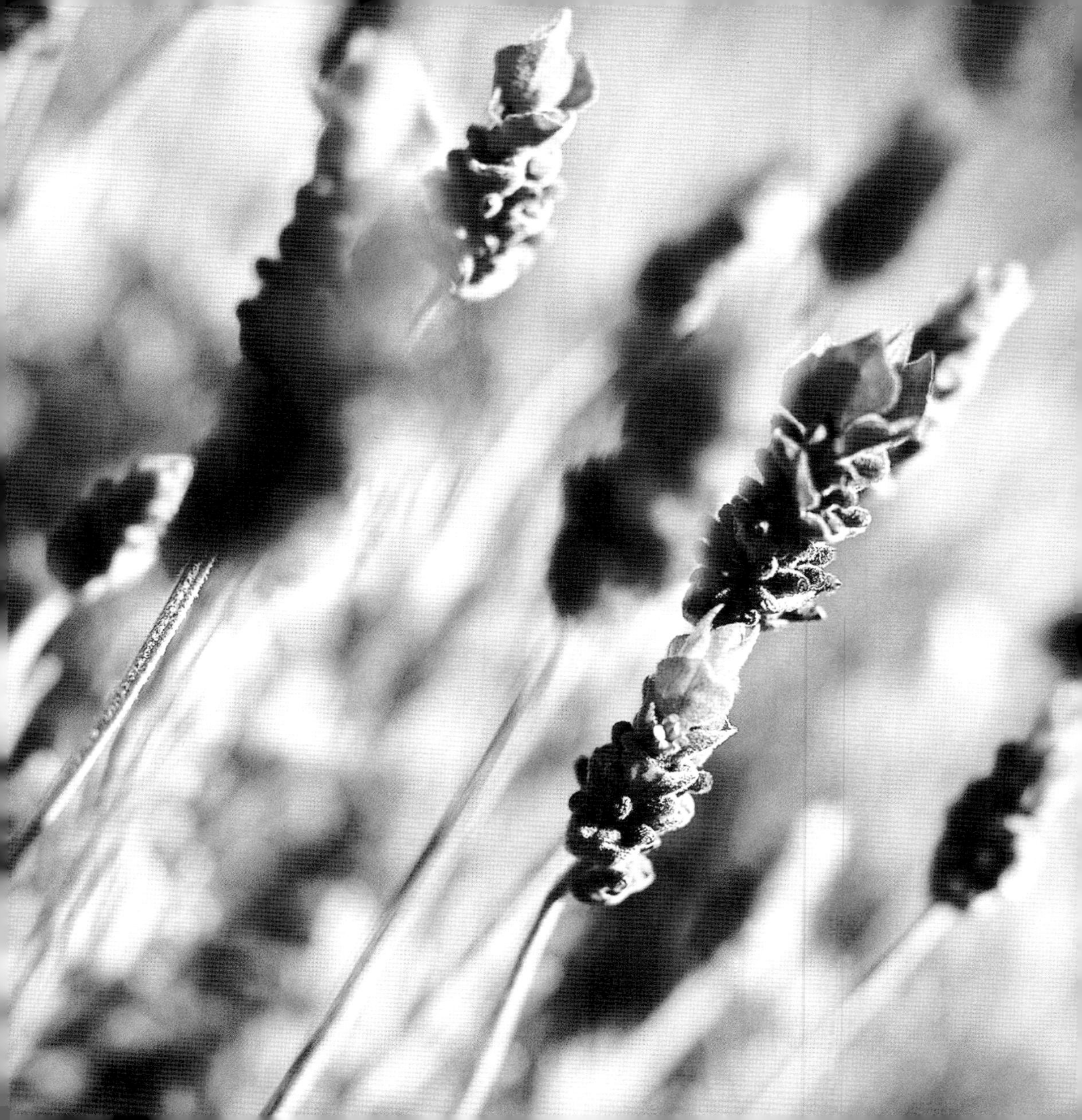

lawns

Although not really appropriate for a continent as dry as Australia, lawns have remained popular. Maintaining a good lawn involves a few simple steps:

1 **Choose the right variety.** For a drought-tolerant lawn, or a lawn in a shady area, use a tall fescue variety. For a very drought-tolerant lawn that also needs to cope with dog urine, one of the new buffalo varieties, such as Sir Walter, is best. Kikuyu and couch are also good at repairing themselves. If you require a manicured, English look, a Kentucky bluegrass–ryegrass blend is likely to be the most appropriate.
2 **Water more, less often.** At the height of summer, most lawns need only two generous waterings (the equivalent of 25 mm of rain) a week. Generous watering less often encourages the deep root-growth essential for healthy lawns. In winter, watering is seldom required except in the driest spells.
3 **Fertilise and weed regularly.** Use a complete lawn fertiliser at least four times a year. Water before and after application. Regular treatments of a broadleaf herbicide will help keep weeds like bindi-eye under control.
4 **Don't mow the grass too short.** In hot climates, lawn roots tend to burn easily, making a good cover on top essential.

Mower maintenance should be carried out in spring to avoid the loss of temper associated with attempts to get a recalcitrant machine to kick into life when the warmer weather arrives.

For a two-stroke mower:
- drain all fuel from the tank and old fuel container (it is likely to be contaminated with water condensation)
- clean and/or replace spark plug
- check and sharpen/replace blades and bolts
- clean/replace air filter
- clean underneath and around cylinder fins for cooling and cutting efficiency
- spray throttle cable with an appropriate lubricant.

For a four-stroke mower:
- check engine oil and top up if necessary
- start and run motor for 2–3 minutes to warm up oil
- with the plug lead removed, tip mower so that spark plug is vertical and, using the appropriate tool, remove sump plug and drain oil and fuel
- with mower still tipped, check and sharpen/replace blades and bolts
- refit sump plug and refill engine with correct oil (generally around 600 ml of SAE 30 – check owner's manual if you still have it)
- check and clean air filter by brushing off muck then washing in clean petrol and re-oiling element
- clean underneath and around fins (as for two-stroke)
- lubricate throttle cable (as for two-stroke).

lemon trees

Of the three lemon varieties commonly grown, 'Eureka' has fewer thorns and a heavier summer crop than 'Lisbon', which is tougher, thornier and produces more lemons overall (throughout the year). 'Meyer' is a smaller, sweeter lemon–orange hybrid that is more cold-tolerant than the others and does well in a pot.

Lemons are incredibly forgiving trees; more often than not it is overzealousness on the part of the gardener that leads to problems. They benefit from a warm, sunny position away from draughts with moist, well-drained soil. Apply a complete garden fertiliser twice a year – but remember that lemons are surface-rooted and, to avoid burning the roots, should be watered prior to and after the application of fertiliser.

Troubleshooting lemon trees:
- Collar rot is one of the most common diseases in lemons and other citrus. It is caused by building up soil or mulch higher around the trunk than the existing surface roots, causing the bark to go mouldy. Keep any mulch around the roots away from the trunk itself.
- Scale is another common problem. It is not terminal but will weaken your tree and, if left untreated, the tree may eventually need to be removed. Black soot on the leaves (sooty mould) is a likely indication of scale. Ants crawling all over your tree are also a warning sign – they are attracted by the scale insects (which secrete honeydew) and spread sooty mould around on their feet. Spray the tree with white oil (but not in extremes of hot or cold weather).

- In spring, citrus leaf miner – a small, burrowing grub – might cause unsightly markings, similar to water stains, on the surface of your tree's new leaves. Leaf miners can cause disfigurement of the leaves in established trees, and might retard the growth of young trees. Thoroughly spray the tree with white oil, including both the tops and bottoms of the leaves.
- Swellings in your tree's stems are a sign of citrus gall wasp – it lays its eggs beneath the bark. There is no cure; the infected branches must be cut off and disposed of to prevent the tree from losing vigour.

Don't expect to harvest lemons from your new tree for at least two years. Instead, pull off any small lemons as they develop to give the tree a chance to grow bigger and stronger.

See also: **companion planting; espaliers; organic garden; pots**

lettuce and other leafy greens

Lettuce primarily refers to the common type *Lactuca sativa*, of which there are four varieties: crisphead or iceberg, looseleaf, butterhead, and cos or romaine. There are also a number of associated cultivars commercially available. Like most vegetables, lettuces prefer a well-prepared bed with plenty of organic matter and benefit from fortnightly applications of a nitrogen-rich liquid fertiliser.

Looseleaf, butterhead and cos lettuces are easier to grow than crisphead because you don't have to wait until a heart has formed before they can be harvested. (Try eating a crisphead before it has formed a heart and you will find the leaves bitter and unpalatable.) These varieties can be eaten as young as you like; just tear off the leaves as you need them. Sow them throughout the year; in fact, when you have finished pulling the leaves off, allow them to run to seed and they will merrily self-seed.

Crisphead lettuces should be sown in early spring or late summer.

Asian greens are now available in mixed punnets from nurseries and the young leaves add a spicy flavour to salads.

English spinach is another alternative to lettuce during the colder months and can be eaten either cooked or raw. Like looseleaf lettuce, you only need to pull off as many leaves as you need. It can be sown from late summer through much of winter.

Rocket is perhaps the easiest salad vegetable to grow; once you have planted it in your garden, you seem to have it forever. To keep it under control, cut back the plants as soon as they commence flowering, to stop them self-seeding everywhere. Rocket is also available in punnets.

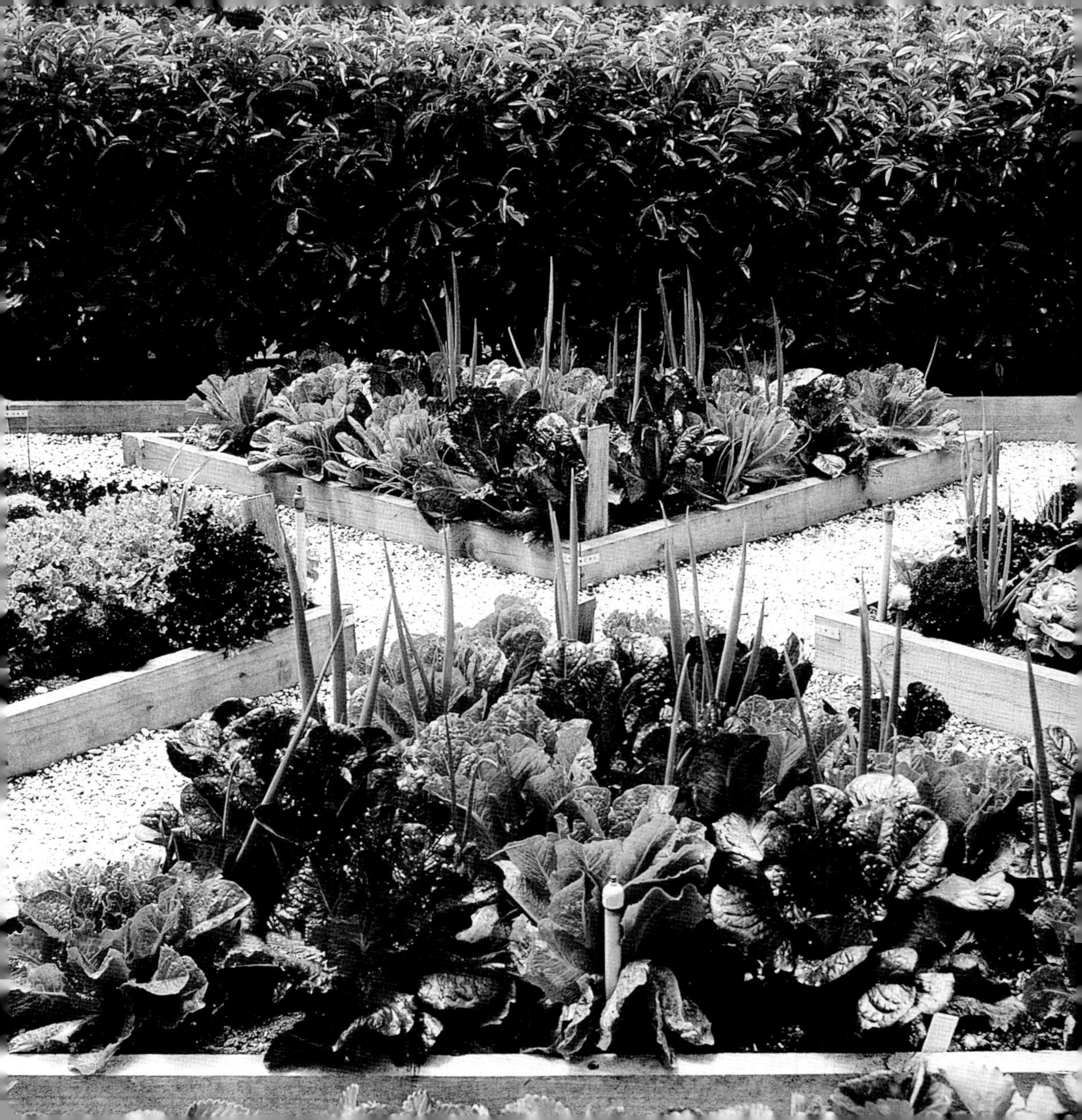

magnolias

A large and varied genus of over 100 species of deciduous and evergreen trees and shrubs, magnolias are one of the loveliest garden plants around. As a rule, the Chinese species are deciduous, cold-climate, spring-flowering plants while those from the Americas are evergreen and bloom in summer.

- Bull bay magnolia (*Magnolia grandiflora*) is a huge, spreading beauty of 18–24 m in height, bearing fragrant, bowl-shaped flowers from summer to autumn. It is slow-growing and takes a long time to flower. Later hybrids, such as 'Exmouth' and 'Little Gem', are less spreading in shape and produce slightly smaller flowers at an early age.
- The *M.* × *soulangeana* cultivars, with their tulip-shaped blooms in a wide variety of colours, are the most commonly grown deciduous varieties.
- Lily tree (*M. denudata*) is slow-growing, but worth looking for, as it will eventually grow to a height of 10 m and makes a spectacular display in spring with its fragrant, creamy-white flowers borne on bare branches.
- Star magnolia (*M. stellata*), a bush to 3 m, produces fragrant, many-petalled, star-shaped white flowers.
- *M. campbellii*, or the cup-and-saucer magnolia, is a slow-growing mountain giant (up to 24 m) said to be one of the wonders of the gardening world.

When choosing a deciduous magnolia, **bear** in mind that they are cold-climate plants and unsuitable for gardens exposed **to wind;** a strong wind will ruin their beautiful floral display in a couple of days.

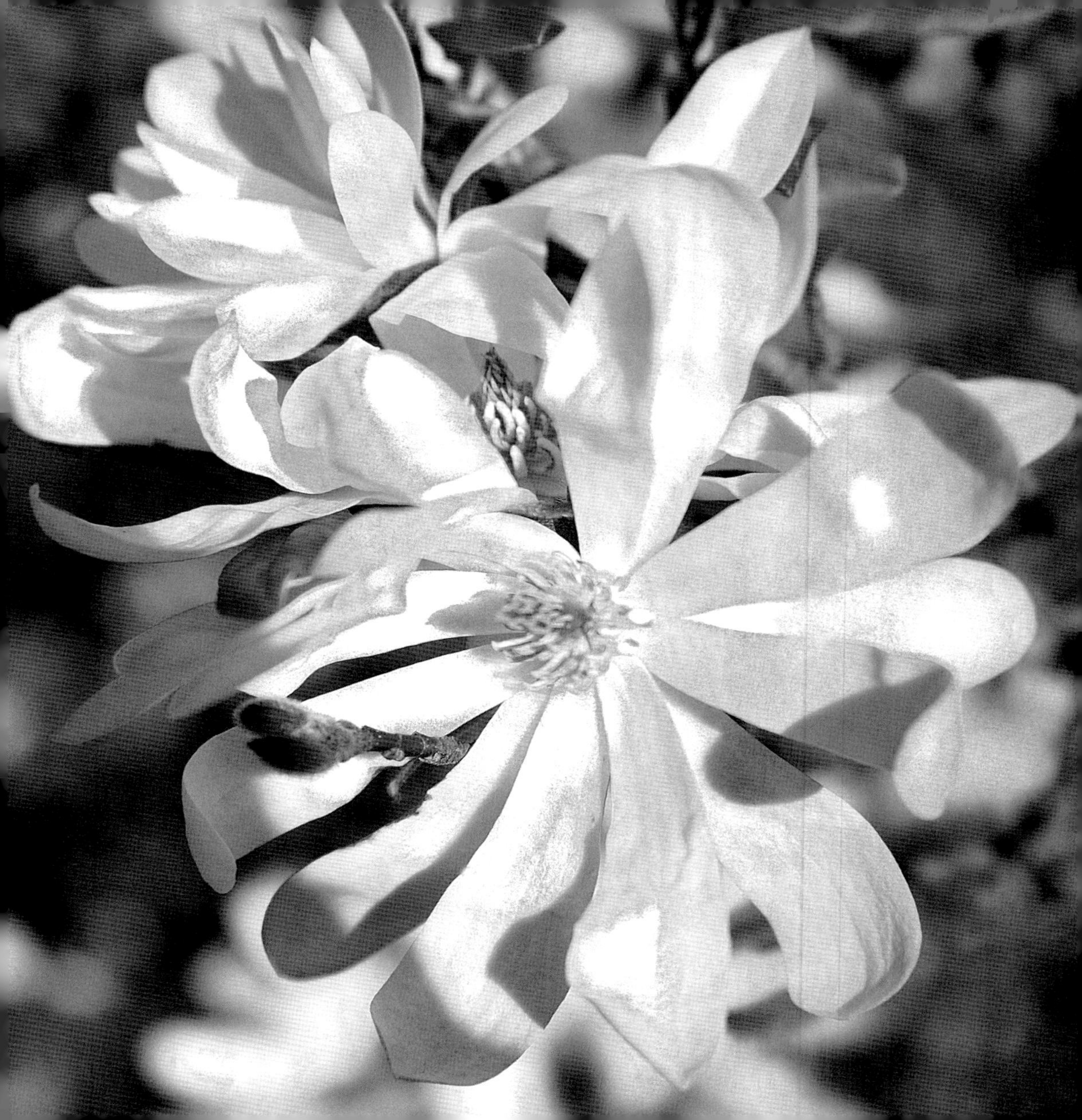

mulch

Mulching brings numerous benefits to your soil and is one of the best things you can do for your garden. It:

- improves the friability of heavy clay soil
- adds body to sandy soil and helps it retain moisture
- helps conserve water, lowering your water bill
- encourages earthworm activity, which in turn adds humus and nutrients to the soil and increases aeration
- helps keeps the soil warm in winter, and moist and cool in summer.

Almost anything can be used as mulch, including compost, pea straw, tan bark, stable manure, mushroom mulch, newspaper and old carpet. (You can even use stones, gravel or glass; although earthworms won't have much luck breaking these down, the other benefits remain the same.) Do not dig your mulch into the soil; simply spread it on the surface and leave it to decay.

> Growing up on a farm, my brothers and I learned the meaning of mulch at an early age; our mother used to pay us five cents a bag for sheep manure procured from beneath the shearing shed. She soon realised, however, that the benefit of raw sheep manure as a mulch was compromised by the hundreds of weeds that it harboured, and which ended up in her garden. So, our job changed to shovelling metres of fine woodchip from the nearby racing stables, whose occupants had a more discerning diet.

See also: **organic garden; soil; weeds; worms**

no-dig garden

A no-dig garden is one where, rather than digging into the soil to plant a crop, you build a garden above the ground. This way, a productive garden can be grown on ground with very poor soil. A no-dig garden is:

- an excellent way to grow organic herbs or vegetables
- a method of saving on water and maintenance
- a means of having a garden even on a small, inner-city property
- ideal for elderly people, or others with limited mobility
- a delight for children.

You can create a no-dig garden almost anywhere, providing the area gets enough sun. I have seen wonderful no-dig gardens created on concrete driveways and even old cast-iron beds! The secret is in the layering and the compost. Here is the simplest method:

1. Use a wooden, brick or other frame to mark out the edge of the garden and to keep it contained. (You can make it any size you like, but 4 m^2 is a good size to start with.)
2. Lay about 10 sheets of old newspaper in the bottom of the garden bed.
3. Add a layer of pea or lucerne straw.
4. Add a layer of compost (or soil covered with a sprinkling of either manure or blood and bone and potash).
5. Repeat these layers until you reach the desired height.
6. Give everything a good soak, plant your seeds or seedlings, and away you go!

native garden

Over the past few years, drought, the soaring cost of water and the increased hybridisation of native plants has caused gardeners to think again about the benefits of planting natives instead of trying to emulate English garden styles. Even the most hardcore exotic-plant lovers are beginning to realise what a diverse range of natives are now available, how they can be integrated into almost any style of garden, and how much more suitable they are to our climate. Natives also have many other benefits:

- You can treat many of the beautiful new hybrids in just the same way as exotics (prune them, shape them, feed them, and so on) and they will reward you accordingly.
- Many natives are available as tube stock and they tend to be fast-growing; if you are on a budget, this can be the most economical way to start a garden.
- Many natives flower during the winter, when a more traditional garden might be lacking colour.
- Most natives encourage birds to your garden.

Some natives that I regularly use to great effect are native hibiscus (*Alyogyne huegelii*), kangaroo paw (*Anigozanthos* spp.), spiny-headed mat rush (*Lomandra longifolia*), white cedar (*Melia azedarach*), coastal banksia (*Banksia integrifolia*), pigface (*Carpobrotus glaucesens*), knobby club rush (*Isolepis nodosa*), native rosemary (*Westringia fruticosa*) and silver princess gum (*Eucalyptus caesia* subsp. *magna*).

See also: **dry spaces; gum trees; seaside garden**

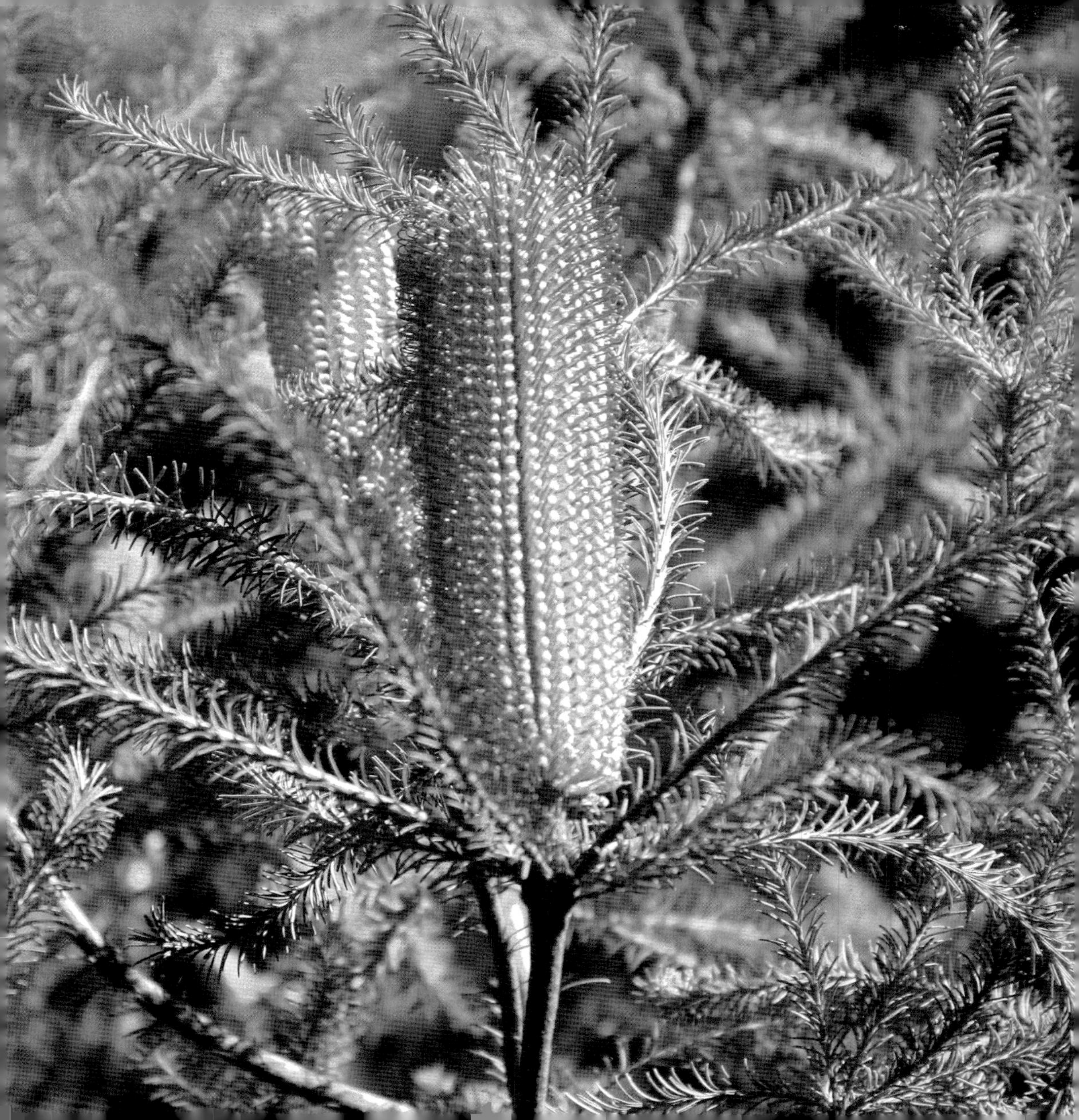

orchids

As far as gardening fashion goes, one plant that has never fallen out of favour — particularly as an indoor plant — is the orchid. An orchid looks good in almost any style of house and nowadays it is possible to have one flowering at most times of the year. There are also an increasing number of scented varieties being bred.

Plant your orchid in a free-draining potting medium or specialist orchid mix and do not leave the pot sitting in a saucer of water. Orchids prefer to be slightly root-bound, and while your orchid is setting flowers, it needs to be watered regularly and fed with a liquid fertiliser. When is has finished flowering, give it a good dose of slow-release fertiliser, and an additional feed of fish-based liquid fertiliser every two weeks during its flower-set period. Don't bring the plant back inside until the flower buds are about to open the following year.

The most popular orchids are *Cymbidium* spp., which are now grown in an endless variety of earthy colours. To ensure that your cymbidium flowers each year, put it outside in a warm, sunny position — but don't let it bake in hot summer sun, which can burn the leaves. It also needs good ventilation, but without wind or cold breezes. Moth orchids (*Phalaenopsis* spp.), which enjoy a warm environment and flower for months, are becoming increasingly popular as more people move into apartments.

To avoid draining your orchid's energy for next year, some people advocate cutting off the flower stems as they bud and pinning them in place. I don't do this and, by caring for my orchids as described above, have never had a problem getting them to re-flower.

See also: **indoor plants; pots**

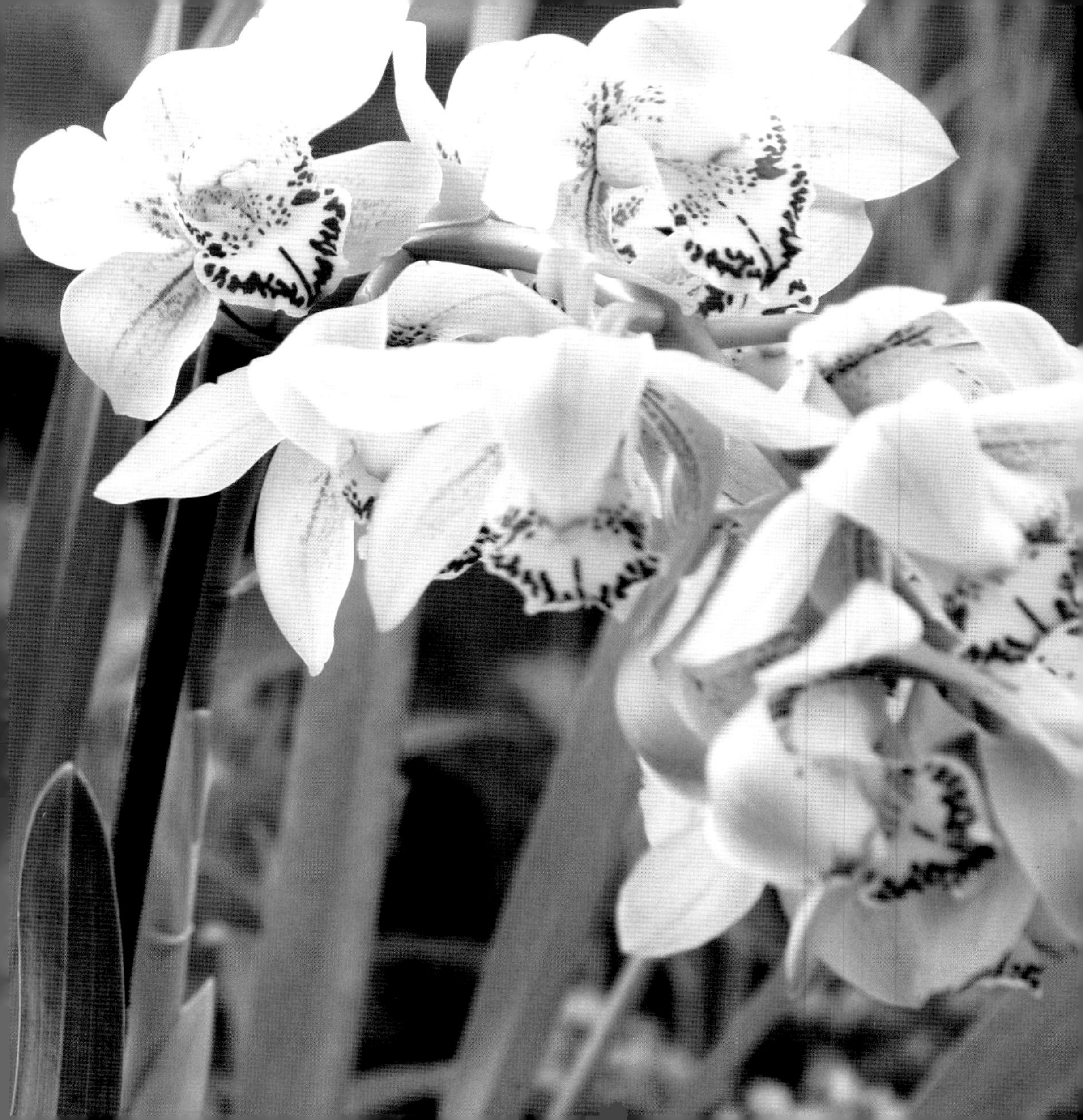

organic garden

As a rule, the nutritional level of home-grown produce is much higher because it goes straight from the garden into the pot. There is also scientific evidence to prove that organically grown fruit and vegetables contain much higher concentrations of many essential minerals and trace elements than commercially grown produce.

Organic gardeners reject the use of toxic chemicals and believe in growing healthy plants by building healthy soil. Plants grown in soil containing living microbes that provide nutritious food are less prone to pests and diseases than those grown in poor soil. Bugs prefer to attack unhealthy or old plants. Recycling is the secret to organic gardening. If you have a pest problem in your garden, improve your soil with mulch and compost rather than spraying; the pests should then disappear naturally.

In most gardens, after crops have finished bearing, the plants are pulled out and thrown onto the compost heap. Organic gardeners, however, often cut off the plants at soil level, compost the tops and allow the roots to rot down to increase the humus in the soil. Then they add a sprinkling of gardener's lime and plant a different crop (never the same as this can lead to pest and disease build-up) directly on top.

If you do need to spray to get rid of pests, use an organic spray like the ones below. They will help deter pests without leaving harmful chemical residues on the surface of the plant or, in the case of a systemic spray, inside the plant itself.

Soap spray kills most insect pests by suffocation and is safe for both us and the environment. Make your own by using the garlic spray recipe below but omitting the garlic.

Bordeaux mixture is an old-fashioned fungicide made from copper sulphate and lime (natural products which are acceptable to most organic gardeners). It can be sprayed at bud swell to prevent apple and pear scab, or curly leaf in stone fruit. It is simplest to buy this ready-made from a good nursery.

Hot chilli spray is an organic insecticide that will deter most chewing insects. It is an easy-to-prepare contact spray that will work for aphids, caterpillars and earwigs. It does, however, need to be reapplied fairly frequently, especially after rain or heavy dew.

hot chilli spray

750 ml vinegar
8 small dried chillies
1 tbsp freshly ground black pepper

Warm the vinegar. Grind the chillies and pepper together, and mix with the vinegar. Leave to stand. Store in a sealed container and use as required.

Garlic spray will repel insects such as thrip, aphids and pear slug. The addition of paraffin adds to the spray's residual qualities.

garlic spray

25 g pure soap
500 ml warm water
2 tsp paraffin
100 g crushed garlic

Grate the soap and dissolve in the water. Add the paraffin and garlic, and mix. Leave to stand. Store in a sealed container and use as required.

Rhubarb spray is an excellent way to control aphids, woolly aphids, caterpillars, pear and cherry slug, and whitefly. Note, however, that rhubarb leaves are poisonous, so wear adequate protection during preparation and use.

rhubarb spray

10 large rhubarb leaves, roughly chopped	1 litre boiling water
	1 litre cold water

Pour the boiling water over the rhubarb leaves, stir, strain, and set aside to cool. Dilute with the cold water. Use within a few days.

Earwig bait is one way to deal with these insects, which eat both live and dead plant and animal material. Earwigs like to crawl into tight spaces and tend to be present in gardens where there is lots of mulch, leaf litter and loose bark. In small numbers they are not often a problem, but in larger numbers they can do considerable damage to plants such as lettuces and gardenias. They will also chew off the stalks of small seedlings and create unsightly holes in the leaves of dahlias, Japanese anemones, chrysanthemums and other similar plants. The bait also helps to control slaters, which will eat the tips off seedlings and can be a particular problem in spring.

earwig bait
> *1 kg treacle*
> *4.5 litres water*
> *2 kg processed bran*
> *200 g sodium fluoride (buy as tablets from the chemist and grind to powder)*

Dissolve the treacle in half the water. When dissolved, add the rest of the water and mix well. Add the dry ingredients and combine into a crumbly mixture. Scatter around the garden as you would snail bait.

An even easier way to get rid of earwigs is to trap them by putting balls of scrunched-up newspaper around the garden. Each morning, simply collect the balls (along with the earwigs, which will have crawled into them) and dispose of them.

> In the past, it was safe to use commercial animal and poultry manure on your garden, and stable straw was a boon to poor soil. But these days, you need to be careful where you get your manure from, as most farm animals are drenched regularly for parasites and many are also treated with growth hormones and antibiotics.

See also: **companion planting**

paths

Imagine Monet's garden without the Grande Allée, rose trellises and spilling nasturtiums, or the Sissinghurst Castle garden without the Lime Walk. Paths, whether straight and formal or meandering and informal, can play a vital role in the creation of an interesting garden, large or small. There are endless possibilities . . .

- paths bordered by lavender or edged with box hedging
- paths designed to lead your eye to some focal point, like a pond or a statue
- access paths that, although functional, do not need to be boring
- paths paved with local stones or laid with local gravel
- the traditional pebble paths of the gardens of China and Provence, which feel as if you are walking in therapeutic sandals, or the bark-chip paths that often lead through Australian native gardens
- memorable walkways such as the Cranbourne annex of Melbourne's Royal Botanic Gardens; wandering through the flowering heath instantly transports you to an unspoilt area of the country, far from the city that exists only metres away.

One small garden I find fascinating has a path that meanders around under a tree and leads to the fence, where the owner has affixed a mirror beneath an arch, with pots on either side. The garden is reflected in the mirror and the path appears to lead through the fence to another garden beyond.

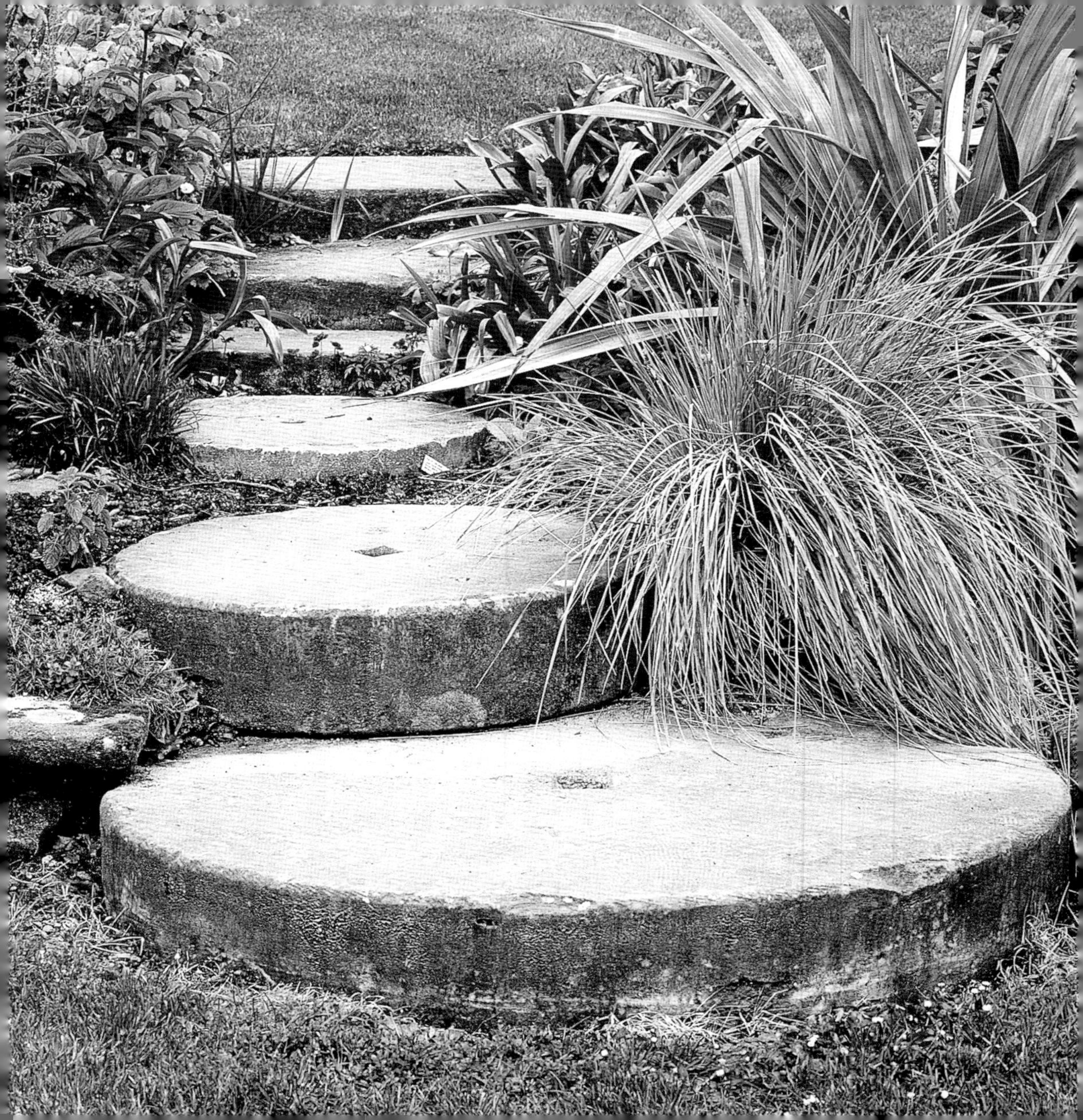

perennials

Perennials are plants that last more than two years and include herbaceous or soft-stemmed plants that become dormant each year and reappear the next, as well as bulbs and rhizomatous plants that, once planted, gradually spread and increase from the root structure. Perennials are rewarding to grow because, as the years go by, the clumps become larger and you can lift and divide them, acquiring lots more little plants – sometimes far more than you want!

When planning your garden and planting perennials, take into consideration:

- when the perennials will be flowering. It is easy to get carried away with a planting scheme. You see it in your mind: the massed planting of purple iris in front of the mauve lavender . . . But alas, in reality they flower at different times of the year.
- the different heights that the plants will grow to. Place low-growing plants at the front of the flower bed and graduate to the taller plants and shrubs at the back.
- the fact that it takes several full-time gardeners, and around 25 ml of rain per week, to maintain those beautiful herbaceous borders seen in large English gardens.

In my garden designs, I regularly use perennials such as New Zealand rock lily (*Arthropodium cirrhatum*) and Lenten rose (*Helleborus orientalis*) in semi-shaded positions, and daylilies, euphorbias and iris in full sun.

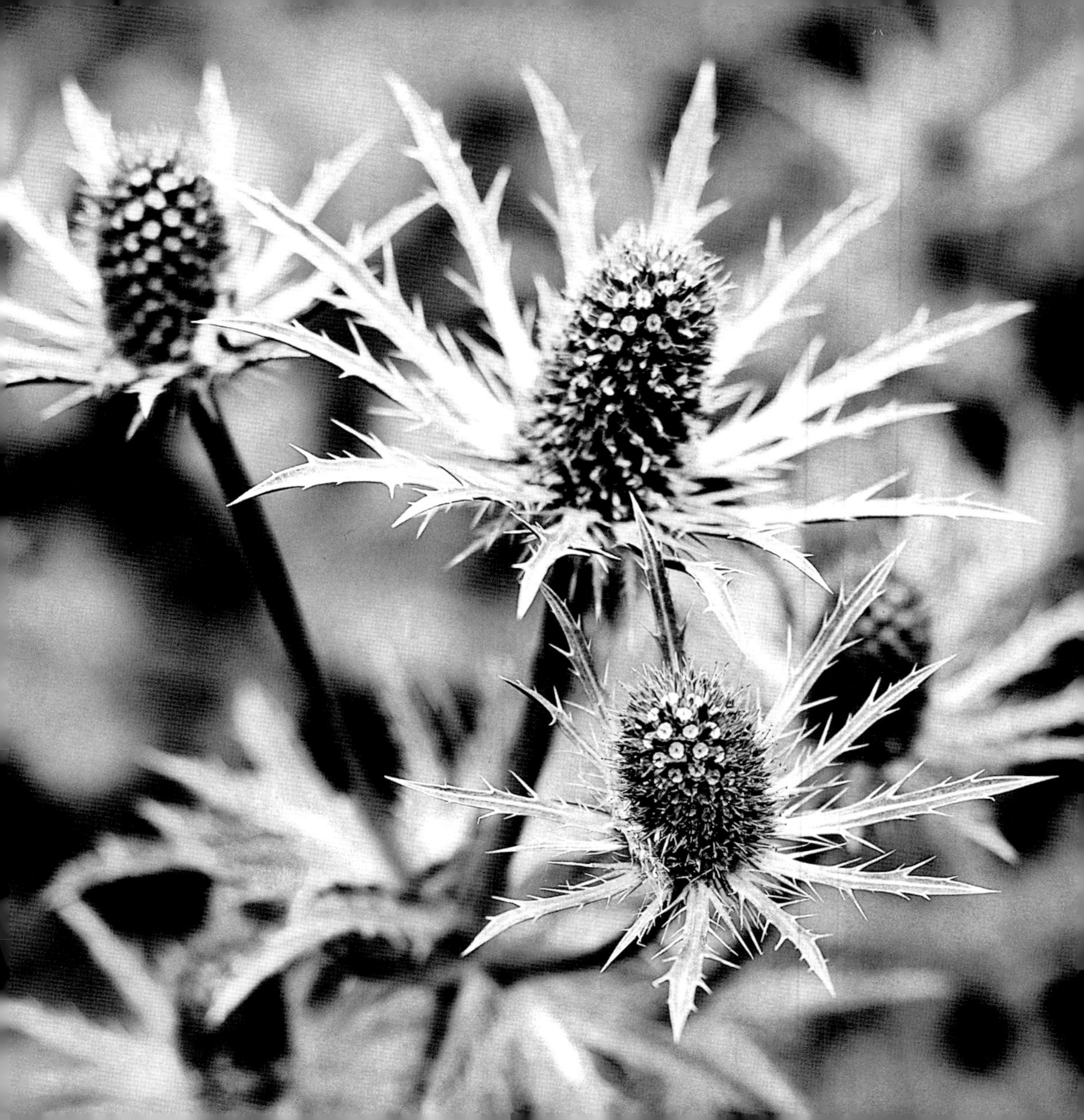

perfumed plants

Perfumed plants fall into several categories . . .

Spicy-scented plants have a perfume that is often stronger on sunny days, when oil is released from their leaves. They include species we think of as cottage-garden plants: honey-scented alyssum; spicy-scented wallflowers and cottage pinks; herbs; and sweet peas.

Exotic plants sometimes reserve their main scent for the night: the magical angels' trumpets or zombie cucumber (*Brugmansia* × *candida*) with its huge white, pink or apricot-scented blooms; frangipani, which always evokes memories of romantic tropical evenings; tobacco plant (*Nicotiana* spp.); and perennial stocks and climbers such as jasmines and honeysuckles.

Winter-flowering plants are, strangely, some of the strongest and most beautifully scented species: the fashionable tree *Michelia doltsopa*, which bears huge, creamy-white magnolia-shaped flowers towards the end of winter; wintersweet (*Chimonanthus praecox*), Chinese witchhazel (*Hamamelis mollis*) and *Luculia gratissima*, which all have the most beautiful scents but, sadly, are now almost impossible to find in nurseries; *Buddleja salvifolia*, which makes a good, hardy, spicy-scented hedge; and daphne.

Perfumed native plants include native frangipani (*Hymenosporum flavum*); brown boronia (*B. megastigma*); mint bush (*Prostanthera* spp.); sweet pittosporum (*Pittosporum undulatum*); and wattles.

Scented spring bulbs include hyacinths, jonquils and freesias.

Blossom trees, roses and lilacs also provide beautiful fragrance.

Scented climbers are a good way of introducing fragrance into your garden, particularly if you don't have much room. There are a number of really lovely climbers that are long-flowering and easy to grow.

- Several species of honeysuckle (*Lonicera* spp.) are fast-growing and do well in shade – but prune regularly to keep them under control.
- Giant Burmese honeysuckle (*Lonicera hildebrandiana*) has much larger flowers than other varieties and grows well in a warm, sunny position.
- *Stephanotis floribunda* is an evergreen climber from Madagascar. Given the right conditions (a warm, sunny position), it will grow to 3 m and flower in late summer, producing white waxy flowers over a long period.
- Star jasmine (*Trachelospermum jasminoides*) starts flowering in the spring and continues into early summer. It is a bit slow to start but makes a very attractive fence cover, with dark-green leaves and tiny, star-like flowers.
- Pink jasmine (*Jasminum polyanthum*) is a vigorous climber that produces spicy-scented flowers in early spring. Prune it back hard each year.
- Summer jasmine (*Jasminum azoricum*) produces white flowers from late spring until autumn and does not need much attention. As a bonus, it does well in seaside locations.
- Of the climbing roses, my favourite is the apple-blossom-like 'Rennae', which has almost no thorns and flowers on and off throughout the year.

See also: **poisonous plants; sweet peas; walls**

poisonous plants

We have many poisonous plants in our gardens. Daphnes, arum lilies, foxgloves, euphorbias and honeysuckle, for example, are all poisonous, but not likely to cause much of a problem because children are not tempted to eat them. It is wise, however, not to include in your garden poisonous plants with brightly coloured berries or dangling pods. There is generally no danger in handling a tree or shrub that is poisonous, but sucking or swallowing the seeds or pods can make you ill. Be aware of the following species:

- golden rain (*Laburnum* spp.) has particularly poisonous seed pods
- golden dewdrop (*Duranta repens*) has poisonous yellow berries
- rhus tree (*Toxicodendron succedaneum*) is related to poison ivy and, in some people, can cause severe rashes and skin irritation
- rue (*Ruta* spp.) and euphorbias have caustic sap that can produce an irritant reaction
- angels' trumpets (*Brugmansia* × *candida*) have poisonous leaves and flowers; you might prefer to chop off the lower branches to force the tree to grow taller, keeping the beautiful scented flowers out of harm's way
- oleander (*Nerium oleander*) is poisonous if ingested, so do not plant an oleander hedge where it is available to livestock.

If you are concerned about planting a poisonous tree or shrub, check with the nursery when making your purchase.

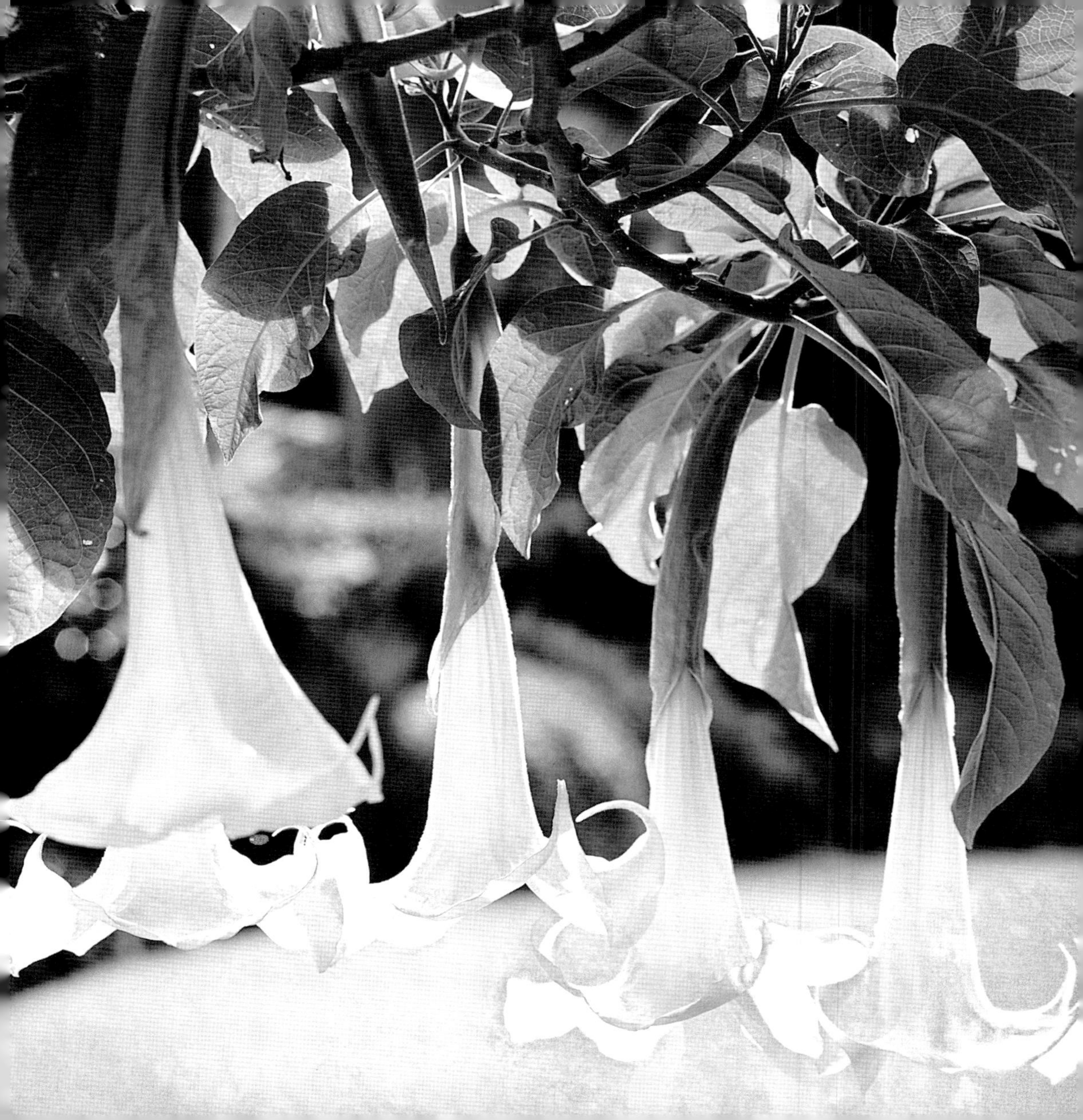

pots

Pots add personality to a garden. Plant them with annuals to add extra colour, clipped balls or spirals for topiary interest, or citrus for year-round greenery and winter colour. But remember that plants in pots are like babies in bassinettes: they rely on you to look after them because they are unable to receive any extra goodness from the soil as plants in the garden can.

In warm weather, pot plants need to be watered every day, or even twice a day if the pots are small and the weather hot. They should also be fertilised regularly. I use a slow-release complete garden fertiliser on all my pots twice a year, alternating fortnightly with liquid applications of a fish-based fertiliser and a seaweed-based plant tonic.

- If you live in an apartment and all you have is a courtyard or a balcony, you can create a mini-garden using pots of all sizes.
- Citrus trees grow well in large pots, but be sure to provide a regular liquid-feed as well as a complete garden fertiliser. An addition of urea, which is high in nitrogen, will also keep their foliage shiny and green.
- You can grow a thriving vegetable garden entirely in pots.
- Bay trees, which often sucker in the garden, make a beautiful pot specimen, particularly if clipped into a standard ball or other shape.
- Gardenias, geraniums, azaleas, camellias, clivias, buxus, and most annuals and succulents all do well in pots.

Re-potting is necessary when a plant outgrows its pot (although some plants, such as orchids and African violets, flower better if they are slightly root-bound). The temptation is to simply pull the plant out of the existing pot and put it in a larger one. The problem is that it will often be root-bound and, when it is watered, all the water will run down the sides of the old root-ball, leaving it dry where it really matters.

Follow these steps to ensure successful re-potting:

1. Tip the plant from the old pot and gently tease out the roots either by hand or with a trickling hose. (If they are totally bound up, you can scratch around the outside with a key or piece of broken pot to fray the edges.) Wet the root-ball of the plant thoroughly – you may even need to soak it in a container of water.
2. Place the plant into a slightly larger pot, fill the pot with good quality potting mix (to the same level as in the old pot), and tamp down firmly.
3. Water in well with a seaweed-based plant tonic or a plant starter and trim the foliage back by around 20 per cent to compensate for any root disturbance.
4. Keep the plant moist, paying particular attention to the root-ball. If you like, you can also use a soil-wetting agent (ask at your local nursery) to help the new pot retain moisture.

See also: **annuals; courtyards; fruit trees; herbs; indoor plants; orchids; succulents**

pruning

The purposes of pruning are to let more light and air into the bush or tree, to preserve its shape, to remove dead wood, and to encourage vigour. This leads to more flowers or, in the case of deciduous fruit trees, more fruit. There is not space here to include instructions on how to prune, since different plants require different treatment. But the pruning question I'm most often asked is when to do it . . .

Prune after flowering is the simplest rule. This way, the plant has the whole year to recover and produce flowers for next year.
Fruit trees, however, should be pruned after fruiting; if you prune after flowering, you cut off the fruits before they form.
Stone fruit should be pruned after fruiting in late summer; the dryer conditions reduce the incidence of bacterial infections.
Shrubs that flower all year such as daisies, native hibiscus and French lavender make pruning tricky. Use common sense here; if the bush looks like it needs pruning, prune it – even if there are still flower buds on it.
Spring-flowering shrubs such as philadelphus, viburnums and early roses (including banksias, 'Lorraine Lee' and 'Wedding Day') should be pruned soon after flowering. If you prune these in winter (the traditional time to prune roses and fruit trees) you will cut off all the flowering canes that produce that year's flowers.
Frost-sensitive plants such as gardenias, plumbago and hibiscus are an exception to the rule. They should be pruned in early spring, after the danger of any late frosts has passed, because any new growth produced after pruning will be burnt off if there is a cold snap.

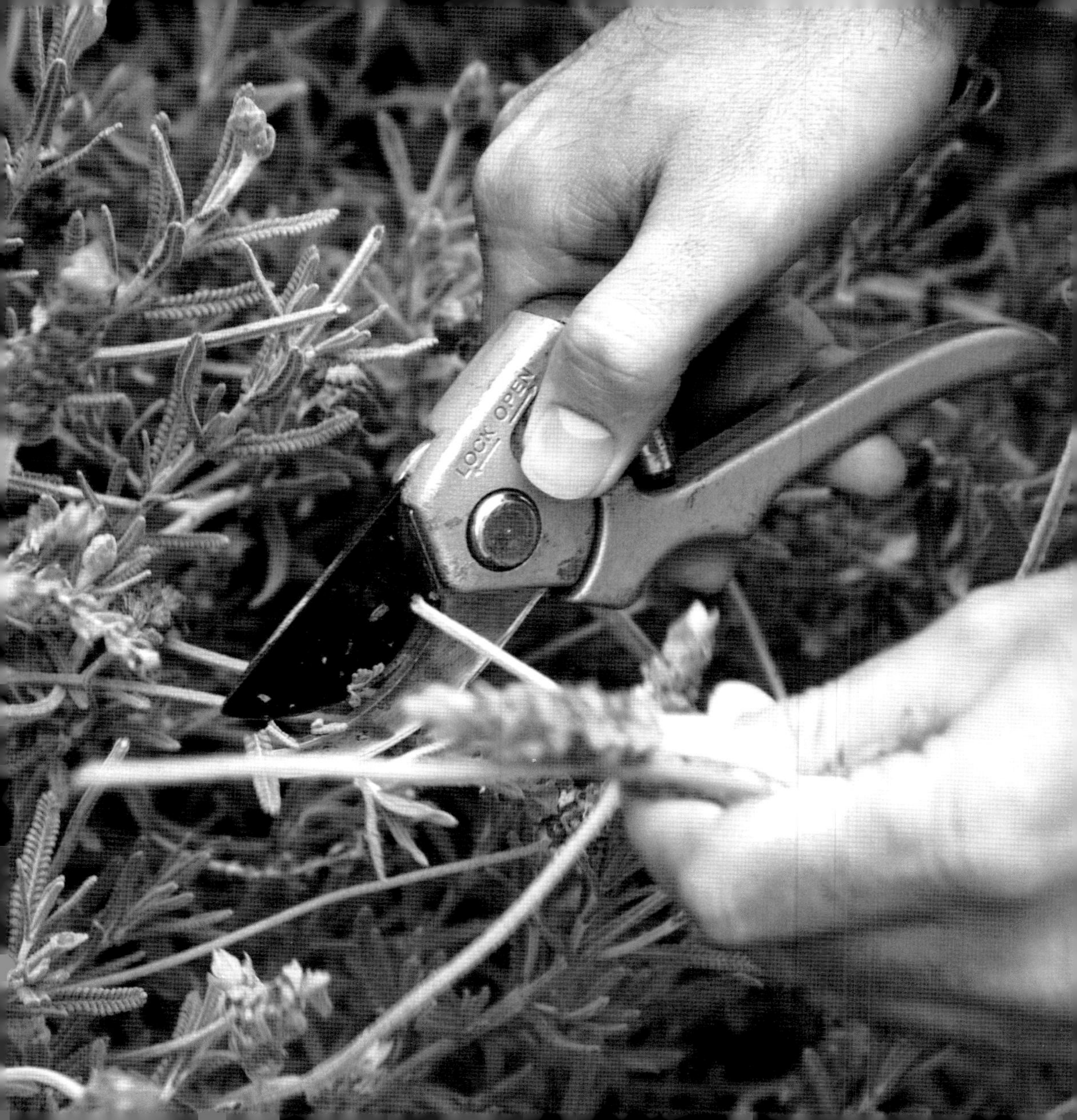
LOCK OPEN

purple flowers and foliage

Encompassing a range from the palest mauve of swamp foxtail grass (*Pennisetum alopecuroides*) to the almost neon tones of purple top (*Verbena bonariensis*), purple can be included in almost any planting combination imaginable.

- 'White' gardens will benefit from a hint of mauve in the form of a soft dusting of catmint (*Nepeta × faassenii*) or the equally attractive purple sage (*Salvia officinalis* 'Purpurascens'). In a larger area, try a copse of purple birch (*Betula pendula* 'Purpurea') with its white trunk and deep-plum foliage.
- Add a touch of purple or mauve to a pastel garden — Jerusalem sage (*Pulmonaria saccharata*) or *Buddleja salviifolia* work well.
- In shady areas requiring a shrub of larger dimensions, include the native mint bush (*Prostanthera melissifolia*).
- For a stunning, bright garden, combine the magnificent bee plant (*Echium candicans*) with a front planting of the maize-coloured, spring-flowering kniphofia 'Zambia'. Or, try a massed planting of *Iris germanica* 'Dusky Challenger' within a sea of yellow chamomile (*Anthemis tinctoria*).
- The purplish foliage of Cootamundra wattle (*Acacia baileyana* 'Purpurea'), New Zealand flax (*Phormium tenax* 'Purpureum') or *Ajuga* 'Catlins Giant' not only makes a statement in its own right but contrasts superbly with its neighbours.

See also: **colour in the garden**

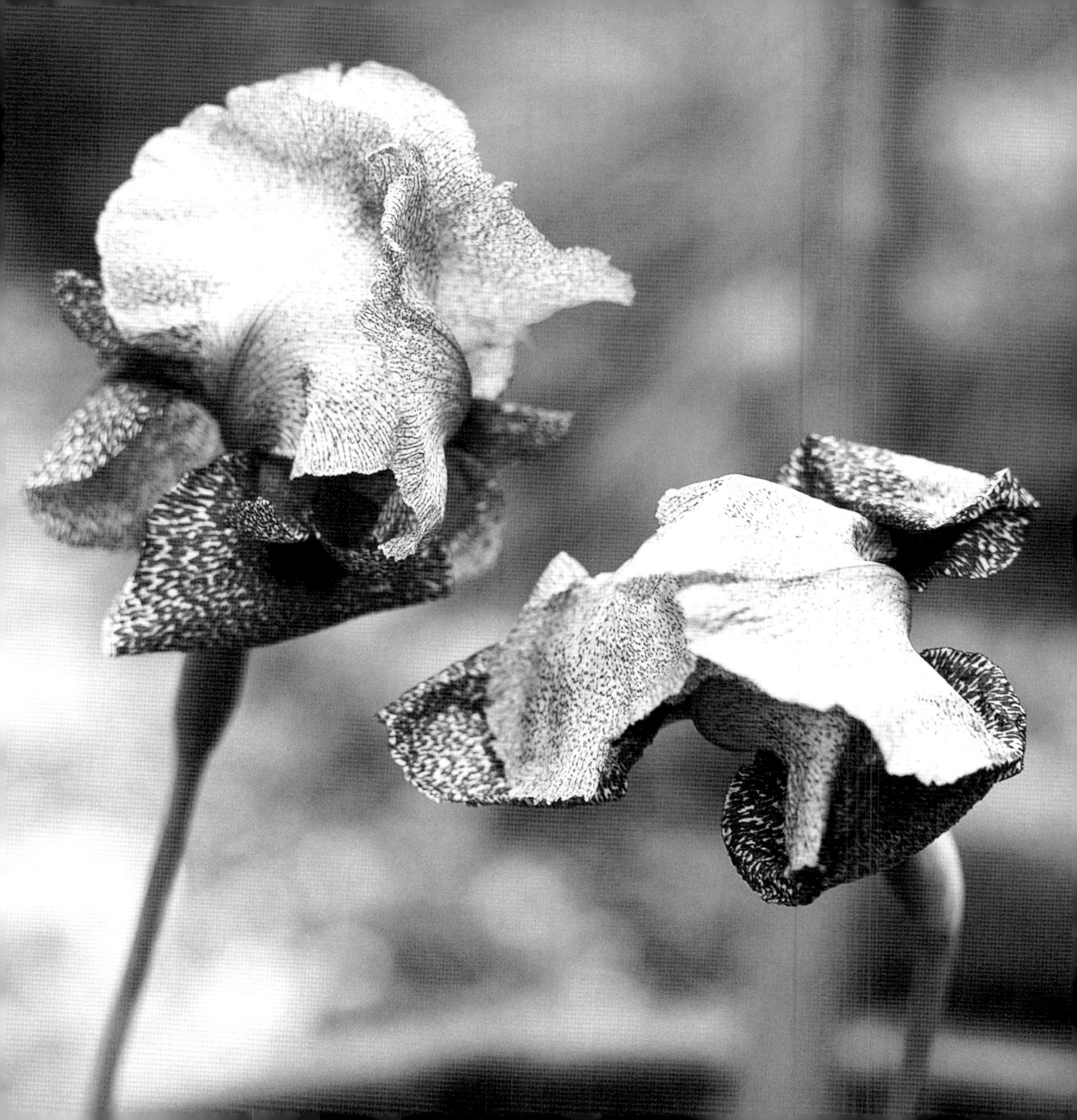

red flowers

Used among other strong colours such as orange, plum and purple, red can be magnificent in the garden. It is not, however, as easy to use successfully as some other colours. If one red camellia or one red rose is planted in a garden with plants of mixed colours, for example, it can throw the whole scheme out of kilter. The following hints will help you to use red creatively.

- Splashes of red can add strength to a colour scheme. The long-flowering climbing rose 'Altissimo' looks fantastic climbing up the posts of a pergola if the paving beneath is a soft sand colour or the house is painted in a pale shade. And pots of red pelargoniums along a balcony or red geraniums spilling over a wall always make me feel good.
- Planters filled with red tulips can be a welcome harbinger of spring. In summer, the same pots could be filled with red arctotis; their silvery leaves offer a softening contrast to the dark-red flowers.
- The dark, plum-coloured leaves of the dahlia 'Bishop of Llandaff' provide another type of contrast to strong red flowers. But if you want to use this species, plant several tubers together to make a real splash of colour and then repeat this planting elsewhere for balance. Against the silver foliage of plants such as artemisia, the effect can be breathtaking.

Although there are exceptions (Nantucket is famous for its red roses), the warmer the climate, the better strong colours such as red work.

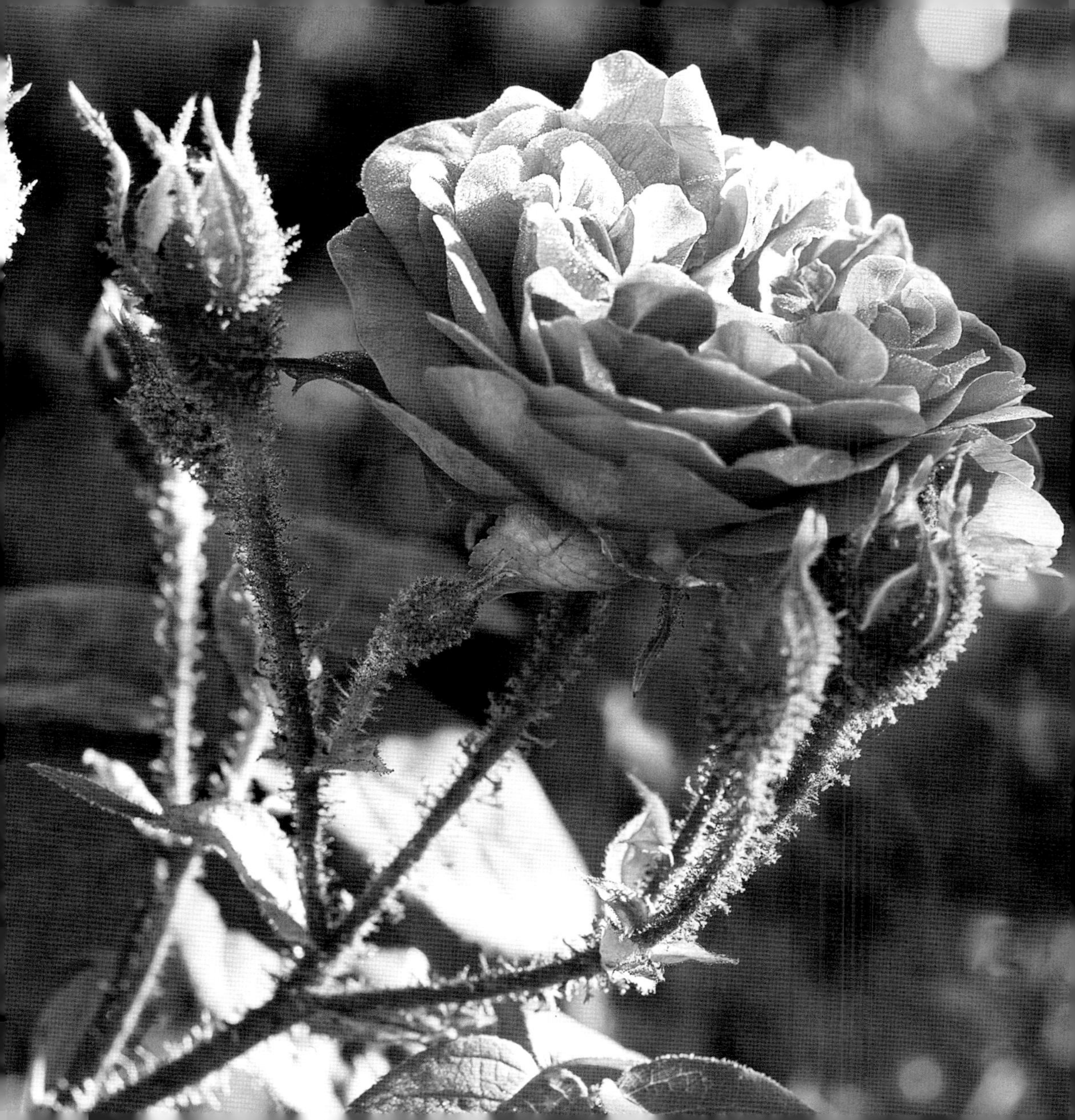

root vegetables

Carrots, radishes and turnips are great for beginner gardeners; not only do they take up little space, but they are also easy to grow and enormously rewarding. Their foliage does not look out of place even in a flowerbed and, along with other root vegetables such as parsnips and beetroot, they grow quickly.

Root crops prefer cool growing conditions. But there are varieties available for planting throughout the year and, given adequate moisture, they will survive in all but the hottest climates.

Soil should not have been recently manured or composted when you plant the seeds; this can cause malformation of the roots and may introduce weeds that will interfere with your crop. Sow carrot and parsnip seed into soil that has been improved with compost and manure for a previous crop of cabbages, cauliflowers or something similar.

Sowing season varies. Radishes and carrots can be planted any time except midwinter. Parsnips can be planted from spring to late summer/early autumn in cooler and temperate areas, and in autumn in warmer areas. Beetroot can be planted from spring to autumn in cooler and temperate areas, and all year round in warmer areas. Turnips prefer to be planted from late summer to early winter.

Care for the crops by applying a complete fertiliser at sowing time and thinning out the plants as required to allow them room to grow.

> In my opinion, beetroot is an underrated vegetable. It is easy to grow and tastes delicious grated raw in a salad, steamed whole with the leaves on, roasted with other vegetables or made into borscht.

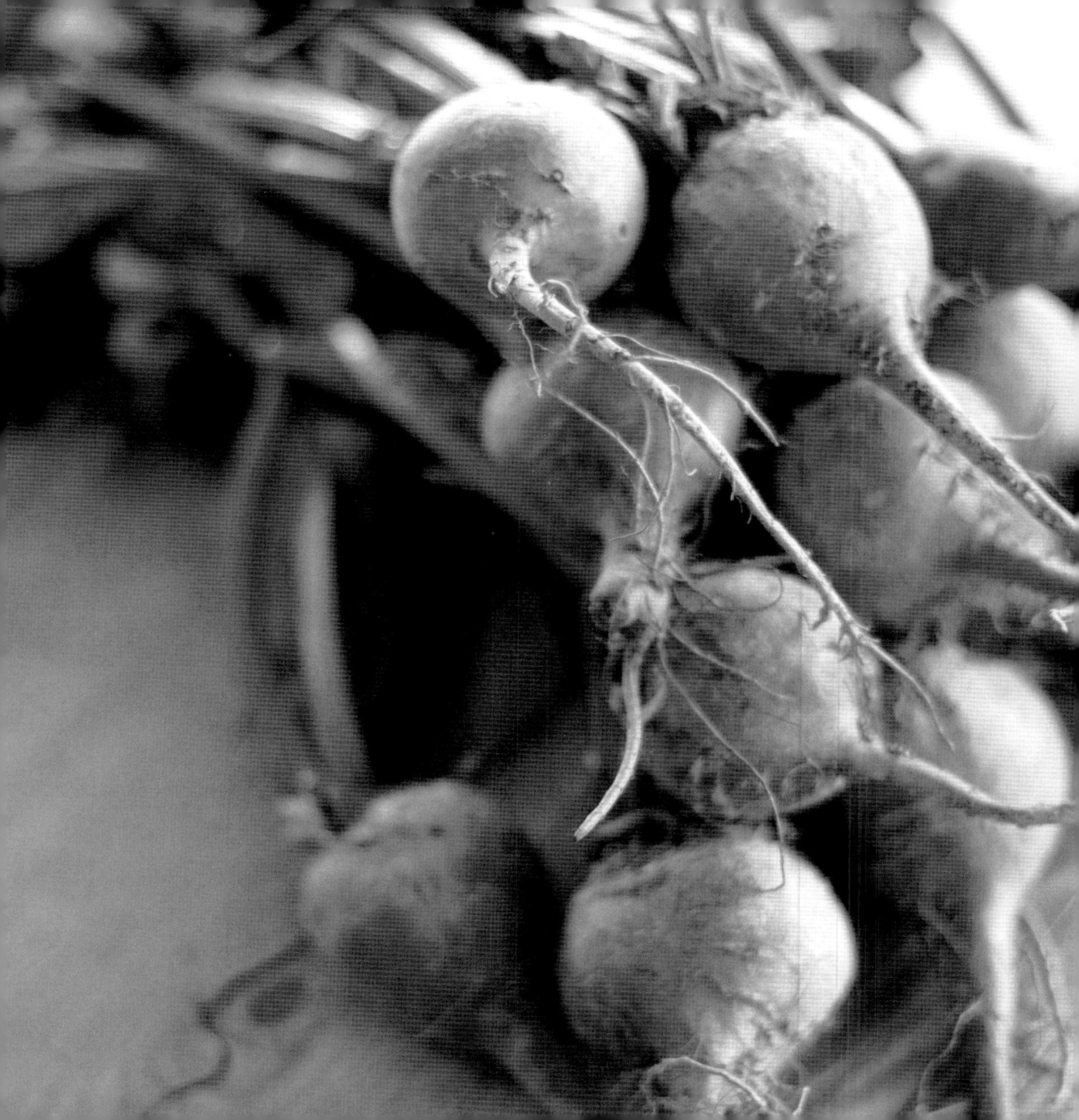

roses

More than 100 species of rose, an equal number of natural hybrids, and who knows how many cultivated varieties, are to be found from the Arctic to the tropics, and each has adapted to its own environment. Contrary to popular opinion, roses are hardy, easy to grow and do not require special treatment. They make ideal garden plants for various situations: garden beds, borders, hedges, pots, rock gardens (miniature roses), walls, arbours and pergolas (climbing roses). As well as their fragrant flowers, borne mainly in summer and autumn, their fruits (hips) can also provide colour in the garden.

Rose cultivation has a long history, beginning with the Romans. At the end of the eighteenth century, repeat-flowering China roses and tea roses were introduced to Europe. Hybrid-teas and floribundas were the common roses of the twentieth century, before English rose-breeder David Austin added a new classification by cultivating roses with the charm and scent of old-fashioned shrub roses combined with the colours and flowering ability of the modern rose.

Perhaps the most popular of all roses in Australia is the white floribunda 'Iceberg'; it flowers continuously but has little scent. 'Just Joey' is another quite beautiful floribunda, pale-apricot in colour and free-flowering. 'Radox Bouquet' is a deliciously scented pale-pink rose with a slightly untidy shape, while 'Graham Thomas', a David Austin rose, is one of the more popular yellow varieties.

You can buy either potted or bare-rooted roses from the nursery. Bare-rooted roses require a little extra attention.

Bare-rooted roses should be planted as follows:

1. Pre-dig the rose bed and mulch it with compost or stable straw.
2. Choose roses with smooth green or reddish-brown stems; any wrinkling, especially towards the top of the stem, indicates that at some stage the roots have been allowed to dry out.
3. Be prepared to plant the roses as soon as you get them home; if this is not practical, at least give them a good soak and heel them in until you can plant them out.
4. With a sharp pair of secateurs, prune any roots that have messy or untidy ends and reprune the stems to an outward-facing bud to ensure a good bush shape.
5. Add a little organic-based liquid fertiliser to a bucket of water and soak the roses for about half an hour.
6. Dig a hole approximately 30 cm in diameter, or slightly larger than the root-spread on your rose. Make a small mound in the bottom of the hole and spread the roots over this mound in much the same way as you would place your hand over an orange. Then mix some of the loose soil back in the hole to hold the rose in place, and fill the hole with the water and fertiliser mix from the bucket. When this soaks away, finish filling the hole with soil and press down lightly, making sure that the soil level comes right up to the bottom of the graft (the lumpy bit at the bottom of the main stem).
7. Finally, water the rose and place a layer of mulch or compost around the base to keep the graft and soil moist.

Drought-tolerant roses include various species that are particularly suited to tough, dry conditions. Rugosa roses are seedlings or crosses of *Rosa rugosa*, a hardy species from Northern Japan and Siberia. They are disease-free, flower over a long period and bear large orange or red hips in autumn. They have a dense, suckering habit of growth and respond well to light pruning, making them excellent hedging plants. Being tolerant of salt winds, they are also appropriate for drought-prone areas and seaside gardens. I particularly like the following cultivars:

- 'Frau Dagmar Hartopp' has single fragrant pink flowers followed by crimson fruit.
- 'Alba' is another fragrant cultivar with large, single white flowers borne in clusters, and large orange–red hips.
- 'Roseraie de l'Hay' is one of the best examples of a double rugosa, with huge, fragrant, plum-coloured flowers and lush, shiny foliage.

Other hardy species include:

- *Rosa sweginzowii* (a spreading shrub up to 4 m tall with pink flowers)
- *Rosa virginiana* (a rose of erect, suckering habit with single pink flowers followed by ruby-red hips)
- *Rosa wichuraiana* (a vigorous, climbing rose often used as ground cover, with shiny green leaves, single white flowers and orange–red hips).

Pruning roses is best done in the middle of winter. But remember that banksia roses (*Rosa banksiae*), which flower early in spring, are different and need to be pruned back soon after flowering – otherwise you'll be cutting off next year's flowers.

Rose pruning is not as difficult as many people think. You want the shape of your rose to be like your hand, palm-up with fingers spread (not too far) as if ready to catch a small ball. Envisage this shape and then follow these steps:

1. Ensure that your secateurs are clean and sharp. Dirty or blunt secateurs will produce a torn, untidy cut that is likely to spread disease and make your rose more susceptible to dieback. Also have a small pruning saw or pair of loppers handy for thicker, woodier stems.
2. Remove any weak, overcrowded or diseased wood (don't put this wood in the compost as it can aid the spread of fungal spores; burn or bin it).
3. As a general rule, dwarf, bush and standard roses should be cut back by about a third, while hybrid-tea and floribunda roses can be cut back by about half. Climbing roses should have their secondary growth pruned back to around 7–10 cm from the main canes (a bit like a fish skeleton).
4. Prune each stem to about half a centimetre above an outward-growing bud, on a slight upward angle.
5. Any growth coming from below the graft should be removed as it is part of the root stock and not the rose you bought.
6. Spray the roses with lime sulphur to help prevent any fungal build-up.

screening

Part of living in the city is existing cheek by jowl with your neighbours. Planting a living screen is one solution if you require a bit more privacy. There are plenty of good screening plants available.

- Maidenhair creeper (*Muehlenbeckia comlexa*) has a fast, compact habit of growth and, given a suitable frame, can easily grow to a height of 4.5 m. Although it is a rather severe-looking plant, it clips well.
- Potato vine (*Solanum jasminoides*) is another quick-growing creeper that also clips well. It is ideal for hiding (in record time!) things such as bins, clothes lines or general service areas.
- Fast-growing trees such as pittosporums and ornamental pears (*Pyrus* spp.) are narrow, easy to look after and will hide the ugly block of flats next door.
- Slower-growing trees such as magnolias and *Michelia doltsopa* are very beautiful and produce huge, scented flowers. Prune them regularly to keep them tall and compact.
- Native options include blackwoods (*Acacia melanoxylon*), native frangipani (*Hymenosporum flavum*) and coastal banksia (*Banksia integrifolia*).
- Non-invasive, clumping bamboos are good if you don't have enough room for a screen of trees down the side of your garden.

To hide a dog kennel, plant Allard's lavender (*Lavandula × allardii*) or westringia around it. Both are fast-growing and will form a hedge to surround the kennel.

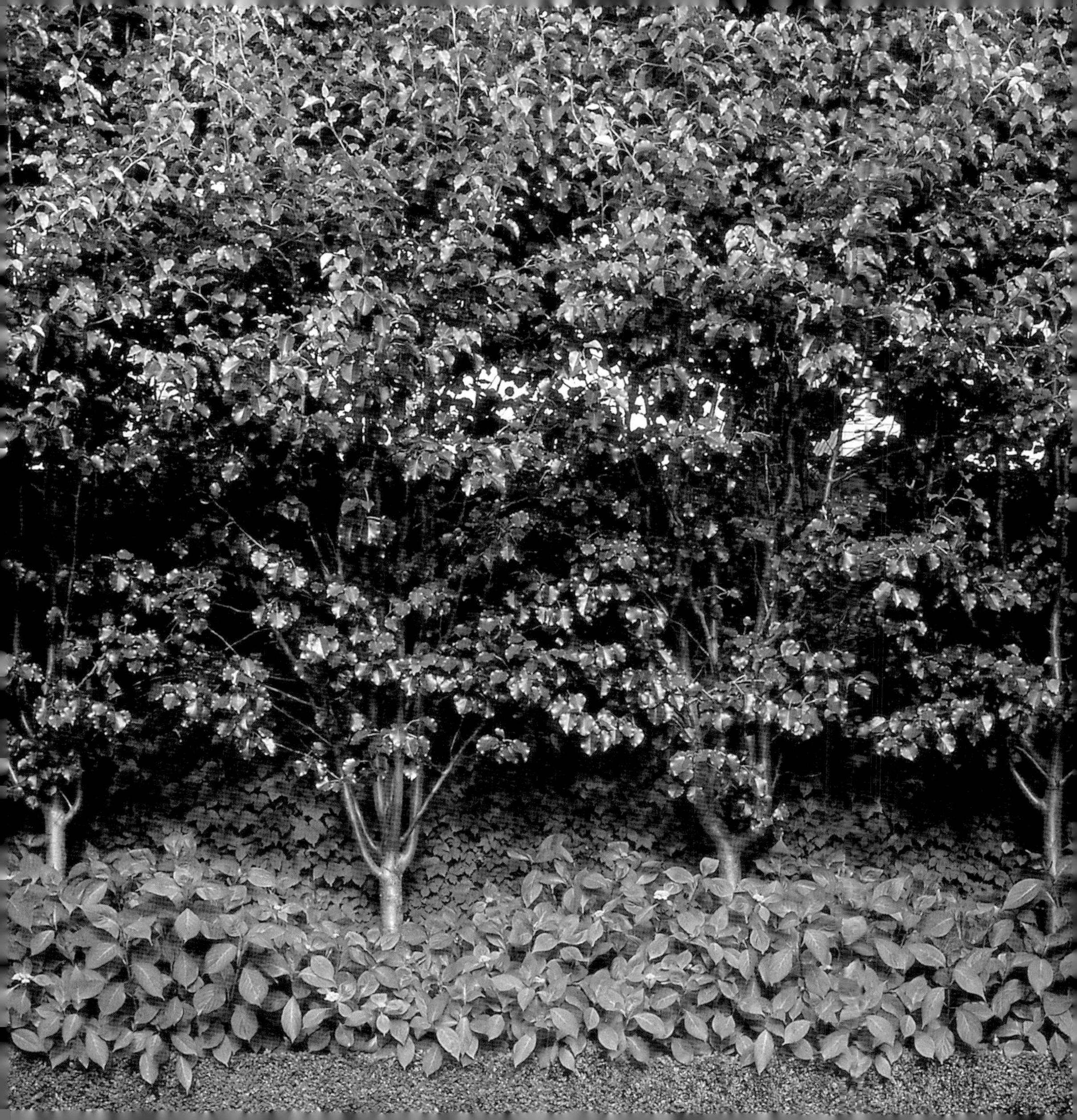

seaside garden

The secret to successful seaside gardening is to choose plants that will thrive in this environment. Forget silver birches, azaleas and camellias; choose hardy plants that will cope with salt winds and little attention, and still look good all year.

- Foliage plants are a good start. Large *Agapanthus praecox* look marvellous edging a drive while smaller varieties are perfect for edging gravel or shell-grit paths. Also, the fine foliage of ornamental grasses such as *Pennisetum alopecuroides* contrasts well with most other plants, giving interest and structure to a garden even when not much is in flower.
- Silver-leafed plants survive well; the hairy covering on their leaves collects salt, protecting the leaf surface, and the leaves also reflect the light, keeping the plant cool and conserving moisture.
- Many Australian natives grow happily beside the sea. *Banksia integrifolia*, which can be grown as a tree or clipped to create a protective hedge for a garden exposed to coastal winds, bears yellow–green flower spikes from summer through to early winter. *Banksia ericifolia* is much-loved by native birds and produces huge orange flower spikes. There are also many good grevillea cultivars as well as the amazing *Alyogne huegelii*, a shrub to 2 m that produces large, blue hibiscus-like flowers also over a long period.
- African daisies (*Arctotis* spp.), gazanias, kniphofias and all species of rock rose (*Cistus* spp.) add colour and blend well.

See also: **grasses; native garden; roses; silver and grey foliage**

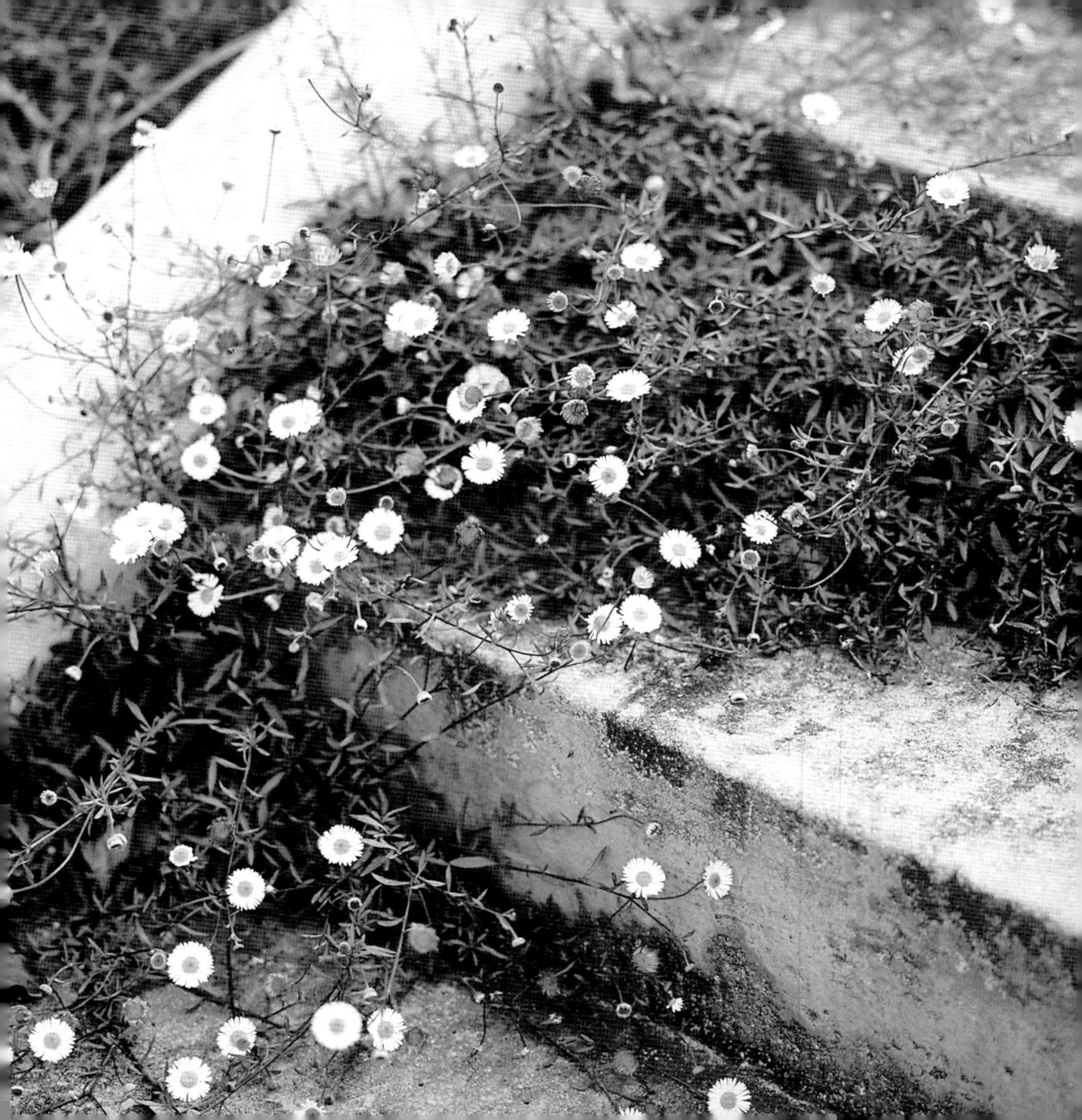

shade trees

A garden without trees would be a very soulless place indeed, but as garden blocks become smaller our choice of trees is also reduced. If you are lucky enough to have a spacious block, you can plant larger deciduous trees or eucalypts. But if you are choosing for a standard block, it is important to consider whether you will be casting your neighbour's garden into shade in a few years' time, or whether the tree's roots might interfere with the drains. Deciduous trees are often the best choice, as they offer shade in summer but allow sunshine in during winter.

- Jacarandas, although not particularly fast-growing, are one of my favourite choices; they do not drop their leaves until late winter and, in early summer, bear a magnificent display of mauve-blue flowers on bare branches.
- Chinese elms (*Ulmus parvifolia*) are fast-growing, attractive trees with beautiful trunks – but keep them away from neighbouring fences and driveways.
- Manchurian pears (*Pyrus ussuriensis*) have become popular for smaller gardens; they are relatively uninvasive, have both spring blossom and autumn colour, and can be pruned to produce a lovely spreading habit.
- If you want evergreen, there are now several smaller varieties of *Magnolia grandiflora* available. Or, *Agonis flexuosa* is a beautiful, weeping native tree.

If you are growing a smaller tree in your garden, prune off the lower branches only to force it to grow taller and give you space underneath for a table and chairs.

shady spaces

One of the biggest mistakes many gardeners make is to underestimate how much sun a plant requires to do well. If a plant label doesn't say 'sunny position', it will almost certainly say 'full sun or part shade'. And this is where the problem lies: 'part shade' doesn't mean 'full shade with the occasional sunbeam filtering through'. Nevertheless, there are some plants that can cope with shade . . .

Part shade — hydrangeas, hellebores, arthropodiums, dogwoods, Japanese anemones, lomandra and dietes will all grow well. Many of these also survive quite happily in full shade but with a reduced flowering capacity. *Plectranthus ecklonii* prefers partial shade and produces masses of tall purple spikes during autumn when nothing much else is happening.

Deep shade — apart from ferns and other shade-tolerant foliage plants that don't have any flowers to speak of, the lovely *Clivia miniata* is my choice. It will produce its beautiful orange, red or yellow flowers with almost no sun whatsoever. Into the bargain, it will cope with dry conditions. *Iris foetidissima* will also grow happily in deep shade and, like clivia, its bright-orange seed heads are very ornamental.

Taller species — arum and green goddess lilies (*Zantedeschia* spp.) survive well in moist shade, as does elephant's ear (*Colocasia esculenta*), particularly the cultivar 'Fontanesii', which has dark leaves and pale-yellow, scented flowers.

Ground cover — winter heliotrope (*Petasites fragrans*) is a shade-tolerant, spreading ground cover with large, waterlily-shaped leaves and, in winter, purple and white toothbrush-shaped flowers with a beautiful vanilla scent.

silver and grey foliage

Silver and grey work well with almost any colour in the garden. Plants with silver or grey foliage can be particularly useful in lightening dark areas, highlighting colours and accentuating plants with darker foliage. Silver or grey colouring is often due to a carpet of fine hairs on the surface of a plant's leaves. These hairs prevent salt and other damaging materials from coming into contact with the leaf's surface and, as a result, grey plants are used extensively in coastal areas.

- Tree wormwood (*Artemisia arborescens*) is good for background planting. It has soft, feathery leaves with an amazing silvery sheen and makes a great hedge – but it does need to be clipped regularly. *A.* 'Powis Castle' has similar foliage, but the leaves have a slightly blue tinge. It spreads quite widely, but you only need to clip the edges.
- *Lavandula × allardii* has quite insignificant flowers without that lovely lavender scent, but it clips beautifully and makes a long-lasting hedge.
- Sage (*Salvia officinalis*) has furry grey–green leaves and is useful in cooking.
- *Helichrysum petiolare* does just as well in sun (where it grows into a shrub 1.5 × 1.5 m) or shade (where it has a more sprawling habit). Under trees, the dappled sunlight reflects off its silvery leaves.
- *Cotyledon orbiculata* also grows well in either sun or light shade. Its fat, glaucous leaves look especially dramatic under trees. In summer, salmon-pink bell-shaped flowers hang down from tall maroon stems.

See also: **red flowers; seaside garden; summer garden**

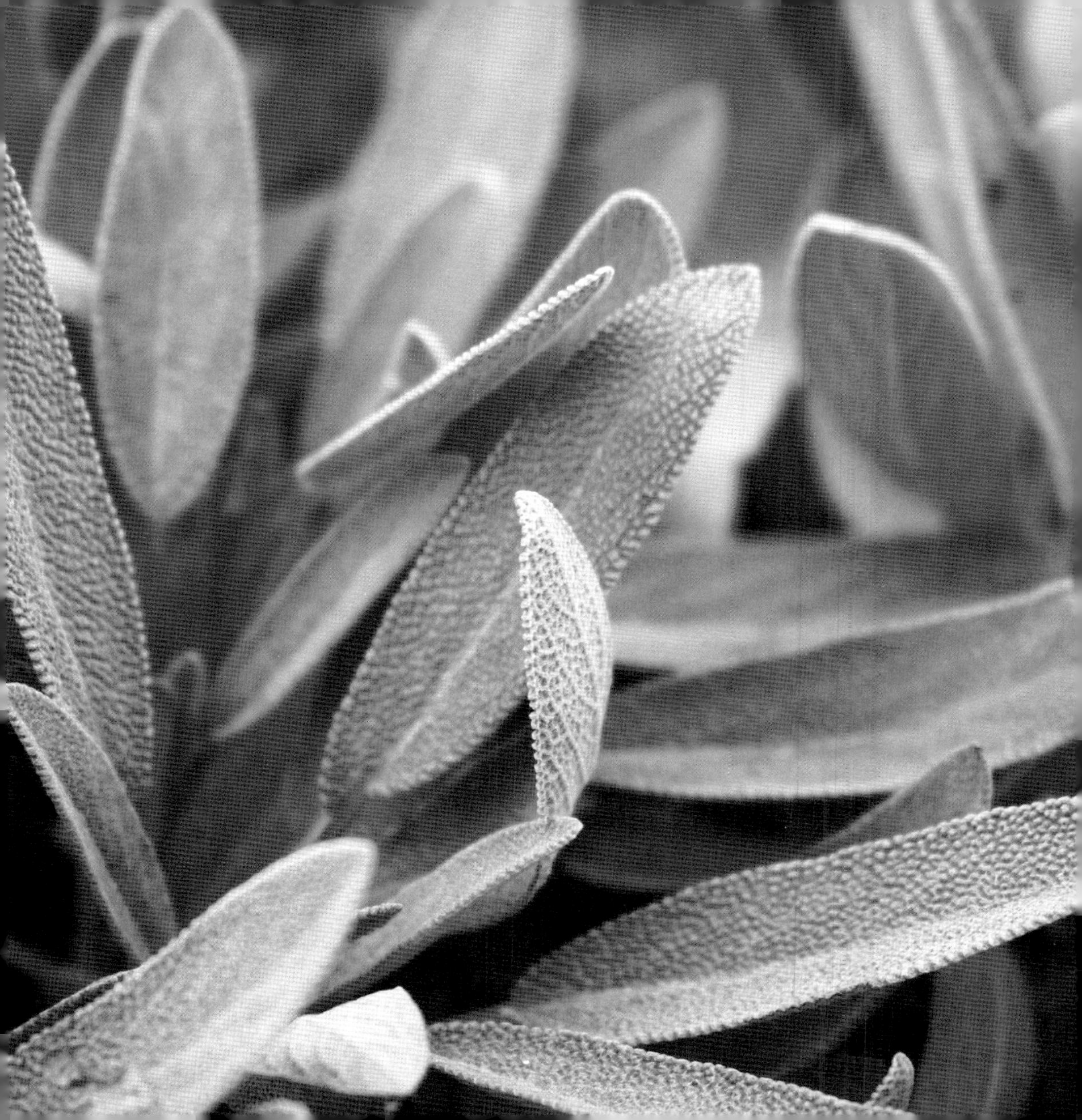

snails

At the end of last winter, when I had not been out in the garden so much, I suddenly realised how terrible my succulents were looking; I couldn't understand what was eating them. Sure enough, it was the snails who were using the nearby kniphofias as high-rise accommodation. I collected them and put out snail pellets for weeks before I even began to win the battle. But the snail battle is never really won; you need to remain vigilant all the time to keep these pests under control.

If you are happy to use snail pellets, put them out at least once a month. There are now products available that use iron (which will not affect dogs, birds or earthworms) as the active ingredient. However, if you prefer not to use any chemicals, you will need to kill the invaders yourself.

- Upturned plastic pots work well if you don't have dogs who will knock them over. Cut a snail-sized entry door in each pot, smear the inside with fat, and leave the pots in unobtrusive places around your garden as permanent snail traps.
- A saucer of beer is another old-fashioned snail bait.
- Nothing beats going out with a bucket of boiling water or lime (instant death to snails). The best times are after rain, when snails are on the march, or early in the morning, when they are returning from their nightly depredations. Or, most rewarding of all, make a night raid with a torch!

See also: **organic garden**

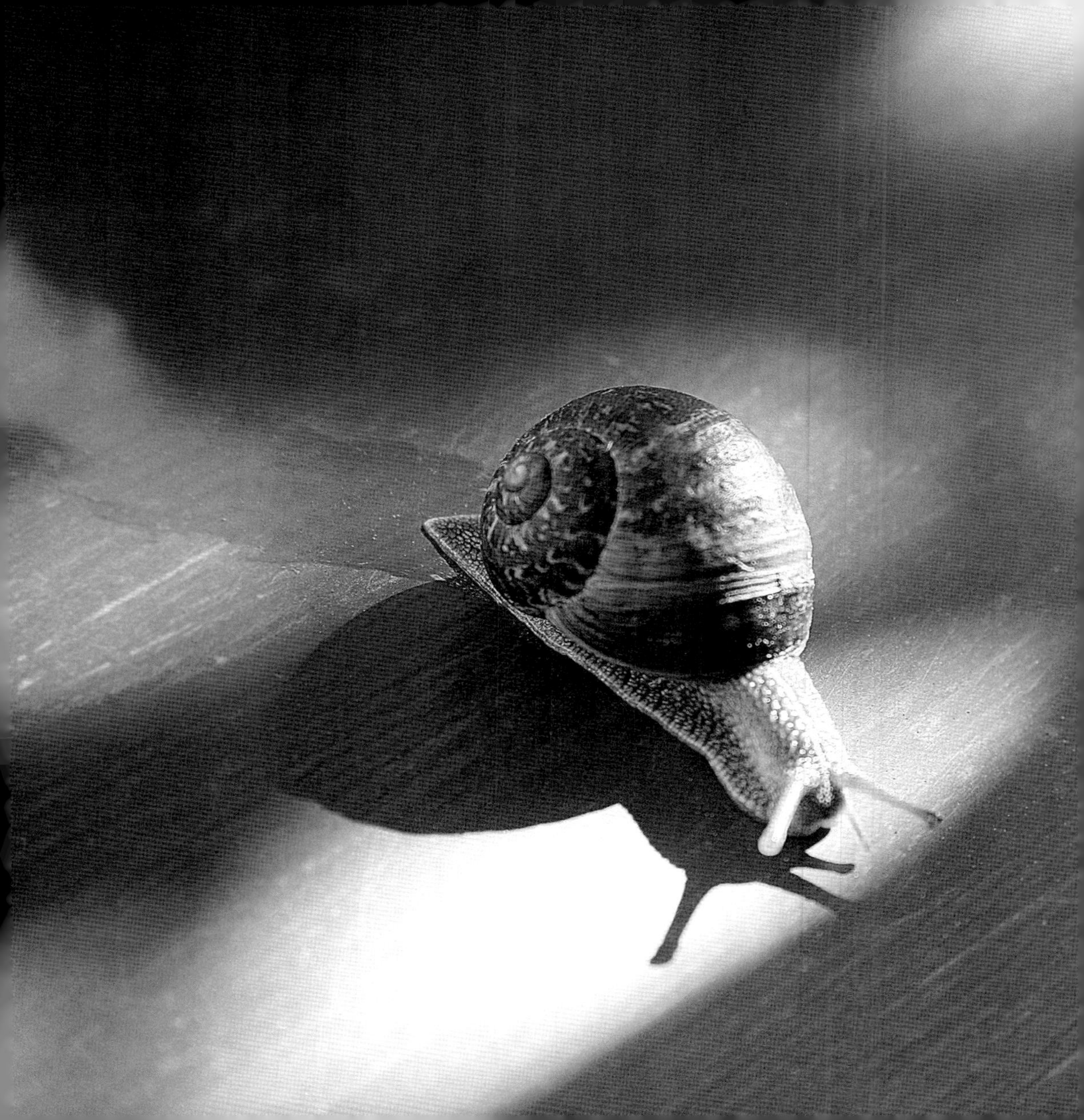

soil

There are many different soil types but, other than inappropriate pH levels (see below), gardeners in temperate regions tend to face one of two main problems:

- **sandy soil** (allows water to drain straight through)
- **clayey soil** (holds water like a sponge in winter while in summer water runs straight off).

Either way, the soil can be improved by adding humus or organic matter in the form of mulch or compost.

Sandy soil can be improved by the addition of rough mulch like pea or lucerne straw, compost, animal manure or stable straw. To begin with, the mulch will seem to disappear into the soil, and it may be several years before the soil becomes really rich and friable. But the effort will be worth it.

Clayey soil in which nothing will grow is often left after a new house has been built. In this situation, drainage is the primary concern. But once the drainage is working, you need to improve the soil before you start planting. Clayey soil will break down and become friable if lime, gypsum, compost and/or good rough mulch are added. Gypsum should be added at a rate of around 1 kg per 1 m^2. It is vital to allow the mulch to break down into the soil; the longer you wait before commencing planting, the better.

pH level is another way in which soils vary. pH stands for 'power of hydrogen' or 'potential of hydrogen'. The logarithmic scale of 1–14 measures the concentration of hydrogen ions in any given substance, and so its degree of acidity or alkalinity.

The higher the acidity, the lower the reading; battery acid has a pH of 0, distilled water is neutral at 7, and drain cleaner is strongly alkaline at around 14. Most plants prefer a neutral or slightly acidic soil with a pH of around 6.5–7; some, such as potatoes, rhododendrons, ericas and azaleas, like it a bit more acidic and others, such as lavender and most coastal plants, lean more towards the alkaline side.

If your plants seem to be suffering ill health generally, it is worth testing the pH of your soil in case a pH imbalance is the cause. Testing is not a difficult job. Most nurseries sell pH testing kits; they usually involve taking a soil sample, mixing it with a powder or liquid, and comparing the colour it turns against a chart. If your soil is too acidic or alkaline, the problem is easy to fix.

To raise the pH (make the soil less acidic) apply ground dolomite lime at a rate of 2.5 kg to 10 m^2. Wood ash or ground oyster shells will do a similar job. To lower pH (make the soil more acidic) add fresh manure at 2.5 kg to 10 m^2 or aluminium sulphate at 600 g per 10 m^2.

> Once you have improved your soil, ensure that you continue mulching and looking after it. Bacteria, fungi, worms and insects all live in the soil and take part in the important processes of aeration and breaking down organic matter.

See also: **mulch; worms**

spring garden

Spring is a time of year when almost everyone's garden looks good, whether it is in Japan and part of the spectacular *sakura zensen* (cherry blossom front), or in Australia where the climate is more benign. The best way to make the most of your spring garden is to plan ahead earlier in the year . . .

- Think about colour and plant species that will look attractive when they flower together.
- Find out how long whatever you plant will flower for. Do you want your whole garden to burst into flower at once, or would you prefer to stagger your flowering season over several months?
- Consider the other nine months of the year. In many cases, a plant that looks good in spring and also adds interest to the garden for the rest of the year is preferable to one that looks spectacular in spring but dull at other times.

Along with the warmer weather and increased growth in spring come a few gardening chores that are best attacked early in the season.

Spring jobs
- **Dig over and prepare your vegie garden** if you haven't already done so. Make sure that you turn the soil to a depth of at least 20 cm and dig in plenty of well-rotted compost or manure. Top off with garden lime (a generous handful for each 1 m^2).
- **Give box bushes a light trim** in preparation for their new spring growth.

This will ensure that they maintain their shape better and give you the benefit of all that new, bright-green growth for longer.
- **Check for bent grass** (*Agrostis* spp.) and other invasive horrors that might start to put on new growth in your garden beds and paths. If you spray them with a glyphosate-based herbicide now, and again in a few weeks, they will be much easier to eliminate than later in the year when their growth will be considerably stronger.
- **Clean lily ponds**.
- **Tidy up frost-bitten plants** (scented-leafed pelargoniums, Japanese anemones and daisies) – cut off any messy old foliage that hides the new growth underneath.
- **Fertilise lawns** with a complete garden fertiliser. You can also fertilise the rest of the garden, provided you're sure that the cold weather is really over. (Like all plants, grass absorbs fertiliser best when it is actively growing.)
- **Check your mower** and carry out any maintenance required, in preparation for the warmer months to come.

See also: **lawns**

succulents

Succulents are one of the most valuable garden plants available. Even when not in flower, their foliage is lush and interesting. They cope quite happily with extended periods of dryness (too much water and they start to rot at the base), making them ideal for pots. Here are some of my favourites.

- Pig's ear (*Cotyledon orbiculata*), especially the silver-leafed variety, looks great growing in full sun or light shade. The large leaves catch the light and stand out magnificently when planted in large clumps under trees. In summer, it bears long-stalked clusters of orange bell-shaped flowers, much-loved by little honeyeaters. In winter, the green-leafed variety puts up even larger, orange blooms on tall, stiff stems.
- Echeverias, with their fat rosettes of leaves, are ideal for edging beds or paths. Both leaves and flowers come in a huge range of shades.
- Blue chalk sticks (*Senecio serpens*) make an amazing ground cover for a hot, dry area. The silvery-blue leaves point upwards like fingers. Small, cream-coloured flowers appear in summer, but this plant should be grown for the foliage alone.
- Agaves and aloes have bold, sword-like foliage. The grey–blue *Agave americana* is an excellent pot specimen, particularly in a dark-coloured stone pot that provides a nice contrast against the leaves. *Aeonium* 'Zwartkop', with its distinctive plum-coloured rosettes, is another that works well not only in pots but massed in the garden against a different-coloured background.

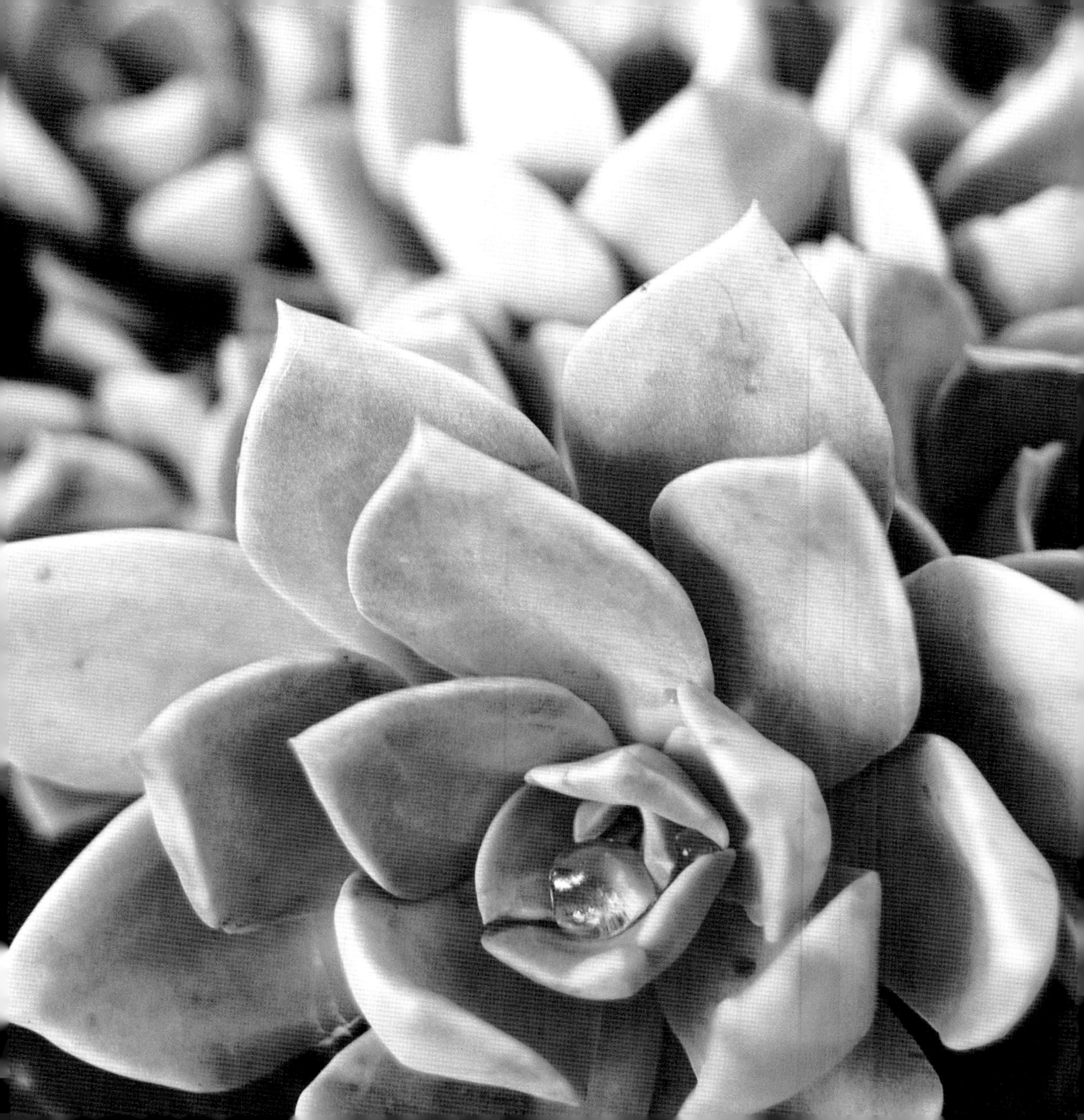

summer garden

Where a spring garden derives most of its strength from its flowering display and a winter garden relies on the more solid structure of trees and hedges, the focus of a summer garden is foliage and form. A good summer garden takes advantage of whatever is flowering at the time, as well as the colour and shape of perennial planting that has five or six months' growth behind it. The garden's beauty can come from the visual strength of the plants themselves.

Grey-leafed plants like lavender, cotton lavender (*Santolina*), *Ballota acetabulosa* and wormwood (*Artemisia arborescens*) can be clipped into structural balls that look fantastic on their own but even better when combined with the pale, sword-like foliage of iris or the green of agapanthus and daylilies. These, in turn, can be augmented by softer background planting of taller perennials such as lion's ear (*Leonotis leonurus*), bog sage (*Salvia uliginosa*) or one of the kniphofias.

Summer is also the time when grasses start to make their presence felt. Soft clumps or sweeps of gently waving tufts interspersed among other plantings provide interest and movement in what might otherwise be a more traditional display.

Summer can be a busy time, but don't ignore what needs to be done in your garden to ensure that it maintains its health and vigour through the months ahead.

Summer jobs
- **Prune *Jasminum polyanthum***, now that it has finished flowering; not only will you get rid of the brown flower remnants, but you will help the plant to maintain a more compact growth habit and discourage one of the bugbears of jasmine – the 'everything up the top and nothing down below' syndrome.

- **Deadhead echiums** if you haven't already. The best way to do this is to imagine that you are cutting off the old flower heads in order to use them in flower decorations.
- **Deadhead roses** to encourage flower growth and extra vigour, ensuring that your summer rose supply will be as good as possible.
- **Watch for thrip on roses** as they are often prevalent at this time of year. Treat thrip in much the same way as you would treat aphids. I find a pyrethrum-based insecticide, or even just rhubarb spray, as good as anything.
- **Remove old flower stalks on irises** as they finish flowering so that the shape of their foliage is not compromised by the tatty remains of their once-beautiful flowers.
- **Start planting basil and tomatoes**.

There is an old English saying, 'When you can put your foot on seven daisies, summer is come'. The common daisy does not hold any place in the handbook of the true lawn aficionado but I love a sweeping lawn with a swathe of white daisies!

See also: **grasses; organic garden**

sweet peas

Gardening folklore says that you should plant your sweet peas (*Lathyrus odoratus*) from around St Patrick's Day (17 March) to May, for stronger and more disease-resistant plants. Sweet peas grow well up tripods, or against a fence in full sun. They generally need encouragement to begin with, as they tend to lie around on the ground, but if you tie them up as soon as you can, they will soon be able to support themselves.

Sweet peas are deep-rooters and require good quality soil. To get the best out of your sweet peas, follow these steps:

1 Into the top 15 cm of soil, fork some well-rotted animal manure or compost, ½ cup of complete fertiliser per 1 m^2 and, except in alkaline areas, twice this amount of agricultural lime. Water well.
2 Allow a week before sowing; most sweet pea germination failures are due to over-watering or soggy soil. When sowing, the soil should be just damp.
3 Water once at sowing time and, unless conditions are very dry, do not water again until the seedlings appear (usually about two weeks later). After that, water fortnightly with liquid fertiliser. The stronger the plants, the better they bloom – and when they do bloom, it is the best scent of all.

I find many of the commercial cultivars available these days lack the perfume of the older varieties. If you can source some seeds from older, more fragrant sweet pea varieties, let them run to seed after flowering so that you have an ongoing supply.

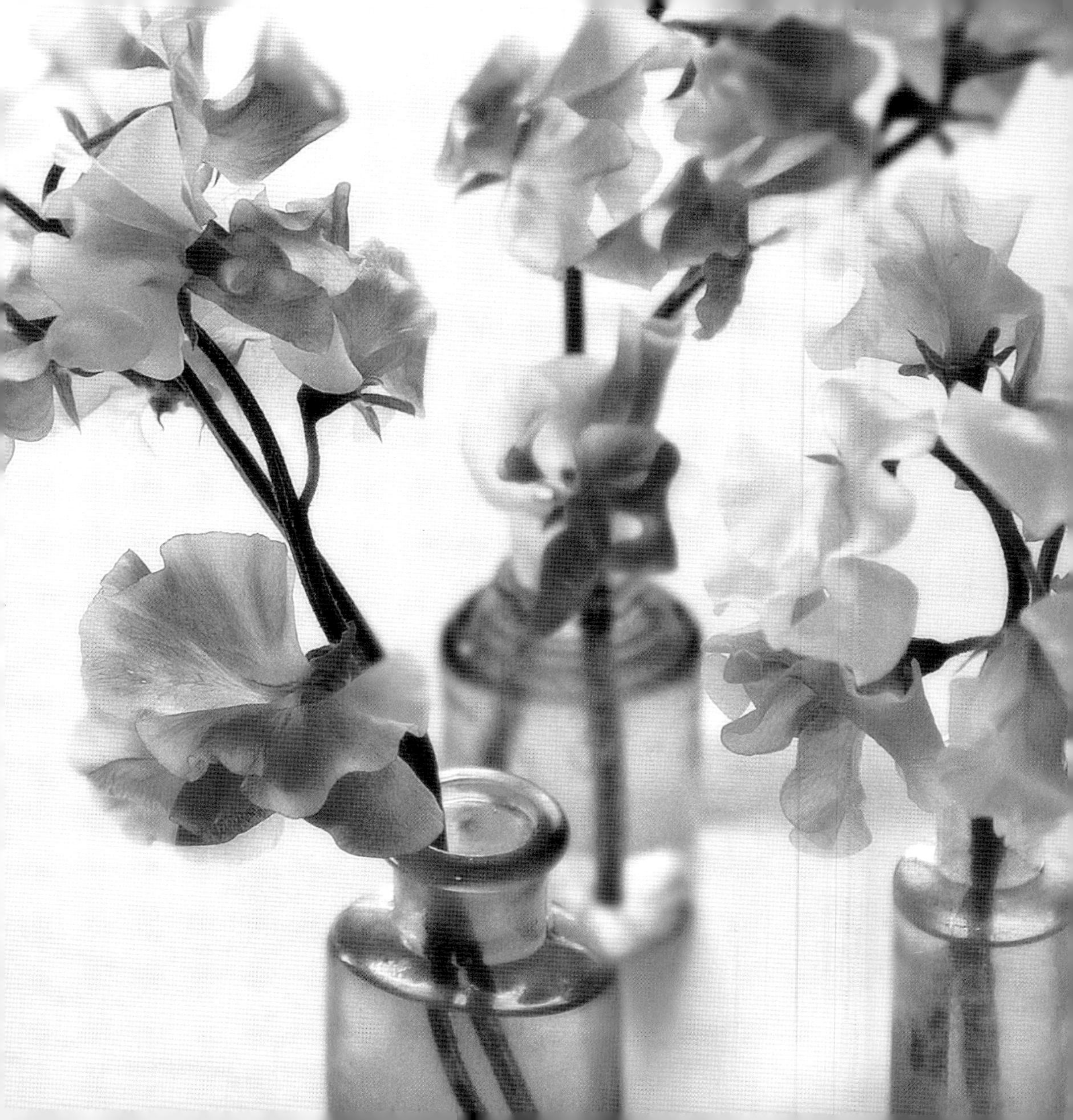

tactile garden

A good garden should appeal to all the senses, including the sense of touch. There are some plants that are almost impossible to walk past without touching.

- Many geraniums have scented leaves, and all the leaves have a slightly different feel. From the soft, downy peppermint-scented geranium (*Pelargonium tomentosum*) to the tight, crinkly, lemon-scented geranium (*P. crispum*) or the slightly coarser rose geranium (*P. graveolens*), each evokes a different sensory reaction.
- Lamb's ears (*Stachys byzantina*) is also wonderful to touch. As the name suggests, the leaves are similar to lambs' ears in shape, colour and feel.
- Bamboo is another wonderfully tactile plant; its smooth, silky canes almost cry out to be stroked.
- If you want to know what it feels like to hug a tree, try one of the smooth-trunked gums such as the lemon-scented gum (*Corymbia citriodora*) or the Sydney red gum (*Angophora costata*). When you wrap your arms around one of these big beauties, you can almost feel its heartbeat.

Don't forget to touch the stuff that gardens are built of and the stuff that grows on them, too: rough and smooth stone, mossy rocks, worn timber, polished metal. All have a beautiful feel in their different ways, especially when the temperature of the material is at odds with the weather on that particular day.

See also: **bark; decorative elements; gum trees**

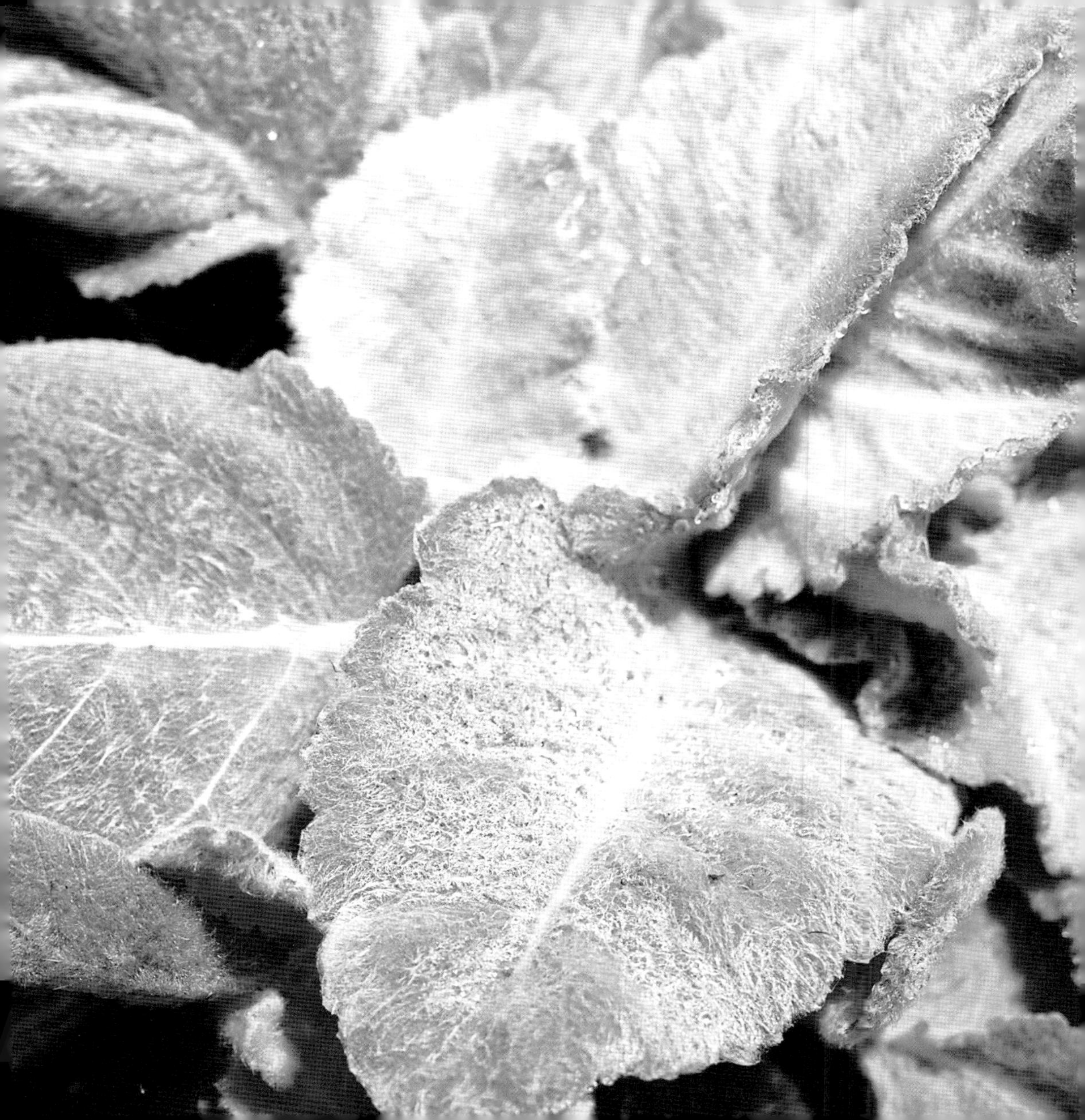

tomatoes

Tomatoes are forgiving plants that can be grown in pots or in the garden, as climbers, shrubs, staked plants or ground covers. They prefer a warm climate so, unless you use miniature greenhouses, wait until the nights are a little warmer before you buy seedlings. By the same token, tomatoes will ripen happily but won't set fruit if the temperature gets too hot, so plant well before the hot summer days begin.

Good health is the secret to successful tomato growing. Plants that are well mulched, fed and watered will be more resistant to pests and diseases. Liquid-fertilise during the growing period. Crop rotation is important as tomatoes do not thrive if continually grown in the same spot. Choose the variety that best suits your requirements:

- 'Tiny Tim' is a miniature, heavily cropping tomato suitable for pots; the tiny fruits are delicious served whole in a salad.
- 'Sweet Bite' is a vigorous, taller-growing variety that also bears tiny fruit.
- 'Grosse Lisse' always produces a good crop, but it is more prone to fusarium wilt (a soil-inhabiting fungus) than other varieties.
- 'Apollo' is long-cropping and will set fruit under cooler conditions.
- 'Rouge de Marmande' is the sweetest tasting of the larger varieties.

As companion plants, basil, shasta daisies, forget-me-nots, lavender and nasturtiums will all help to keep your tomatoes healthy by variously assisting pollination, repelling harmful insects and attracting beneficial ones.

See also: **greenhouses**

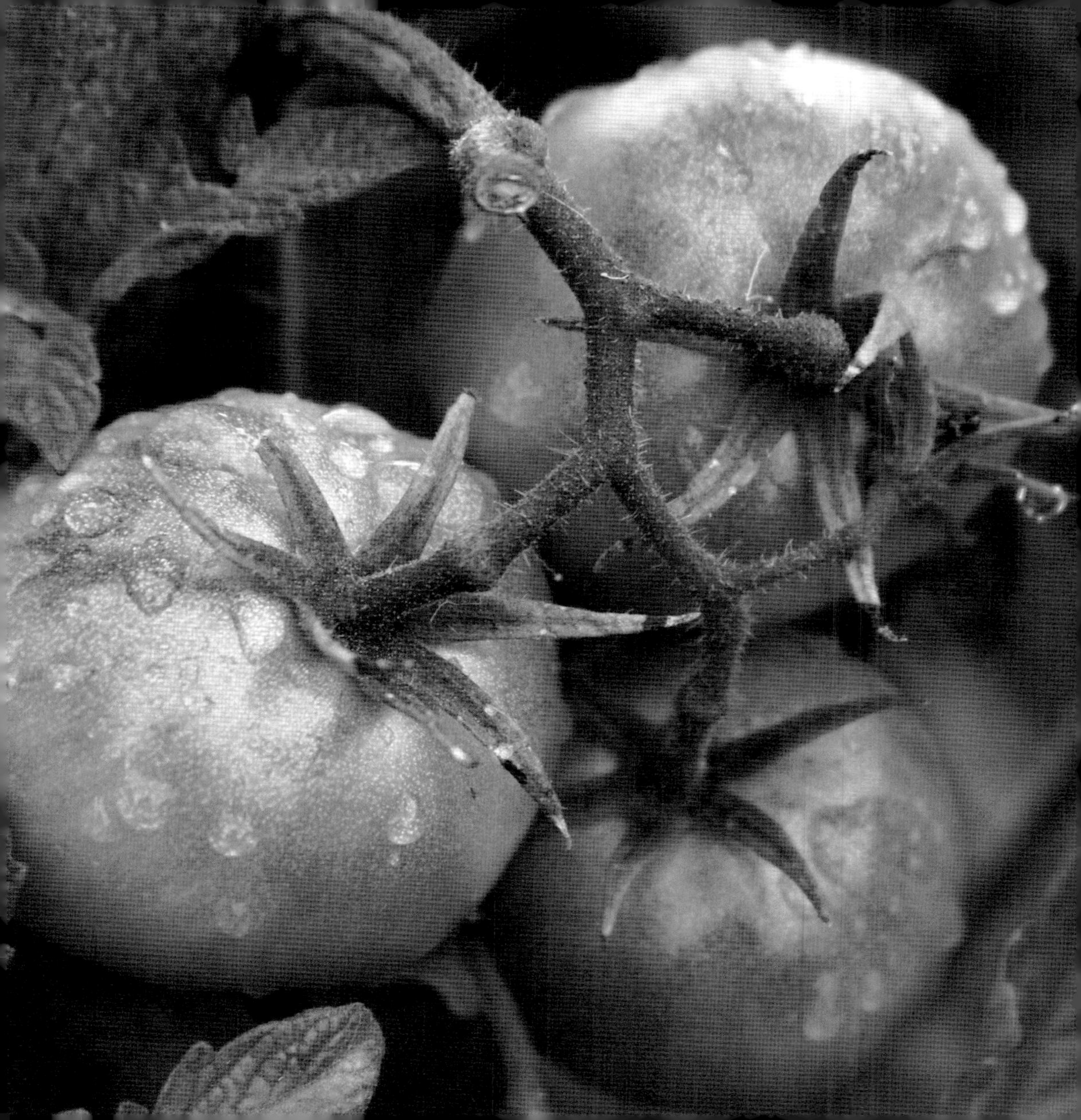

tool maintenance

Keeping your garden tools clean and sharp not only makes gardening more pleasant, it also prevents injury.

Secateurs, loppers, saws and other cutting tools can be sharpened at most nurseries and hardware stores. Otherwise, sharpening stones are available to buy from good hardware stores. The one I use is a small diamond file with a plastic handle, like an emery board. It is inexpensive, easy to use and small enough to get in between the secateurs' blades.

Spades and forks will last much longer if they are well looked after. One old nurseryman I knew had a large drum of coarse sand soaked in engine oil just inside the tool shed. When his workers returned a spade or fork at the end of the day, they were required to plunge the tool up and down in the drum, which both protected and sharpened the implement. (He also drilled small vertical holes in the end of each tool's wooden handle and periodically filled these with linseed oil to keep the handles strong and supple.) In my landscaping business, we have a large copper filled with gravel and disinfectant where we clean all tools at the end of each day. The disinfectant ensures that if we come across anything nasty in the garden, there is no chance of spreading it.

Electric hedgers need to be kept clean and oiled. Canola oil is available in a spray pack from the supermarket and can simply be sprayed on the blades after each use.

> Happiness is a sharp pair of secateurs.

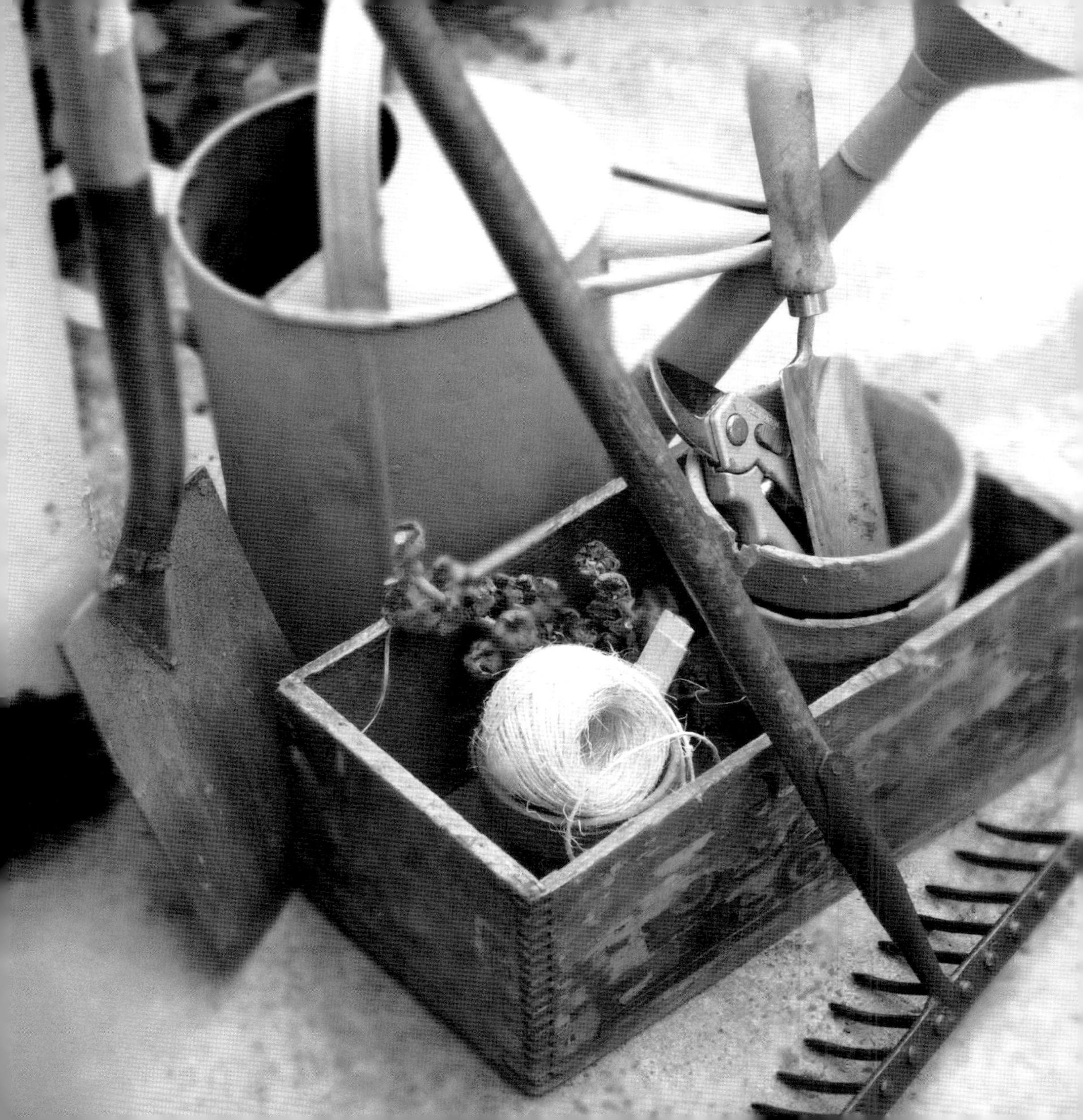

topiary

Topiary, the art of clipping trees and shrubs into shapes other than their own, has been around for over 2000 years. It can take many different forms and is much more popular in formal European gardens than in Australia, where it is not often evident except in clipped balls or cones of box, conifer spirals in nurseries, or the name of a farm clipped into its front cypress hedge.

Topiary can be as simple or as flamboyant as you like. (In Ladew Topiary Gardens in Maryland, retired millionaire Harvey Ladew created acres of topiary, including an entire fox hunt of clipped yew!) But some species take to clipping better than others. It is a good way of dealing with many grey-leafed plants that, left to their own devices, tend to become sprawling and untidy. Also, many gardeners prefer not to allow grey-leafed plants to flower, as the leaves are often prettier than the flowers.

Remember that topiary is time-consuming and a long-term project. But the results can add great interest to the garden. For more adventurous shapes, it is best to use a wire frame (available from good nurseries) of the shape you wish to achieve. In a more informal setting, simply clip plants into standard balls, either edging paths or in large swathes in garden beds. These soft balls or rounded contours contrast beautifully against the sword-like foliage of iris or kniphofia, for example.

Standard plants are really just balls of foliage on sticks. But they can look very attractive in pots on either side of a door or path, or simply as details in the garden.

In most cases, commercial standards are grafted onto an existing straight stem. But, with some patience, it is not difficult to grow your own. The following method can be applied to plenty of plants but works particularly well with gardenias, marguerite daisies (*Leucanthemum vulgare*), rosemary, azaleas, fuchsias and roses.

1. Select a plant with a strong, straight leading shoot and remove any side shoots or other branches.
2. Insert a wooden stake into the ground at the base of the plant and tie the plant to the stake.
3. Continue to grow the single shoot till it has produced at least three pairs of leaves above the desired height of your finished standard, then pinch out the growing tip. This could take anywhere between three months and three years, depending on the plant and how high you want the stalk.
4. As the side shoots grow, pinch out the tips of each shoot to encourage further branching. Repeated several times, this will produce a large bushy head.
5. Once the head is of sufficient size, it only needs to be pruned back after each flowering season.
6. Sometimes the head of the plant can get too heavy for the stem, so keep the stake in place.

One of my favourite styles of topiary is used in the south of France, where lavender bushes are clipped into acres of soft, round balls after the flower heads have been harvested. This form appears to have developed out of necessity rather than for aesthetic reasons.

walls

Walls are an integral part of almost any garden. Those designed purely for aesthetics usually look good, but more often they are built for a reason and can remain a missed opportunity to add interest to your garden. Here are some ideas:

- Use a tall brick wall in an inner suburban garden to espalier a tree or grow a climber, or as the backdrop for a water feature. If the wall is an eyesore, render or paint it, or plant something that will hide it. Boston ivy (*Parthenocissus tricuspidata*) is a fast-growing deciduous creeper, and potato vine (*Solanum jasminoides*) creates the most magnificent flowering hedge.
- The walls of a house can also be ideal for espaliering fruit trees, camellias or crab apples, or for growing climbers.
- If you prefer the look of stone over timber, line your standard paling fence with cement sheets and then clad it with sawn stone pieces – a very economic way to create what appears to be a stacked stone wall.
- Plant a living wall. There is a huge variety of shrubs that make excellent hedges to contain your property, hide neighbours or create 'garden rooms'.
- If you are hiding a view by growing a hedge or building a wall as a windbreak, offer a peep of the view by cutting one or more windows in the hedge or wall, or inserting a doorway with a seat.
- A walled courtyard can be claustrophobic; transform it with the addition of a water feature or a beautiful antique door fixed to a wall.

See also: **climbers; espaliers; water features**

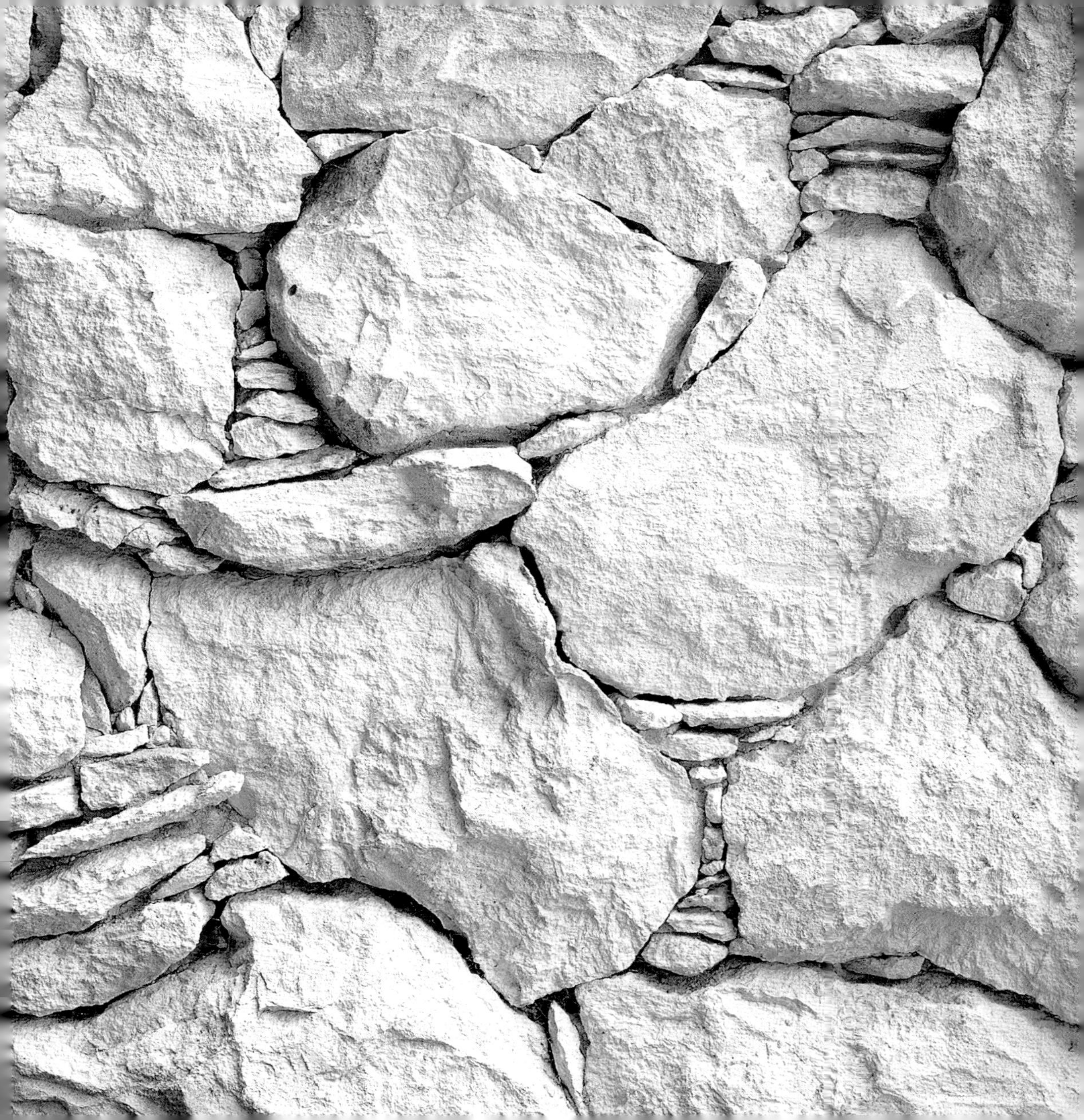

water features

Originally included out of necessity, water quickly became a decorative element in gardens almost everywhere. Virtually all of the world's classic gardens feature water in some form. But even the smallest garden can benefit from the lyrical sound of running water, the tranquillity of a still pond, the joy of birds in a bath or somewhere to watch fish swim. Before you decide on a water feature, consider the scale and style of your garden.

- Small freestanding or wall-mounted fountains are great for courtyards or as a focal point from a window. The water is usually recycled using a quiet pump (low-voltage pumps are available).
- Pools range from naturally inspired ponds with stones and waterfalls to swimming pools that are incorporated into the landscape design. Whenever I incorporate a pond or swimming pool into a garden design, I take great care to match the style and colour of the pool to the style of the garden. You can buy small, ready-made pools from nurseries, or create your own using a pool liner. Remember, though, that any kind of pool can be dangerous to children, who can drown in a few centimetres of water.
- A feature as simple as a beautiful water bowl on the ground or on a stand, or a decorative pot fitted with a bubbler, may be ample for a small garden.

Modern designs, funnily enough, will often work just as well in a classically designed garden as in a modern one. However, a classically designed water feature in a modern setting is more likely to look ridiculous than elegant.

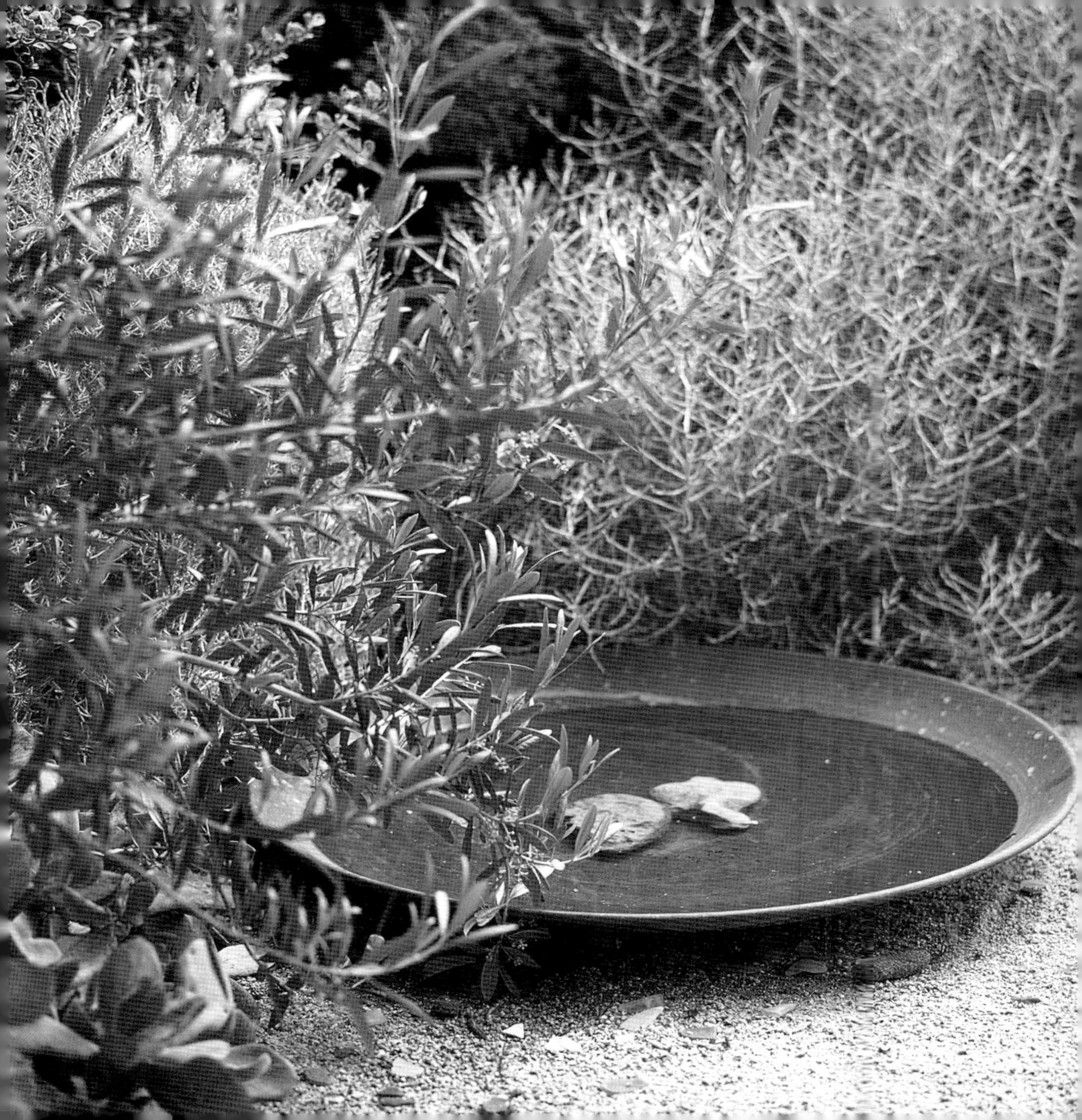

watering the garden

With the cost of water rising and restrictions increasing, it is time to look seriously at how much water we're using compared with how much we really need to use. There are several simple steps you can take to reduce your garden water usage:

1. Group plants not only for aesthetic appeal but according to their water requirements so that water can be directed to where it is needed without being wasted where it is not.
2. Mulch all areas of your garden heavily with organic mulch to prevent the soil from drying out; to keep plant roots cool in summer and so reduce heat stress; to prevent run-off; and to encourage microbacterial activity. This will produce strong plants with more drought-tolerant root systems.
3. Water more, less often, and at appropriate times of the day (early morning is best, before it gets hot). Give the areas of the garden that need watering a good soak every three or four days for half an hour rather than every day for a few minutes. Periodic deep watering is more effective because the deeper the plants put their roots down, the better. If your garden is on a slope and you find that after 10 minutes the water starts to run off, set your sprinklers to water three times, for 10 minutes each time, with a break of about 30 minutes between each watering. This way, you get the same penetration as on a flat bed.
4. Pipe grey water from your washing machine out onto your garden (a plumber can arrange this for a relatively small cost). Alternatively, install tanks to collect the run-off from the roof.

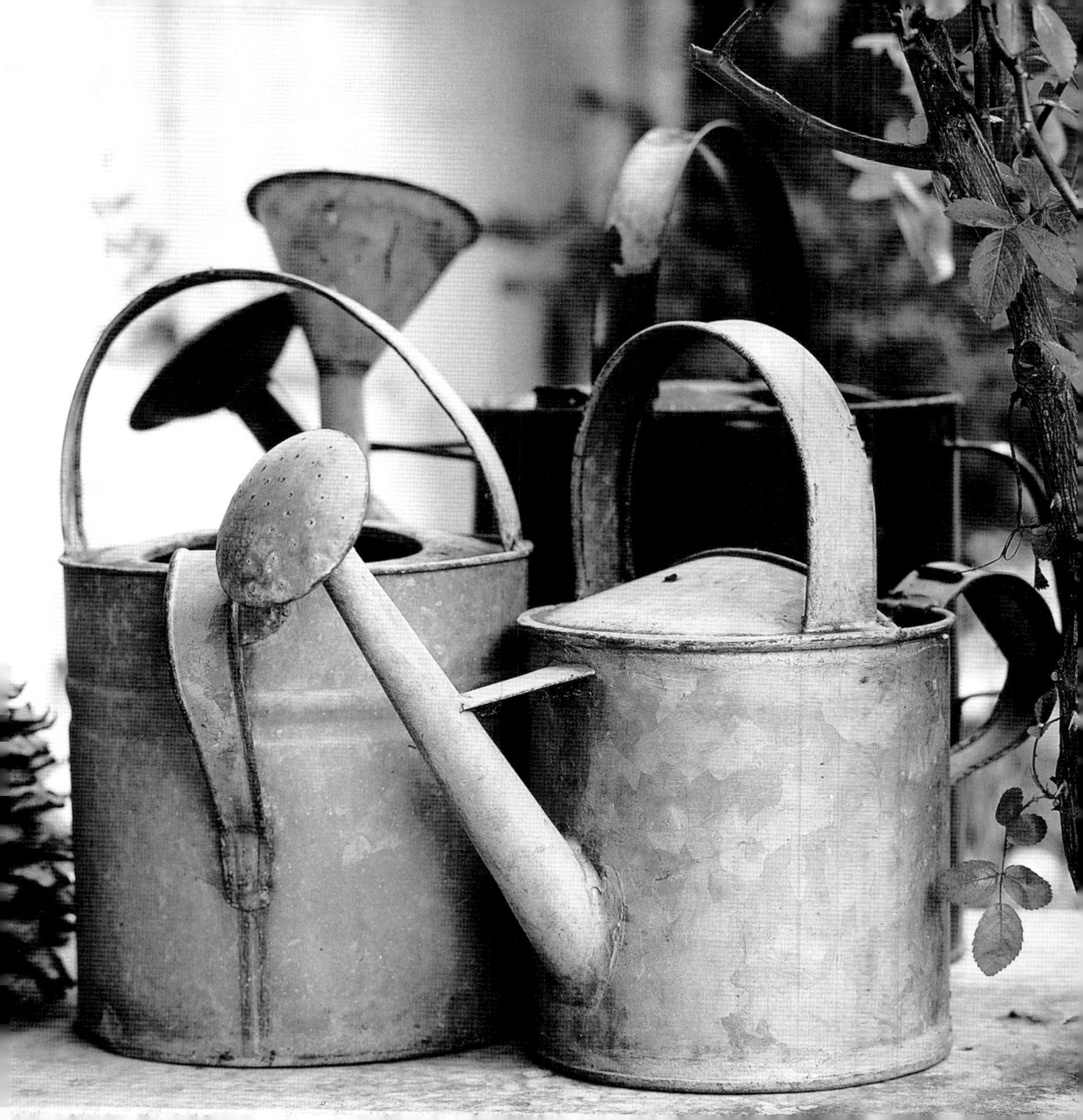

weeds

A plant regarded as a weed in some regions can be a valuable member of the eco-system in others, and vice versa. Plants that in their own regions are kept in check by climate or natural predators can quickly get out of control when introduced to another region. For example, native daphne (*Pittosporum undulatum*), Cootamundra wattle (*Acacia baileyanna*) and bluebell creeper (*Sollya heterophylla*) have been introduced to and thrived in many regions of Australia to the point where they are considered environmental weeds.

But weeds are part of a gardener's lot and, although it involves extra work to keep them under control, there is something quite therapeutic about weeding the garden on a warm, sunny day and standing back at the end to survey your handiwork.

- The best protection against weeds is a good mulching regime; even just spreading mulch over weeds will generally contain them.
- Removing weeds while they are still small and before they set seed is the best way to keep your work to a minimum. You can dig them out by hand, pour boiling water over them (this is especially good on paths), or use a glyphosate-based contact herbicide.
- Glyphosate herbicide has the benefit of breaking down in the soil after use and only killing what it touches. It is, however, imperative that you complete your spraying before there is a breath of wind or the weather gets hot; otherwise, you run the risk of spray-drift, resulting in yellow shrivelling and even death of surrounding plants.

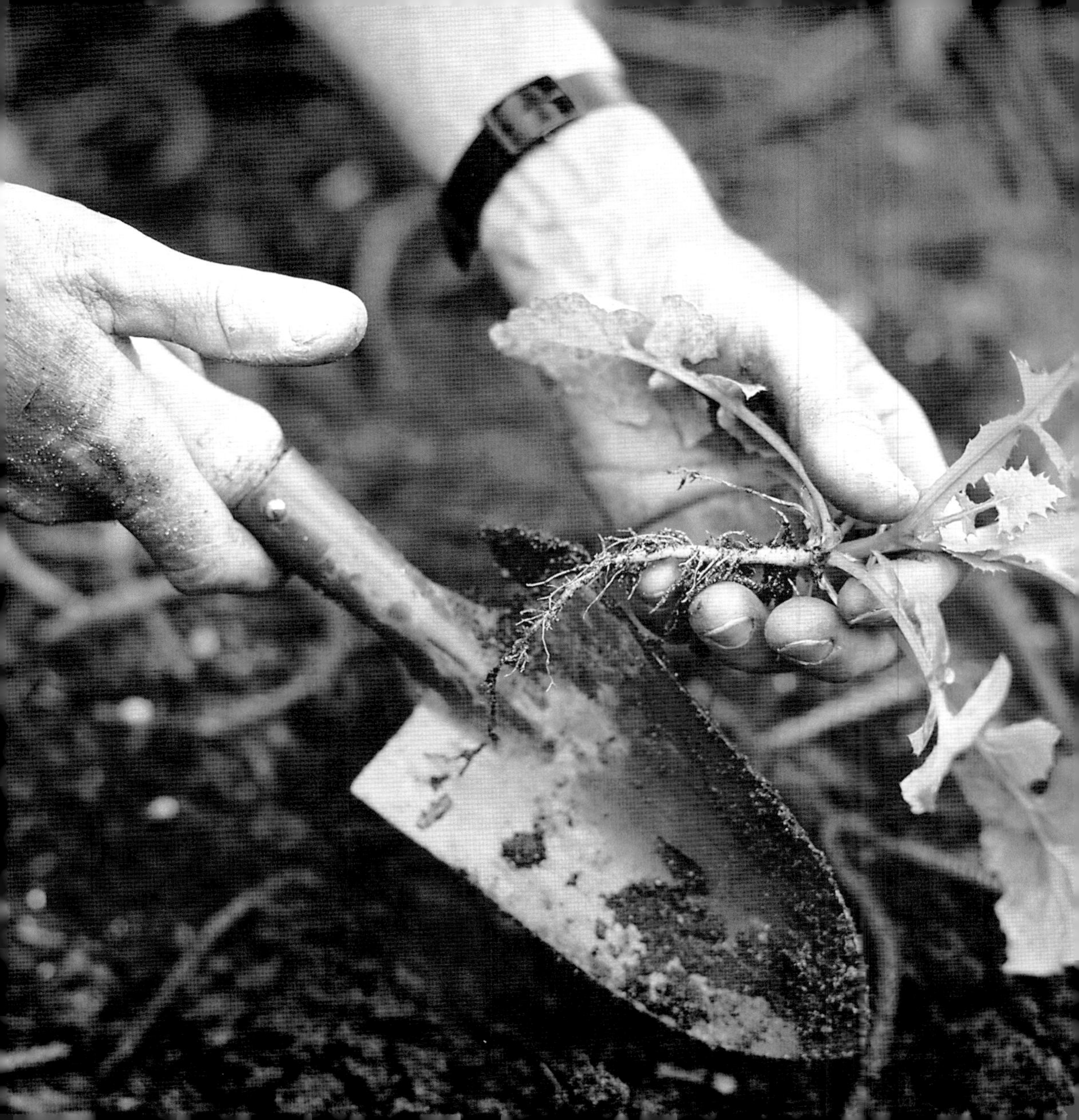

wet spaces

With so much talk about drought-tolerant gardens and 'zero-scaping' (no landscaping it all), it may seem strange to talk about wet spaces. But in some gardens they are a fact of life, whether they are caused by a small soak coming out of the ground, water running down a hill, or a neighbour's overenthusiastic use of a sprinkler system. And there are many species that enjoy wet, boggy conditions.

- Arum lilies (*Zantedeschia aethiopica*) make a wonderful display throughout the winter but the plants tend to die down and can look a bit of a mess during the summer. That is when you need *Z. aethiopica* 'Green Goddess'; it blooms almost throughout the year and its huge white flowers look as if goblins have come in the night and splashed them with green paint! When picked, these lilies will last for up to three weeks in water.
- Several varieties of iris thrive in boggy conditions: *Iris laevigata*, a native of Eastern Asia, English water iris (*I. pseudacorus*) and the Louisiana hybrids native to the southern states of the US.
- Giant ornamental rhubarb (*Gunnera manicata*) is grown mainly for its enormous leaves, but it also produces long spikes of rather strange-looking greenish-red flowers in summer.

In England, bog gardens are popular. They are not often seen in Australia, with its drier climate, but you might like to try creating one if you have a wet area in your garden.

See also: **drainage; irises**

white flowers

Planted thoughtfully, a white garden can be subtle and soothing to the eye, especially if white-flowering species are placed amongst different shades of green, or against a green background such as a painted fence or a hedge. White flowers such as hydrangeas, arum lilies, impatiens and azaleas all flower well in light shade and can brighten dark spots in your garden like nothing else can.

White can act as a full stop or break in the garden, enabling other colours that don't otherwise go so well together to be used in the same area. The following white-flowering species come top of my list:

- The huge, pendulous, almost surreal blooms of angels' trumpets (*Brugmansia* × *candida*) can fill a whole garden with their scent.
- Christmas lilies (*Lilium regale*) are also beautifully scented but disappear underground in winter and are best used in combination with other white-scented plants such as gardenias, *Azalea* 'Alba Magnifica', camellias, roses, philadelphus and osmanthus.
- In sunnier areas, roses are often the white flower of choice. Although the ubiquitous 'Iceberg' is clearly the favourite, I prefer 'White Spray' as it is beautifully perfumed and lasts better as a cut flower.

Carefully lit, a white garden can look particularly beautiful at night. The white flowers take on a luminescent quality and the garden appears like some wonderful stage setting. If the flowers are also night-scented, the effect is even more dramatic.

winter garden

In winter, all of spring's flowers, summer's green camouflage and autumn's fiery foliage is gone and only the bare bones of the garden remain – including any imperfections hidden during the rest of the year. But a garden with good 'bones' (design structure) will be beautiful at any time of year.

In winter, walls, hedges, larger trees, the shapes of garden beds and the placement of paths become more prominent. In a temperate climate, we are lucky that we have plenty to work with: evergreens, and plants that flower and provide colour (and often perfume), as well as deciduous trees that display the fine tracery that typifies winter. Keep this in mind next time you look at making some changes in your garden.

Unless you live in the mountains where it snows, there is always something to do in the garden – even in winter.

Winter jobs
- **Cut back dahlia foliage** by half (late autumn/early winter).
- **Divide and replant liliums and strawberries** (early winter).
- **Keep collecting autumn leaves** for your compost heap or to use as mulch.
- **Start spraying oxalis** with a glyphosate-based herbicide while it is growing strongly and before it starts to flower. (You will probably need to spray a few times to get it all.)
- **Move rhododendrons, azaleas, camellias or deciduous trees** if you need to (early to mid-winter is the best time).
- **Plant bare-rooted roses** (mid-winter).

- **Plant deciduous trees and shrubs** (mid-winter).
- **Prune hydrangeas, wisterias, roses and any fruit trees not pruned after fruiting**.
- **Lift and store dahlia tubers** once the foliage has totally died off (late winter). Store them with whatever dirt they have on them to prevent them from drying out.
- **Take hardwood cuttings**.
- **Lime garden and lawns**.
- **Plant out vines** such as grapes, raspberries and Chinese gooseberries (kiwifruit).
- **Fix and sharpen tools** on the wet days.

See also: **berryfruits; irises; paths; pruning; roses; tool maintenance**

worms

Worms play a hugely important part in the garden. They aid in the breakdown of organic material and in soil aeration, water penetration and fertilisation. Studies conducted by none other than Charles Darwin show that they bring incredible amounts of subsoil to the surface, effectively tilling it for us and enriching it as they go. Over time, they can also help to bring acid or alkaline soils towards a more neutral pH.

There are two types of worms: earthworms (which renew fertility in the soil) and compost worms (which recycle organic waste). Earthworms prefer similar conditions to most plants – humus-rich, well-drained, moist soil – so the more earthworms you entice to your garden, the more attractive it will be and your soil will improve exponentially. Compost worms, on the other hand, prefer warmer and moister conditions. Unlike earthworms, they are not deep burrowers and will not survive in normal garden conditions so do not buy a bag of them to put in your garden. (You can add them to your compost heap though, if you like.)

Worm castings, or vermicast, are one of the best natural fertilisers; they are said to be four times more beneficial to plants than compost and up to ten times more beneficial than cow manure. Vermicast can be purchased from good nurseries. Or, better still, keep your own small worm farm and as you dispose of your kitchen scraps, your compost worms will be making vermicast for the garden!

See also: **compost; mulch; soil**

Compost feeds plants

yellow flowers and foliage

Like white, yellow and gold bring light into the garden and are a marvellous contrast to green foliage. In early spring, when the wattles burst into bloom and then the daffodils begin to flower, yellow is glorious. At the height of summer, yellow works best toned down a little by blues, purples and whites, or by grey-leafed plants. To make the most of yellow, introduce other soft splashes of colour or use it as a foil for different colours.

Early spring – the soft, butter-yellow flowers of the yellow banksia rose (*Rosa banksiae* var. *lutea*) look lovely underplanted with blue forget-me-nots. The pale-yellow flowers of the climbing Kordes rose 'Leverkusen' appear only in spring and look delightful alongside English lavender.

Summer – the lemon-yellow flowers of *Anthemis tinctoria* 'E.C.Buxton' make a perfect foil for the mauve-blue flowers and silvery grey leaves of *Nepeta* × *faassenii* 'Six Hills Giant'. Flag irises come in every imaginable shade of yellow; plant large, bold clumps beside lavender, santolina or *Helichrysum italicum*.

Autumn – as the days grow shorter and cooler, yellow is easier to place again. Chrysanthemums come in a variety of yellow and russet tones and always seem just right in an autumn garden. The leaves of the deciduous trees start to change colour and suddenly the whole garden becomes a wonderful scene of red, yellow and gold.

Throughout the year – except in the middle of winter, the little yellow daylily 'Stella d'Oro' just keeps flowering; with its bright-yellow flowers, brilliant green leaves and long-flowering habit, it has to be one of my favourites.

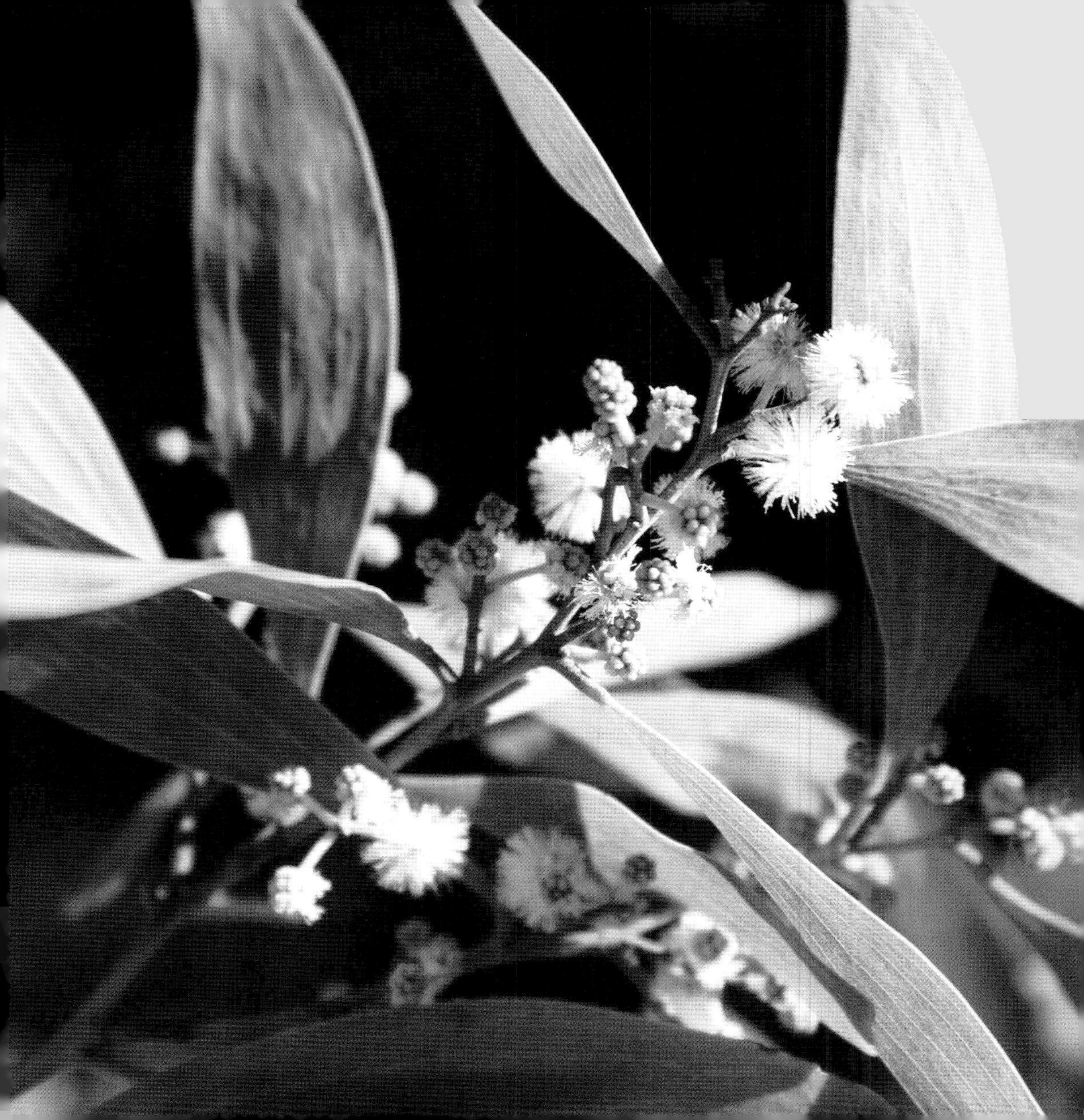

glossary

annual a plant that completes its life cycle in one year, i.e. grows, flowers, seeds and dies in the space of 12 months

biennial a plant that, under normal conditions, completes its life cycle in two years, flowering and fruiting in the second year

cultivar ('cultivated variety') an artificially bred plant that retains the same distinguishing features of flowers, foliage and form when propagated

genus the major subdivision of a plant family, consisting of a group of closely related species; the genus name forms the first part of the two-part name of a plant (e.g. 'Eschscholzia' in *Eschscholzia californica*)

glyphosate herbicide the commercial name for N-(phosphonomethyl)glycine, a relatively environmentally friendly, growth-inhibiting contact weedkiller used in products such as Roundup and Zero

heel in to plant temporarily

herbaceous not woody, i.e. soft-stemmed (usually refers to green, leafy, flowering garden plants or herbs)

humus	decomposed organic matter found in soil
mushroom mulch	the discarded straw and manure mix that has been used for growing mushrooms; excellent as garden mulch
naturalised	refers to an introduced plant that enjoys a particular situation to the extent that it has spread into the surrounding countryside as if it were native
pendent	pendulous (hanging)
perennial	a plant (generally herbaceous) that lasts for longer than two years and that dies back, or is cut back, each year to regenerate from the base
pyrethrum	an organic insecticide derived from the flower heads of pyrethrum daisy (*Tanacetum cinerariifolium*)
rhizome	a stem growing horizontally, at or below ground level, with lateral shoots and adventitious roots
set	to begin to form (flower buds, fruit, etc.)

sp.
(species)

(plural **spp.**) the plant classification below genus, referring to a group of plants unified by structural and genetic characteristics; the species name forms the second part of the two-part name of a plant (e.g. '*californica*' in *Eschscholzia californica*)

subsp.
(subspecies)

the plant classification below species, referring to a naturally occurring variant of a species

sucker

a secondary shoot from the roots or lower part of the stem of a plant

tripod

a triangular growing-frame consisting of three or more metal or wooden sticks

urea

a high-nitrogen fertiliser

var.
(variety)

a naturally occurring variant of a species not different enough to warrant further classification

variegated

exhibiting light and dark variations in foliage

weed   a plant growing wild or where it is not wanted, especially to the detriment of desired plants or the disfigurement of a garden design

white oil   a petroleum- or vegetable-oil-based pesticide used for the control of scale, citrus leaf miner and the like

× (hybrid)   a plant produced by the crossing of two different varieties or species, resulting in a new plant with different (preferably advantageous) characteristics to both parents

index

Plants are indexed by common name. Major references are indicated in **bold**.

African daisies (*Arctotis* spp.) 20, 48, 132
African violets 117
agapanthus **2**, 20, 132
agaves 144
almond (*Prunus dulcis*) 18
aloes 48, 144
aluminium plant (*Pilea cadierei*) 72
alyssum 4, 112
anemones 68, 135
angels' trumpets (*Brugmansia* spp.) 38, 112, 114, 167
annuals **4**, 116
aphids 13, 35
apples trees **6**, 50, 118
arum lilies (*Zantedeschia* spp.) 114, 135, 166, 167
Asian greens 94
Asiatic lilies 24
asters 20
autumn garden **8–9**, 172
azaleas 116, 167, 168

bamboo **10**, 130, 150
banksias 16, 100, 132
bark **12**, 45
basil 35, 78, 61, 147, 152
bay trees 116

beans **13**, 61
bee plant (*Echium candicans*) 120
beetroot 124
begonias 61, 70
bent grass (*Agrostis* spp.) 143
berryfruits **9**, 14, 28, 61
birds **16**, 74, 160
blackwoods (*Acacia* spp.) 130
blossom **18**, 56, 112, 142
blue chalk sticks (*Senecio serpens*) 72, 144
blue fescue (*Festuca glauca*) 66
blue flowers **20**, 34
bog gardens 166
Bordeaux mixture 105
boronia 112
borrowed landscape **22**
Boston ivy (*Parthenocissus tricuspidata*) 158
box (*Buxus* spp.) 55, 68, 116, 142–3
bud drop 64
bulbs 9, **24**, 112
butterfly bush (*Buddleja* spp.) 16

Californian poppies (*Eschscholzia californica*) 4, 20
camellias 16, **26**, 68, 167, 168
campions (*Silene* spp.) 4
Carex spp. 66

carrots 124
catmint (*Nepeta* × *faassenii*) 120
children's garden **28**, 99
Chinese elm (*Ulmus parvifolia*) 12, 134
Chinese lantern bush (*Abutilon* spp.) 16
Chinese witchhazel (*Hamamelis mollis*) 112
chives 79
Christmas lilies (*Lilium regale*) 167
chrysanthemums 61, 172
citrus trees 38, 116
climbers **30**, 113, 130, 158
clivias **32**, 48, 116, 135
collar rot 92
colour in the garden **34**
    see also particular colours
companion planting 13, **35**, 152
compost 9, **36–7**, 99, 104, 168
Confidor (insecticide) 42
convolvulus 72
coriander 60, 79
correas 16
cottage pinks 112
courtyards **38**, 158, 160,
crab apple (*Malus* spp.) 6, 8, 18
crepe myrtle (*Lagerstroemia indica*) 8, 12
crimson glory vine (*Vitus coignetiae*) 30
cut flowers **40**, 76
cyclamen 60, 82

daffodils (*Narcissus* spp.) 9, 24, 60
dahlias 40, 60, 61, 122, 168, 169
daphne 113, 114
daylilies (*Hemerocallis* spp.) 34, **42**, 55, 110, 172
deciduous trees 8, 134, 168, 169, 172
decorative elements **44–5**
dietes 48
dogwood 18, 135
drainage 9, **46**
dry spaces 9, **48–9**
    grasses 66
    ground covers 72
    native garden 48, 100
    roses 128
    see also seaside garden

earwig bait 166–7
echevaria 48, 144
echiums 147
elephant's ear (*Colocasia esculenta*) 135
espaliers **50**
euphorbias 20, **52**, 110, 114
evergreen trees 134

fences 30
fertiliser **54**
    lawns 90, 143
    pots 116

root vegetables 124
vermicast 170
flowers
    blue 20, 34
    green 68
    purple 120
    red 122
    white 167
    yellow 172
foliage **55**
    autumn 8
    green 68
    purple 120
    silver and grey 132, 136
    yellow 172
forget-me-nots (*Myosotis* spp.) 4, 20, 152, 172
fountains 160
foxgloves 114
frangipani (*Plumeria* spp.) 38
freesias 9, 112
fruit trees **56**, 60, 118, 169
fuchsia 16
furniture 38, 44

garden bounty **58**
garden calendar **60–1**
    see also particular seasons
garden layout **62**

gardenias 55, **64**, 116, 118
garlic spray 105–6
gazanias 20, 48, 72, 132
geraniums (*Pelargonium* spp.) 60, 116, 122, 150
gladioli 61
glass elements 45
golden ash (*Fraxinus excelsior*) 8
golden dewdrop (*Duranta repens*) 114
golden rain (*Laburnum* spp.) 114
grasses 4, 8, 16, **66**, 134
green flowers and foliage **68**
green goddess lilies (*Zantedeschia aethiopica* 'Green Goddess') 68, 135, 166
greenhouses **70**
grevilleas 16, 72
grey and silver foliage 132, **136**
ground covers **72**, 135
gum trees (*Eucalyptus* spp.) 12, 45, **74**, 134, 150

ha-ha 22
hawthorn 8
hedges 8, 28
hellebores (*Helleborus* spp.) 40, 68, **76**, 135
herbs 4, 35, 61, 72, **78–9**, 112, 147
hibiscus 61, 118
honeysuckle (*Lonicera* spp.) 38, 112, 113, 114
hot chilli spray 105
hyacinths 112

hydrangeas 20, 40, 60, 135, 167, 169

Iceland poppies (*Papava nudicaule*) 40
identifying plants **80**
impatiens 61, 167
indoor plants **82**
insects 35, 152
irises 8, 20, 49, 55, 60, **84–5**, 110, 120, 135, 147, 166, 172

jacaranda 20, 34, 134
Japanese blood grass (*Imperata cylindrica* 'Rubra') 66
Japanese maple (*Acer palmatum*) 8
jasmine (*Jasminum* spp.) 30, 38, 112, 113, 146
jonquils 112

kangaroo paw (*Anigozanthus* spp.) 16, 100
kiwifruit 30, 169
kniphofias 16, 20, 49, **86**, 132, 146

lamb's ears (*Stachys* spp.) 150
landscape, borrowing 22
lavender (*Lavandula* spp.) 55, 60, **88**, 118, 130, 136, 146, 152, 157, 172
lawns 9, 60, 61, **90–1**, 143
lawnmowers 90, 91
leafy greens **94**

lemon cordial 58
lemon grass 79
lemon trees **92–3**, 116
Lenten rose (*Helleborus orientalis*) 110
lettuce (*Lactuca* spp.) 60, 61, **94**
lilacs 18, 20, 40, 61, 112
lilies (*Lilium* spp.) 9, 60, 168

magnolias 18, **96**, 130, 134
Manchurian pear (*Pyrus ussurensis*) 63, 134
marguerite daisies (*Leucanthemum vulgare*) 157
marjoram 78
Michelia doltsopa 112
mint bush (*Prostanthera* spp.) 112
mirrors 22
Miscanthus spp. 66
Mount Fuji cherry (*Prunus* 'Shirotae') 3, 18
mulch 8, 9, 61, **98**, 104, 162, 164

nasturtiums 35, 152
native frangipani (*Hymenosporum flavum*) 112, 130
native garden 16, **100**
    for dry spaces 48
    perfumed plants 112
    seaside garden 132
    screening 130
native hibiscus (*Alyogyne huegelii*) 20, 100, 130
native rosemary (*Westringia fruticosa*) 100

native violet (*Viola hederacea*) 72
New Zealand rock lily (*Arthropodium cirrhatum*) 110
night-scented flowers 38
no-dig garden **99**

oleander (*Nerium oleander*) 114
orchids 60, 61, 70, **102**, 116–17
oregano 78
organic garden **104–7**
ornamental grasses 4, 8, 16, 34, 143
ornamental pears (*Pyrus* spp.) 130
oxalis 9, 168

palm grass (*Setaria palmifolia*) 34
parsley 58, 76, 78
passionfruit 30, 61
passionvine hoppers 9
paths **108**
paving 46
pelargonium 28, 122
perennials 9, **110**
perfumed plants 28, 38, **112–13**, 150
periwinkles (*Vinca* spp.) 72
pests
    aphids 13, 35
    leafminer 93
    passionvine hoppers 9
    scale 92

snails 9, 78, 138
pest control 104–7
petunias 4, 61
pH of soil 140–1
pig's ear (*Cotyledon orbiculata*) 136, 144
pigface (*Carpobrotus* spp.) 72, 100
pin oak (*Quercus palustris*) 8
pittosporum 112
plumbago 48, 118
poinsettia (*Euphorbia pulcherrima*) 52, 70
poisonous plants **114**
polyanthus 60
pools 160
potato vine (*Solanum jasminoides*) 30, 130, 152
pots 4, **116–17**
    bulbs in 24
    in courtyards 38
    herbs 79
    orchids 102
    succulents 116, 144
    vegetables 116
primulas 4, 60
pruning **118**, 129
purple plants and foliage **120**
purple top (*Verbena bonariensis*) 120

radish 124
ranunculus 60

raspberries 14, 61, 169
red flowers **122**
repotting 117
retaining walls 46
rhododendron 168
rhubarb spray 106
rhus tree (*Toxicodendron succedaneum*) 114
rock rose (*Cistus* spp.) 132
rocket 94
root vegetables **124**
rosemary (*Rosmarinus* spp.) 20, 35, 78–9
roses (*Rosa* spp.) 8, 35, 60, 61, 112, 113, 122, **126–9**, 147, 167, 168, 169, 172
rue (*Ruta* spp.) 114

sacred bamboo (*Nandina domestica* 'Nana') 10
sage (*Salvia* spp.) 120, 136, 146
salad greens 94
scale 92
screening 30, **130**
seaside daisy (*Erigeron karvinskianus*) 72
seaside garden **132**
shade trees **134**
shady places 72, 76, **135**
shasta daisies 152
shrubs 118
silver and grey foliage 132, **136**
smoke bush (*Cotinus coggygria*) 66

snails 9, 78, **138**
snowball tree (*Viburnum opulus* 'Roseum') 68
snow-in-summer (*Cerastium tomentosum*) 72
soap spray 104
soil 124, **140–1**
spinach 60, 94
spiny-headed mat rush (*Lomandra longifolia*) 100
spring garden
    bulbs 24, 112
    colour in the garden 20, 172
    jobs 118, **142–3**
star jasmine (*Trachelospermum jasminoides*) 113
Stephanotis floribunda 113
stone elements 44
stone fruit 56
storm lilies (*Zephyranthes candida*) 24
strawberries 9, 14, 28, 35, 168
succulents **144**
    dry spaces 48, 66
    in pots 116, 144
summer garden
    bulbs 24
    colour in the garden 172
    jobs **146–7**
    shade 30
swamp foxtail grass (*Pennisetum alopecuroides*) 66, 120
sweet peas (*Lathyrus* spp.) 8, 60, 112, **148**

tactile garden **150**
thrip 147
thyme 78
tobacco plant (*Nicotiana* spp.) 112
tomatoes 61, 147, **152**
tool maintenance 154
topiary 55, 116, 146, **156–7**
tree wormwood (*Artemesia arborescens*) 136, 146
trees
    bark 12, 45
    blossom 18, 56, 112, 142
    deciduous 8, 134
    espaliered 50
    fruit 56, 118
    pruning 118
    for screening 150
    shade 134
tulips 9, 20, 24, 60, 122

vegetables 142
    children's garden 28
    companion planting 13, 35, 152
    planting 60, 61, 147
    in pots 116
    see also particular vegetables
veldt daisy (*Osteospermum* spp.) 48
vermicast 170
violets 9, 60, 72

wallflowers 112
walls 38, 46, **158**
water features 38, 45, **160**
watering
    bulbs 24
    garden **162**
    indoor plants 82
    lawn 90
    pots 116
watsonia 68
wattle 112
weeds 4, 8, 9, **164**
wet spaces 9, **166**
white cedar (*Melia azedarach*) 100
white flowers **167**
'windows' 158
winter garden
    colours in the garden 20, 172
    jobs **168–9**
    scented plants 112
winter heliotrope (*Petasites fragrans*) 135
wintersweet (*Chimonanthus praecox*) 112
wisteria 30, 169
wood features 44–5
worms **170**

yellow flowers and foliage **172**
yellowing leaves 64

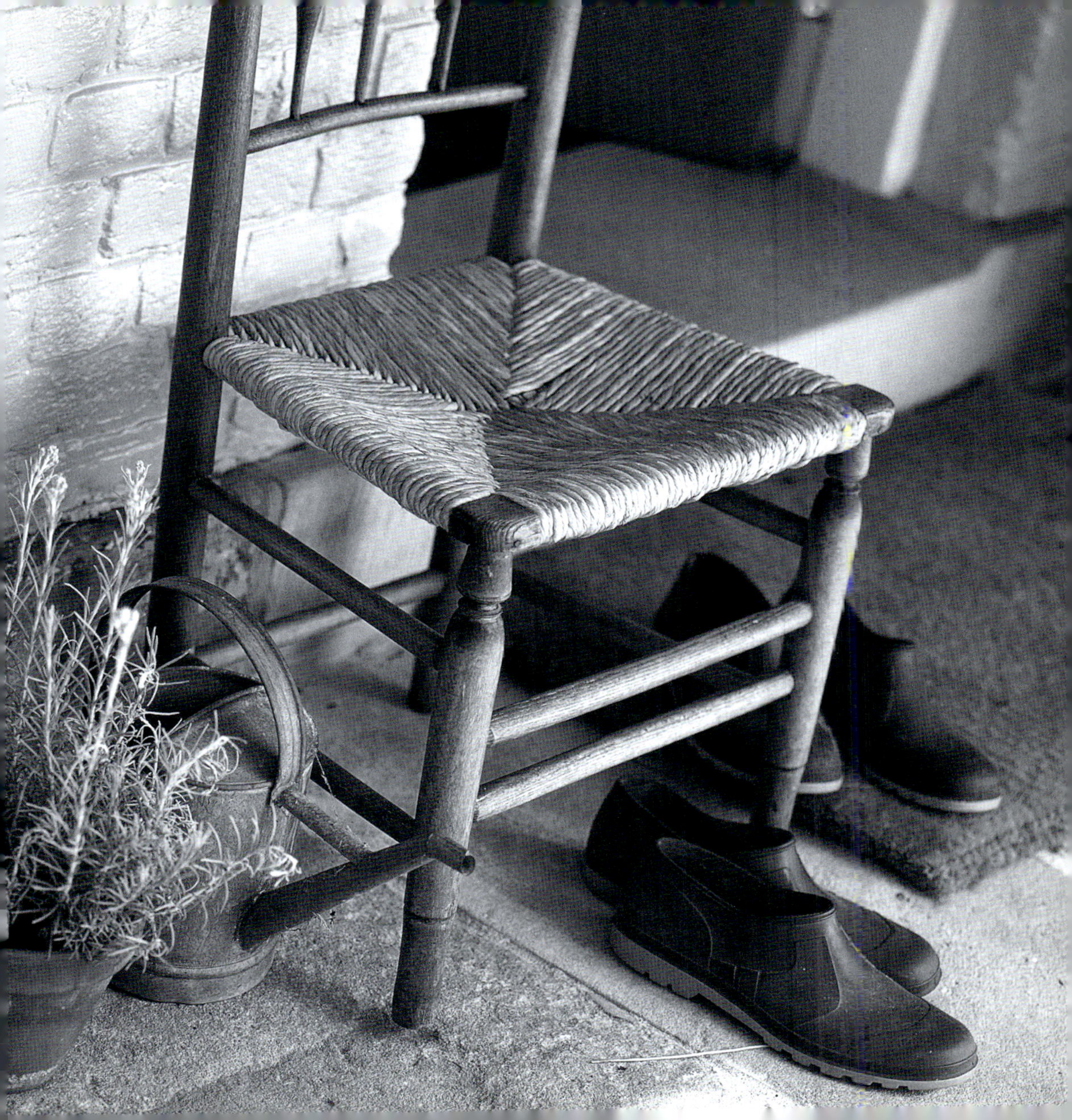

acknowledgements

I would primarily like to thank my publishers, Julie Gibbs and Kirsten Abbott, without whom this book would not exist. I would also like to thank Simon Griffiths for his beautiful photography and for accepting the challenge of illustrating what is generally accepted as a colour medium in black and white. In particular I would like to thank Nicci Dodanwela for all her help, endless patience and always being in a good mood.

For you,
Happy Reading!

ISBN: 9798363823442

Growing Readers

All rights reserved

My Mom

T. Paris

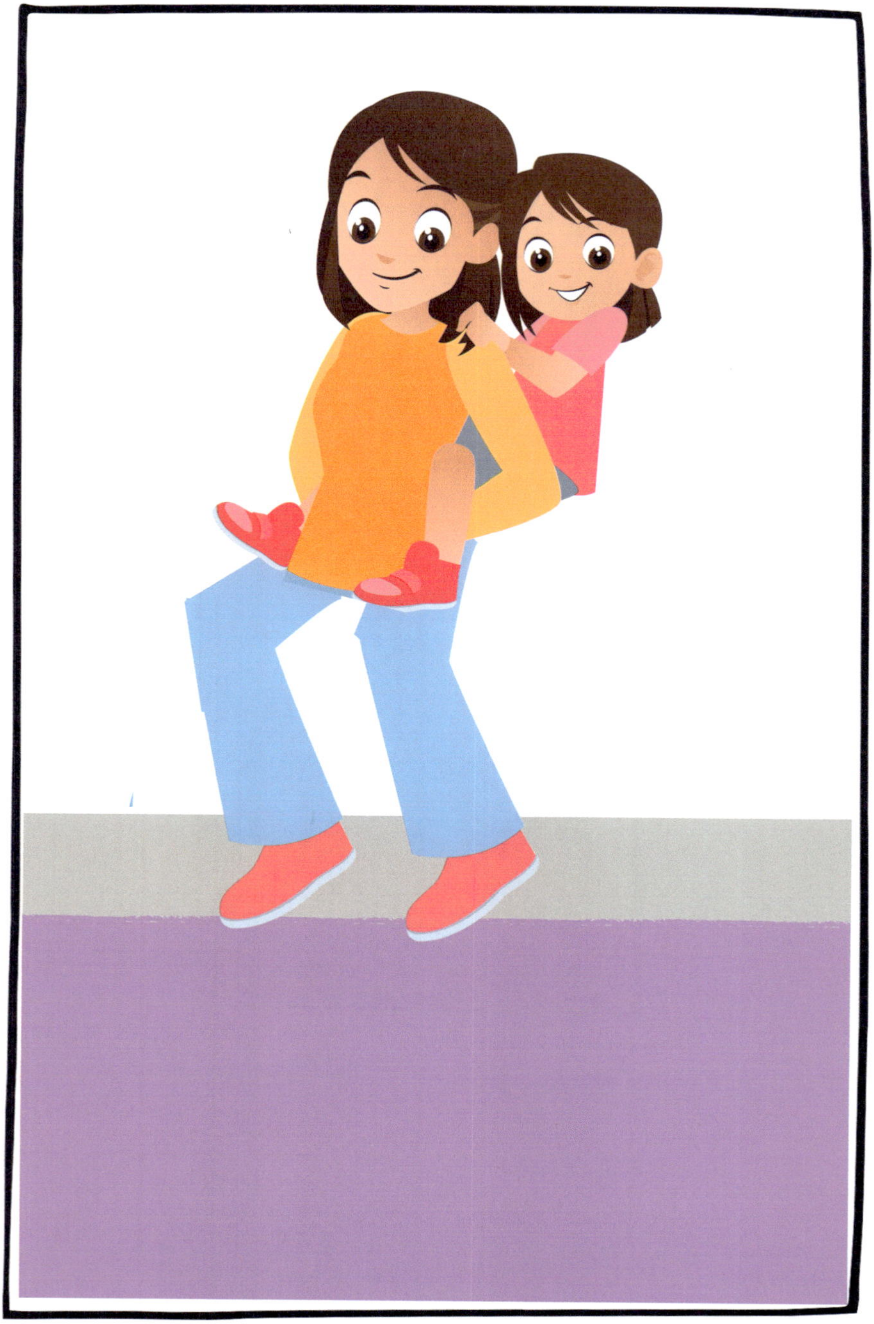

I run with my mom.

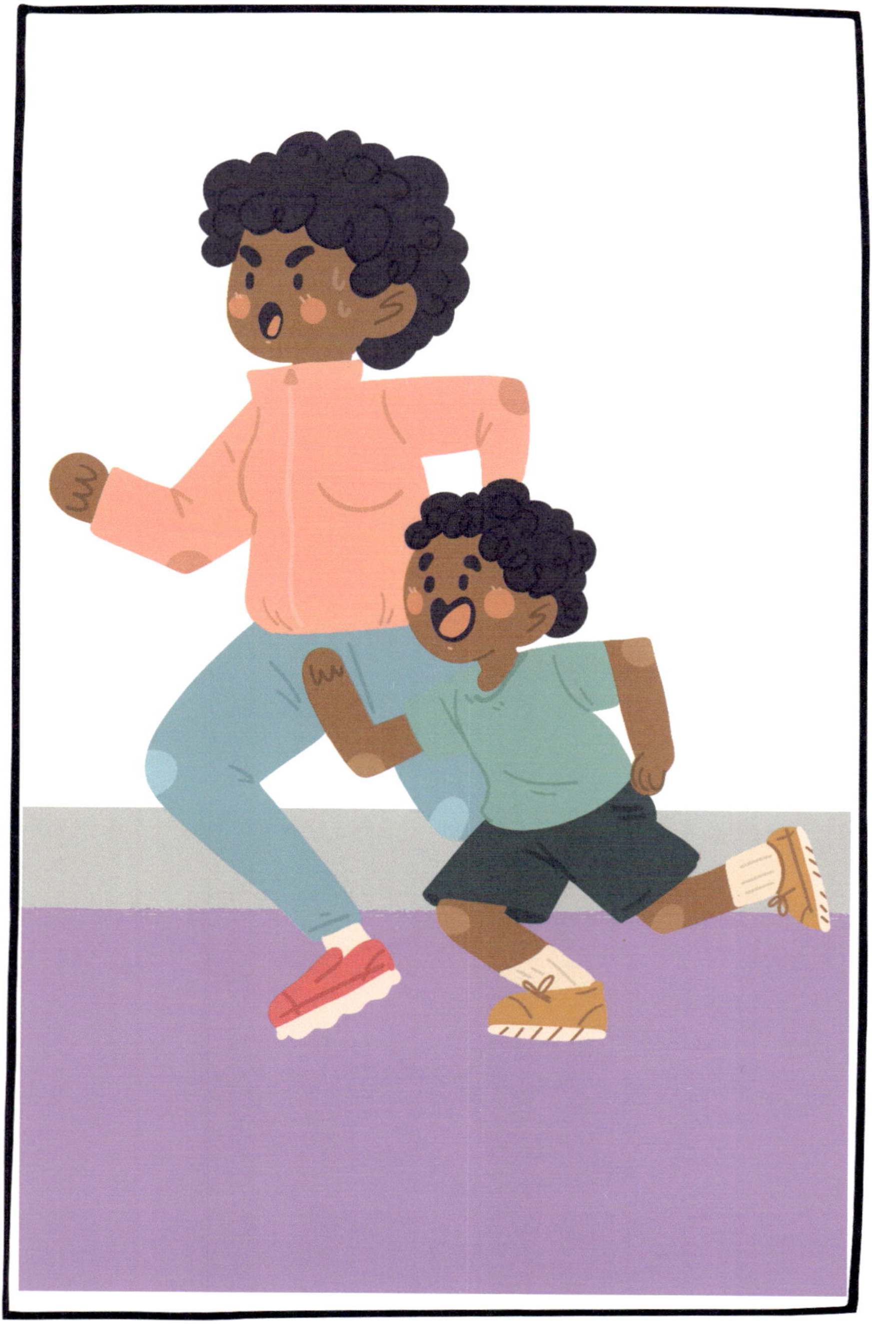

My mom runs with me.

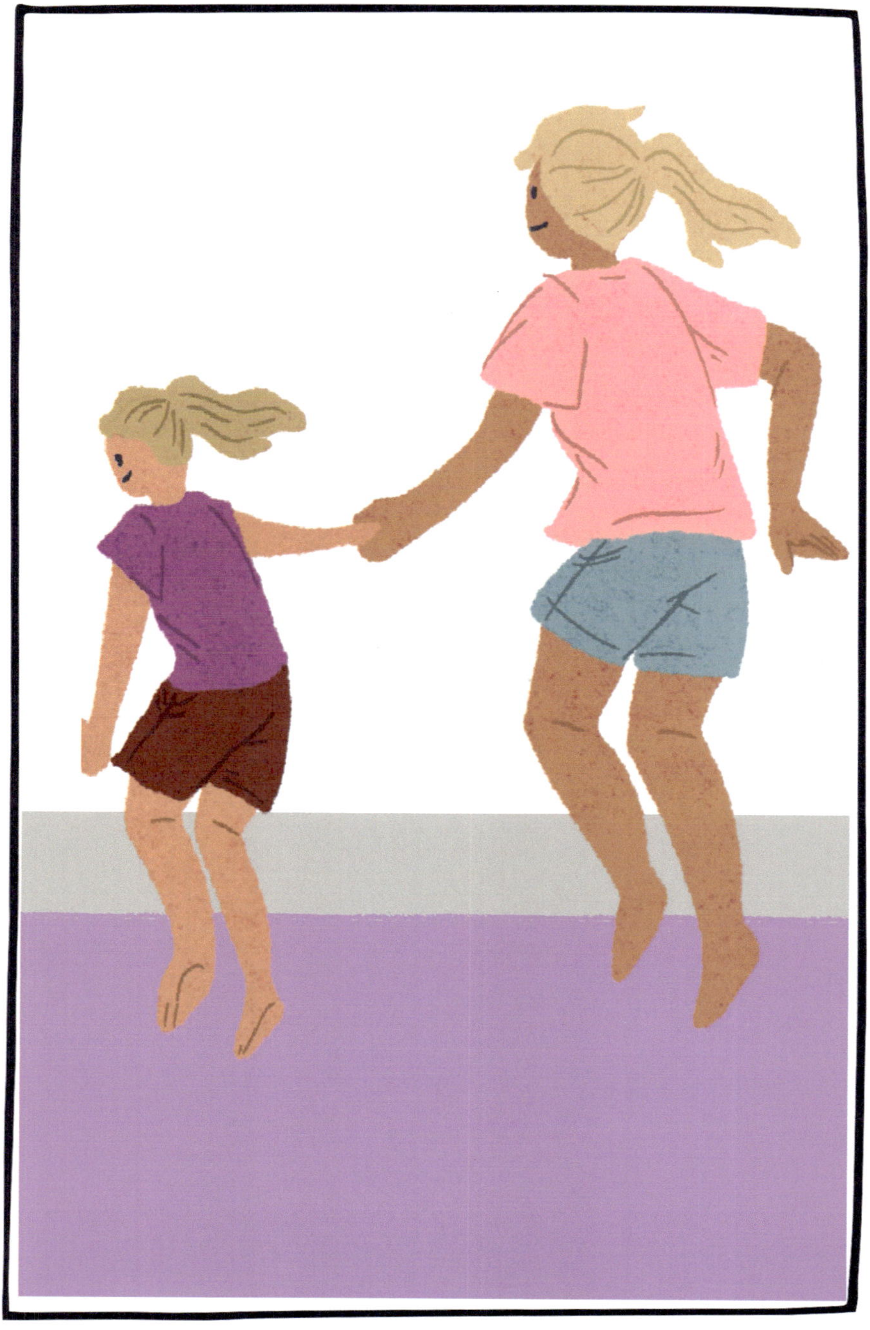

I hop with my mom.

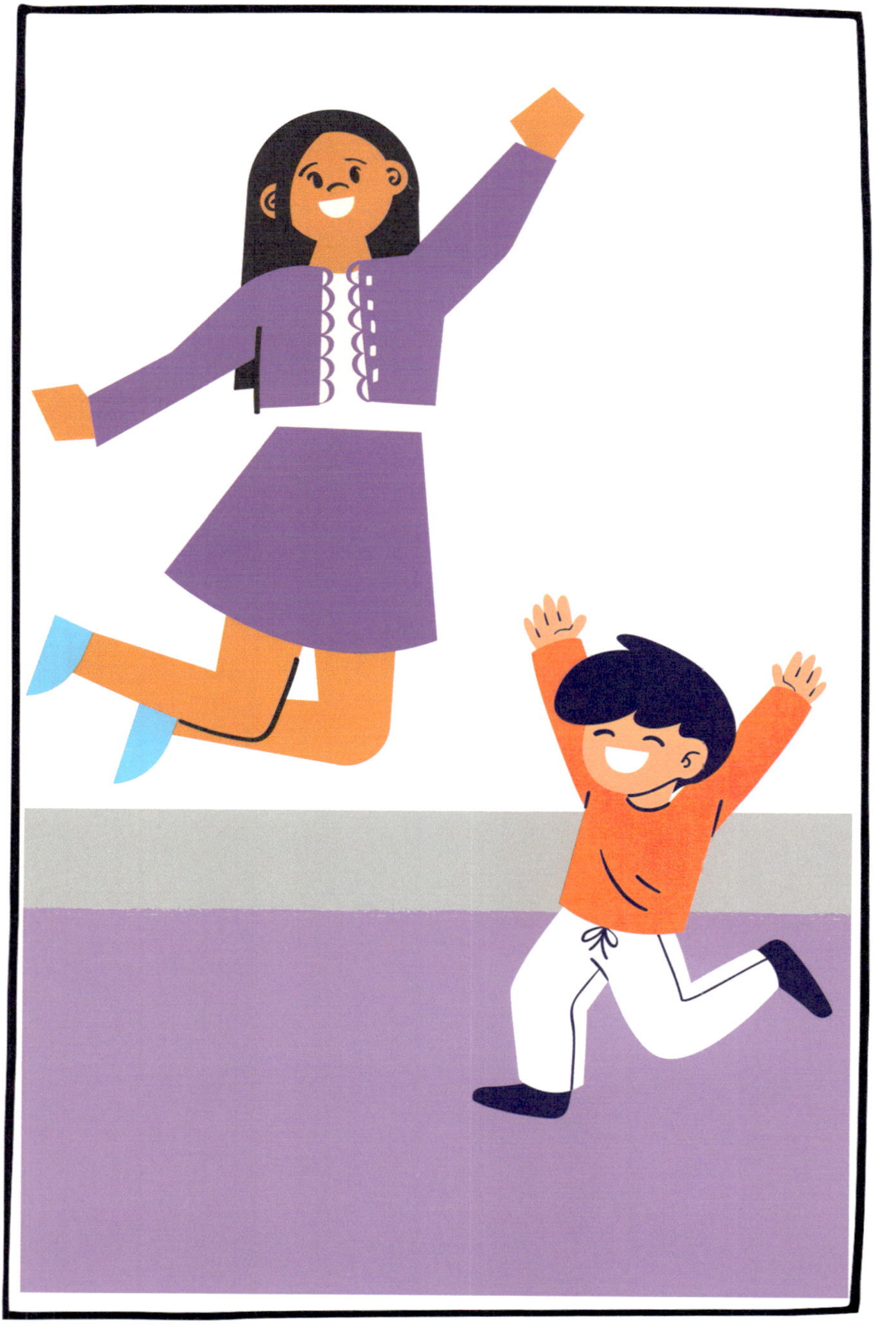

My mom hops with me.

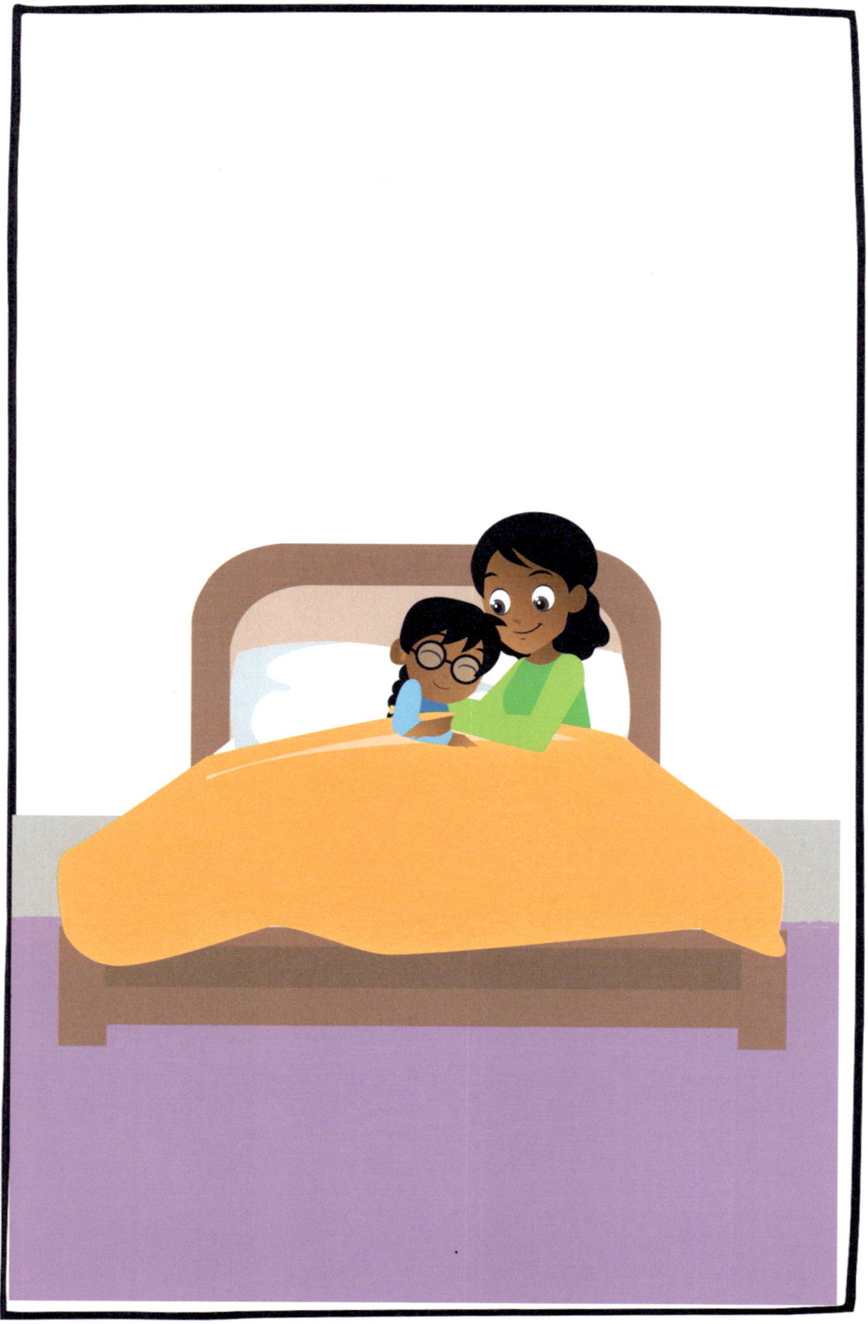

I nap with my mom.

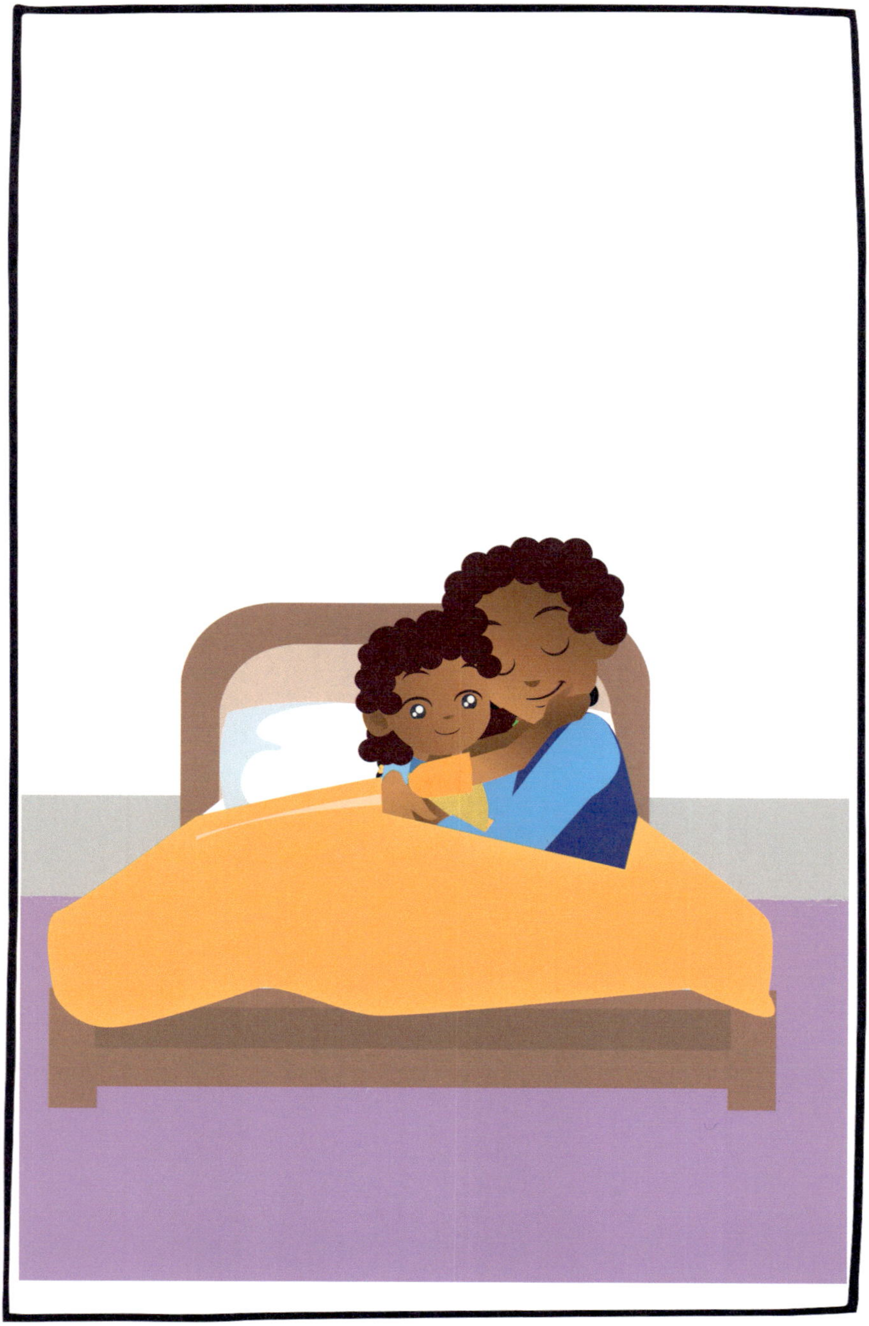

My mom naps with me.

14

I hug my mom.

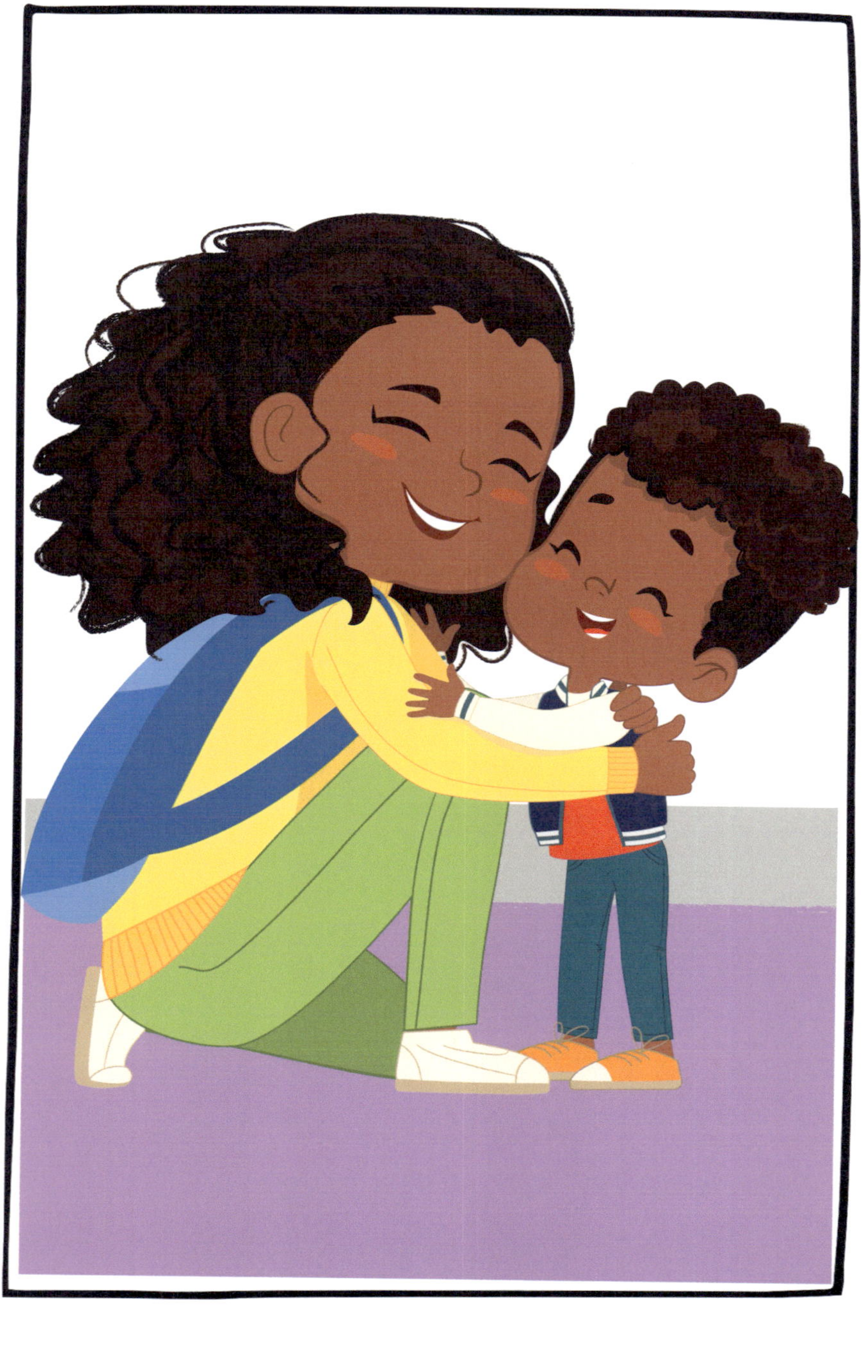

My mom hugs me.

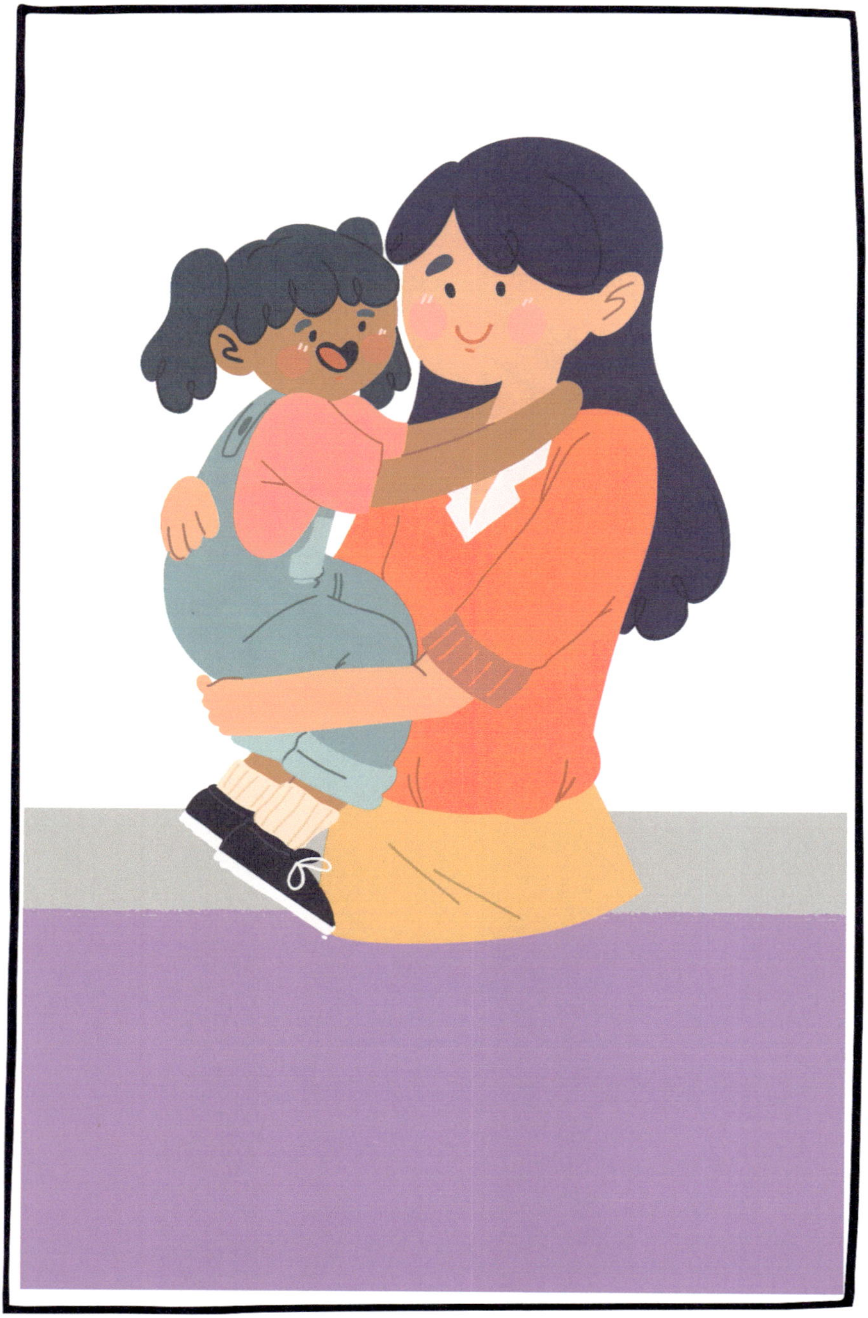

I have fun with my mom.

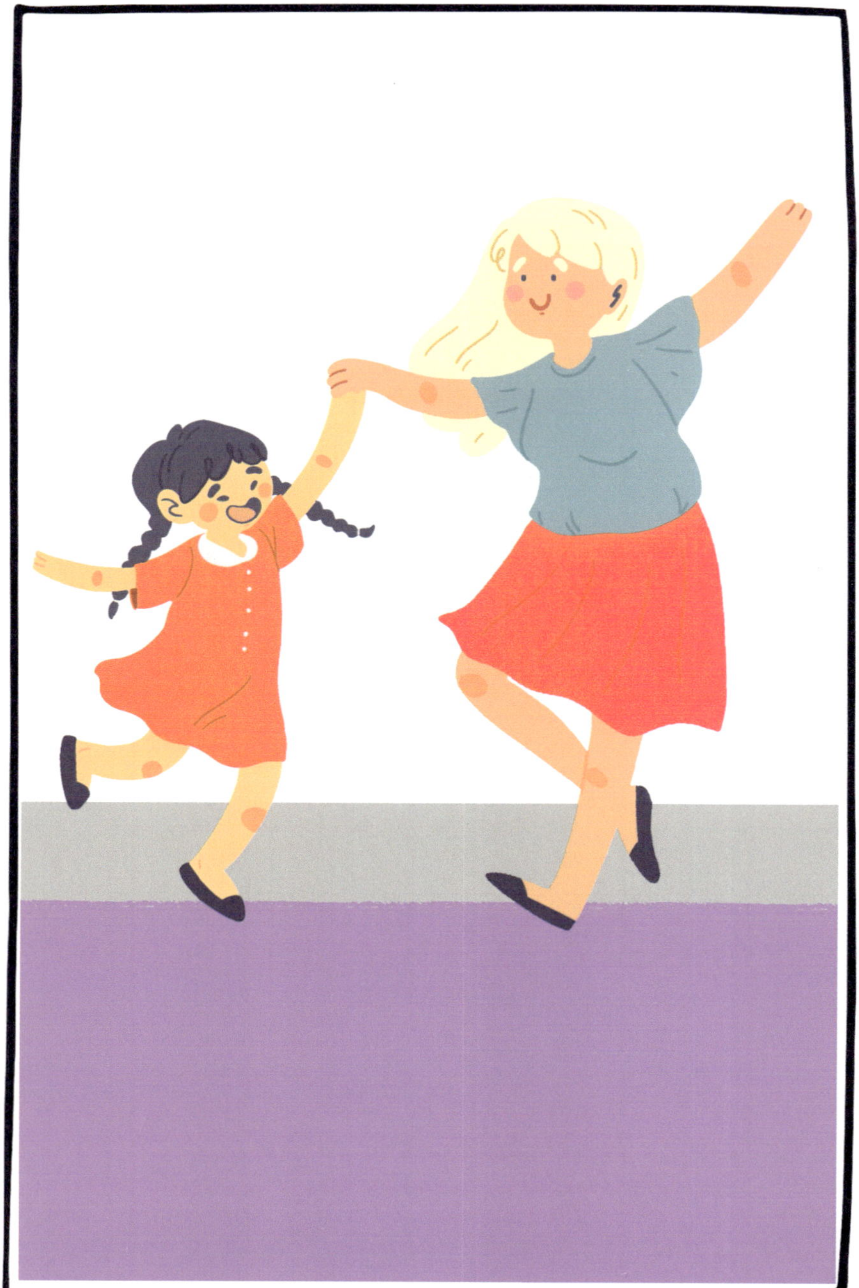

My mom has fun with me.

Made in the USA
Columbia, SC
05 March 2024